Around the Tuscan Table

Around the Tuscan Table

Food, Family, and Gender
in Twentieth-Century Florence

Carole M. Counihan

ROUTLEDGE
NEW YORK AND LONDON

Published in 2004 by
Routledge
29 West 35th Street
New York, New York 10001
www.routledge-ny.com

Published in Great Britain by
Routledge
11 New Fetter Lane
London EC4P 4EE
www.routledge.co.uk

Routledge is an imprint of the Taylor & Francis Group.
Printed in the United States of America on acid-free paper.

10 9 8 7 6 5 4 3 2 1

Library of Congress Cataloging-in-Publication Data

Counihan, Carole, 1948–
Around the Tuscan table : food, family, and gender in twentieth
century Florence / Carole M. Counihan.
p. cm.
Includes bibliographical references and index.
ISBN 0-415-94672-7 (hardcover : alk. paper) — ISBN 0-415-94673-5
(pbk. : alk. paper)
1. Food habits—Italy—Florence—History—20th century. 2. Florence
(Italy)—Social life and customs—20th century. I. Title.
GT2850.C683 2004
394.1'2—dc22
                                                      2003017144

This book is dedicated to
My husband, children, and grandchildren
Jim, Ben, Willie, Marisela, Julian, and Kristina
For the long haul

Contents

List of Illustrations

Preface and Acknowledgments

Writing this book has been a long journey. I spent the period from 1968 to 1984 immersed in Italian culture and the Italian family described here, the twenty-three living relatives of a Florentine I call Leonardo, my former boyfriend, *fidanzato,* and briefly husband. I had been a student at Stanford-in-Italy in 1968, and after college graduation in 1970, I returned to Florence and lived for the next three years in Via S. Ilario a Colombaia, just off the Via Senese, a few hundred yards south of the Porta Romana. I met Leonardo in September 1970 and we spent the next thirteen years living together in Florence, Sardinia, and Massachusetts, while I pursued a doctorate in anthropology and he a bachelor's and master's in fine arts. During the summers of 1982 and 1984, I tape-recorded formal, food-centered life histories with all of Leonardo's living relatives (see Figure 1). I am grateful for the openness and affection they showed me during the project and throughout all the years of our acquaintance. They cooperated fully in the interviews and gave me permission to write about them. When I returned to Florence in March 2003, they again welcomed me warmly and shared memories and thoughts about their everyday lives.

My experience in Italy contributed to my life in many ways. After traveling to Sardinia in the early 1970s, I became fascinated with the land and the people and decided to become an anthropologist to explore Sardinian culture further. I began graduate school in anthropology at the University of Massachusetts in 1974 and benefited from the European Studies Program and a Fulbright Grant to conduct doctoral dissertation research in Bosa, Sardinia, in 1978–79. In 1982, I inaugurated the food-centered life history research in Florence that has finally resulted in this book. I owe my fortuitous decision to study food to the Italians' constant confabulations about eating, which have resulted in years of good eating, spirited talking, rich memories, and fruitful scholarship.

As I was embarking on a career in cultural anthropology, the study of food and culture was simultaneously flowering. I am grateful to many scholars whose work has contributed to my own, and I particularly want to recognize Joan Jacobs Brumberg, Penny Van Esterik, Amy Bentley, Warren Belasco, Sidney Mintz, George Armelagos, Françoise Sabban, Silvano Serventi, Martin Bruegel, Steven Kaplan, Maurice Aymard, and Alberto Capatti.

Many people contributed to this book. My husband, anthropologist Jim Taggart, read and commented on several drafts, and for his wisdom, fine critical ear, and years of support, I am deeply grateful. Carol Helstosky, Sabina Magliocco, Gigliola Panico, and Betsy Whitaker read the complete first draft of the manuscript, gave invaluable feedback, spurred me onward, and made this a far better book. Any remaining lacunae are no fault of theirs, and for their exceptional generosity, I am deeply grateful. I give special thanks to Gigliola Panico for the title. At Routledge, I thank my editor, Ilene Kalish, for her insight and encouragement, and Salwa Jabado, Donna Capato, and Brandy Mui for their cheerful attention to detail.

I am indebted to many at Millersville University whose support has enriched my work: all my sociology-anthropology department colleagues and especially chairs Sam Casselberry and Mary Glazier; the Faculty Grants Committee whose continued support has been a lifeline for scholarship; the Women's and Latino Studies programs and all their faculty who have kept ideas flowing; my former dean, Dr. Rita Marinho, who granted release time at a critical moment; Dr. Chuck Geiger of the Geography Department's Geo-Graphics Laboratory for the maps; president and former provost Dr. Francine McNairy; and Barb Dills, Derek Shanahan, John Short, Ed Shane, Tracey Weis, Barb Stengel, Darla Williams, Nancy Smith, Aida Ceara, and Beverly Skinner. I thank my student assistants, Justin Garcia, Rebecca Gray, Megan Kirkpatrick, and Lauren Schaller and out of gratitude to many remarkable Millersville students, I am donating a portion of the royalties of this book to the Sociology-Anthropology Department Student Research Award.

Over the years I spent in Florence and Sardinia many people gave me their friendship and insights. Deepest thanks go to Chris Streit and Massimo Guerrini, Lorenzo and Caterina Pezzatini, Beppe Lo Russo and Gabriella Bianchini, and their families. I warmly thank all of my Florentine relatives without whom my life would be far less rich and this book would not exist. I thank many people I knew in Florence including Tina and Mario Barsanti, Loretta and Roberto Cellini, Scilla Cuccaro, Damianos Damiankos, Sandra and Rolando Fossi, Maria Teresa Traversi and Carlo Guarnieri, Angela Jeannet, Giuseppe Mammarella, Cinzia and Sergio Meriggi, Maria Luisa and Renato Pezzatini, Samuela Ristori, Elda Seminara, Dora and Sergio Traversi, and Alessandro and Marta Tozzi. I thank Prof. Christine Streit Guerrini at the Scuola Interpreti in Florence and Dr. Paolo Ventura at the Istituto di Urbanistica at the University of Florence for inviting me to their classes in March 2003, and I thank the following students for sharing their thoughts with me: Luca Belati, Alice Bellia, Seraina Biscione, Chiara Ferrari, Elisa Fiorini, Chiara Franzini, Eva Gertzner, Beatrice Giacometti, Sara Giunchi, Elena Grifoni, Emanuela Lembo, Francesco Molinari, Elena Molteni, Jessica Nieri, Chiara Pacini, Mariagiulia Bennicelli Pasqualis, Valentina Pini, Christian Schreinert, Nicoletta Serrais, Silvia Sopranzetti, Caterina Tesi, and the others who wish to remain anonymous.

I thank Giovanna Pezzatini for one day in 1973 giving me a dish cloth that I still have. It was made from an old flour sack inscribed with "Gift from the People of the United States of America to the People of Italy." She had saved it since 1944 when the U.S. government distributed food to the starving Florentines after the Allied liberation of Florence. The flour sack turned dish cloth that traveled from the United States to Italy and back again encapsulates the power of food to create ties that bind. To Italy, I am grateful for the many kindnesses of strangers, the generosity of friends, and the knowledge that there are many ways of being.

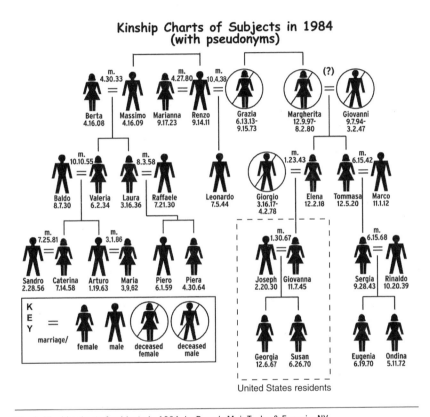

Fig. 1 Kinship chart of subjects in 1984, by Brandy Mui, Taylor & Francis, NY

Map 1 Italy showing Regions and Florence, by Dr. Chuck Geiger, Millersville University Geographics Laboratory

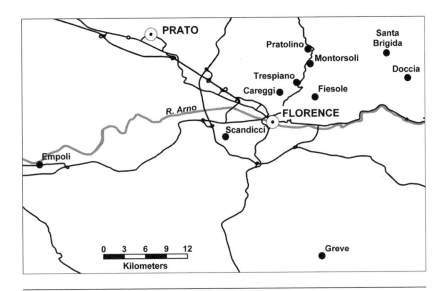

Map 2 Province of Florence, by Dr. Chuck Geiger, Millersville University Geographics Laboratory

I
Food as Voice in Twentieth-Century Florence

Introduction

Non è nemmeno che s'abbia più desideri, fifty-year-old Valeria commented in 1984: *It's not that we have any more unfulfilled desires. We eat whatever we want every day. If we have any desires it's to eat the old cheap foods like **minestra di pane** (bread and bean soup), or cornmeal **gnocchi** (dumplings). We eat meat all the time. Instead, in the old days, we really craved meat and we ate it enthusiastically. Now when we go out, what do we eat? More or less the same things that we always eat at home. When Sunday comes, it is a day like every other. . . . You no longer have any yearning for anything. **Non hai mica più voglia di niente.***

Valeria touched on a major accomplishment of Italian society in the second half of the twentieth century, which was to overcome centuries of food scarcity and to provide dietary abundance for most people. Yet she also touched on the bittersweet side of that abundance, which was the loss of longing. As she and other Florentines spoke about food, they revealed rich dimensions of their lives. Eating played an important role in people's family life, sociability, celebrations, and pleasure. Everything to do with food was important and interesting. Tastes were rich and delicious, smells fragrant and pungent, hungers strong and deep. Florentines bonded and argued at meals, and renewed or ruptured relationships through giving, receiving, or refusing food. The division of labor around food revealed gender roles and relations. Cooking for some women was an expression of creativity and caring; for others it was a burdensome obligation. In pregnancy and breast-feeding, women created relationships with their children. In eating, Florentines connected to their environment, ensured their survival, and affirmed a variegated cuisine and culture. Their foodways expressed values and habits central to their lives. This book uses food as a lens to describe Florentines' changing family, gender relations, and ideology throughout the massive transformations of the twentieth century.

Food-Centered Life Histories as Voice

For many people, food is a powerful voice,[1] especially for women, who are often heavily involved with food acquisition, preparation, provisioning, and cleanup. Food-centered life histories have fit my desire to use ethnography to give voice to traditionally muted people—people not part of the political-economic or intellectual elite, especially women. I began my study in Florence on women, and conducted multiple interviews with some, but eventually also included men to have a full picture of gender. My goal is to make the food-centered life histories carry the purpose of the *testimonios*, which the Latina Feminist Group (2001, 2) defines as "a crucial means of bearing witness and inscribing into history those lived realities that would otherwise succumb to the alchemy of erasure."

The food-centered life histories of the twenty-three Florentines I interviewed between 1982 and 1984 speak out against "the alchemy of erasure," for the lives they describe are already gone due to the rapid pace of change in the second half of the twentieth century. The core of Tuscan cuisine rooted in *mezzadria* peasant farming persisted at the dawn of the new millennium, but there were changes in daily meal routines, diet, cuisine, and food labor that revealed significant changes in Italian culture.

In the food-centered life histories, I asked questions about experiences and memories centered on food production, preservation, preparation, consumption, and exchange. I asked about past and present diets, recipes, everyday and ritual meals, foods for healing, eating in pregnancy, breast-feeding, eating out, and processed foods. As Florentines spoke about these topics, they provided rich data on individual perceptions of food and culture in twentieth-century Italy. This book uses their interviews to contribute the largely missing voices of the consumers themselves to the burgeoning social science literature on Italian foodways conducted by historians, ethnographers, and sociologists.[2] As much as possible, this book foregrounds Florentines' descriptions of their lives, and my words provide context and structure.

I first came to Florence as a student at Stanford-in-Italy in 1968 and returned after college graduation in 1970. I spent the next fourteen years living off and on in Italy, spending about six years total there, first holding a variety of temporary jobs and later conducting ethnographic fieldwork in Sardinia and Florence (see Figure 1.1). I had a long-term relationship with a Florentine I call Leonardo,[3] and the principal data for this book come from fifty-six hours of food-centered life histories tape-recorded in Italian with Leonardo's twenty-three living relatives in 1982–84. I interacted with Leonardo's relatives on many occasions between 1970 and 1984 and did participant observation of many meals. In 1984, two of my subjects recorded all their family food expenditures for one week. Eight kept weeklong daily food logs, recording what, when, and where they ate as well as their feelings before and after eating, covering a total of fifty-three days. I collected approximately two hundred recipes through observation, informants' descriptions, and two women's handwritten cookbooks.

I returned to Florence in March 2003 and visited many of my previous informants, met the several new additions to their families, caught up on family

Fig. 1.1 The author heading off for an interview in summer 1984

history, and asked about current food habits. I did focus group interviews at two university-level classes: one in Italian at the University of Florence and one in English with third-year students at the Scuola Superiore per Interpreti e Traduttori, also in Florence.

The heart of the book consists of the edited interview transcriptions. It took me several years, but I eventually transcribed the tapes into over one thousand pages of text. I sorted my interviews into themes, selected representative passages, translated them into English, and wove them together. Creating a coherent narrative was a complex process and involved shaping the original flow of words in three main ways. The first was through translation. Interviewees spoke to me in colloquial Florentine Italian, and I have tried to stay as close to the original as possible while also providing idiomatic equivalents of untranslatable Florentine expressions.[4]

The second way I have shaped Florentines' words has been through the process of editing their spoken narratives into a coherent written text. This editing has involved eliminating repetition; deleting unnecessary expressions like "I don't know," "You see," and "Understand"; adding occasional words for clarity and context; and sometimes changing the order of sentences or paragraphs to construct a more logical progression of ideas. To indicate our different voices, I interweaved their words in italics with mine in Roman type.[5]

Finally, I shaped the many diverse interviews into a narrative about modernity, family, and gender. In the twentieth century, Florentine foodways evolved from a centuries-old, localized, sharecropping system toward a global market economy, revealing a changing cultural philosophy in beliefs and practices of consumption. My subjects described a set of gender relationships and self-definitions grounded in the extended, closed, male-headed family. They ate a "Mediterranean" diet, scantily in the first half of the twentieth century but with increasing abundance in the second half. This diet, however, was already being modified by the postmodern, ever-larger agro-food industry that continued to grow in 2003, but which Florentines and other Italians shaped by alternative food practices.

Food as Voice of Modernity

This book looks at how Florentines spoke through food about the complex changes in their lives that I consider together as "modernity." By modernity, I mean the processes of social and economic change engendered by capitalism, technology, and informational and bureaucratic complexity that transformed Italy (and the globe) in the twentieth century. Modernity involved a transition from a localized subsistence and market economy that provided most people with barely enough to survive to a fully market, wage labor economy of conspicuous consumption, with altered social relations and meaning systems viewed here through the lens of food.[6]

The transition to modernity in Italy was born out of the rubble of the two World Wars and the intervening years of Fascist rule. It was jump-started by the massive U.S. aid that poured into Italy through Marshall Plan funds and private investment after World War II. It was marked by increasing abundance as the war receded and the economy rebounded. It was an abundance that the children born after the war took for granted in ways that still astounded their parents in the 1980s. *We should have talked about the past more,* said Baldo, born in 1930, lamenting his children's lack of understanding of the conditions of his childhood when he had only two outfits, and if they were dirty, he stayed home, because he had nothing else to wear. His family ate watery soup and ate it willingly, because that's all there was, and it staved off hunger. After the war, most Florentines achieved a much higher standard of living, and they gradually lost some of the traditional foods of their hungry childhoods. They lived farther from the land in urban apartment buildings or row houses, participated in an ever more fully commodified economy, and increasingly ate foods produced primarily for exchange and profit rather than for subsistence.

These changing foodways accompanied a changing Florentine value system.[7] My older subjects grew up taking great pleasure in food but avoiding gluttony. Eating brought deep feelings of pleasure and consolation, but also concerns about immoderation. Medical and nutritional beliefs stressed balance in types and quantity of foods. Too much food disturbed the equilibrium between desire and satiety, and between measure and excess. When my older

Fig. 1.2 McDonald's in Florence, frequented heavily by young people, in March 2003

subjects were young before and during the Second World War, consumption was highly valued because it was scarce and precarious. Yet their children, born after the war in the context of the Italian economic miracle, grew up in a world where consumption was obligatory, taken for granted, and essential to full personhood—a transformation lamented by the older people.

In the 1980s, children were fussy about food and strangers to the parsimony that their parents espoused, as were their children in 2003. They ate what they wanted, demanded variety, and brooked no expense in going out to eat. They ate some of the foods of the past out of nostalgia and genuine appreciation, but rejected others as distasteful. They ate and invented new foods, further from the traditional roots of Tuscan cuisine, dependent on processed ingredients, quick to make, easy to clean up, higher in meat and fats, and lower in vegetables, fiber, and legumes. In the last two decades of the twentieth century, they began to consume more junk food, and by 2003, there were four McDonald's outlets in Florence (see Figure 1.2). Florentines ordered take-out pizza and could choose from over four hundred restaurants, of which approximately fifty-five offered foreign cuisines from ten different countries. From a value on highly pleasurable but measured consumption of quintessentially Tuscan foods emerged the commodification of food, its reflection of an ever-wider world, and a growing commitment to consumption for its own sake.

Food as Voice of Family and Gender

In talking about foodways, Florentines not only opened a window into their experiences of social change, but also revealed family and gender relations through men's and women's roles in production and reproduction. By production I mean the work involved in making the raw materials, products, and money that ensured survival. By reproduction I mean the labor involved in having offspring, feeding and clothing them, and socializing them to be capable members of society. Engels (1972, 71) defined the relationship between production and reproduction as "the determining factor in history" in regard to gender relations—an insight that has been pursued by several recent feminist scholars.[8] Engels underscored how the privatization of the reproductive labor so universally associated with women was a key force in their subordination. He noted that in the "old communistic household" women's work was "public" and "socially necessary," but in the monogamous, nuclear family "household management lost its public character. It no longer concerned society. It became a *private service*; the wife became the head servant, excluded from all participation in social production" (Engels 1972, 137).

Throughout the twentieth century, peasant and working-class Florentine women had almost total responsibility for reproduction, and some may have felt like "the head servant." Although women consistently participated in production, their labor was often undervalued and underpaid. Men gained status by performing socially valued production, their main role. They worked hard outside the home, but most were largely free of responsibility for reproductive labor in the home. Having primary responsibility for home and food contributed to Florentine women's low status, as it has historically done for women the world over.[9] This gender division of labor persisted throughout much of the twentieth century, and only at the turn of the millennium were there signs that young men and women were coming closer to parity in work inside and outside the home. This study hopes to contribute to feminist anthropology by using food as a conceptual lens to show how diverse arrangements of production and reproduction affected gender power in evolving twentieth-century Florence.

Chapter 2 describes the overarching structure of Florentine cuisine and its reflection of class, culture, and ideology. Chapter 3 locates the roots of Florentine foodways in history, beginning with the *mezzadria* peasant mode of production, which under rare optimal conditions produced a diversified, delicious, and healthy cuisine. But the peasants' ability to have adequate food competed with landlords' efforts to squeeze maximum surplus out of them, making scarcity a chronic threat. Women crossed the boundaries between production and reproduction because they worked in the fields, courtyard, and garden, as well as in the house. Their work was visible and recognized, but valued economically lower than the work of men who were legal heads of households. Two world wars and twenty years of fascism dealt a deathblow to the *mezzadria* system and its family structure, and launched the "Italian economic miracle" and transition to a fully capitalist mode of production.

Chapter 4 describes the Florentine diet and principal foods eaten by my subjects in the 1980s, and differences both from the first half of the twentieth century and from its close. Their foods still showed their roots in the peasant cuisine of the past but evinced changes due to prosperity and urban residence. These changes accelerated in the last two decades of the twentieth century, and by 2003 major changes had occurred in food, diet, and meals.

Chapters 5 and 6 describe how Florentine production, reproduction, and gender relations shifted as peasants migrated to the city and became laborers, artisans, and entrepreneurs. When families left the land, women's chores were privatized and lost social value, yet they were still a compelling component of women's identity and interfered with their ability to work outside the home. In the 1950s, '60s, '70s, and '80s, many Italian women were full-time housewives— a relative historical anomaly that the close of the millennium was reversing. In the 1980s, men accepted their privilege of irresponsibility in the home and women complied in the imbalance in domestic chores by defining themselves as *sacrificate*—"sacrificed." The production-reproduction division of labor caused imbalances and tensions in gender relations centered on disparate economic power and social value, and Florentines used a variety of strategies to cope with or minimize them, which they continued in the new millennium.

Chapter 7 explores the links between family and the broader community through food. It explores the meanings of commensality—eating together— and its role in defining the family and closing or opening its borders to outsiders. The most important way family members stayed in touch with each other was sitting around the table over and over again, twice a day, enjoying good meals together. Eating alone most gravely signified social isolation. My subjects' families were quite private, and both informal and ritualized food events were a major means of forging broader social ties. Eating together after the official engagement or *fidanzamento* incorporated in-laws into their new affinal families and involved a serious commitment to a lifelong relationship. Shopping for food was a daily activity for many women and a way of participating in the community, although it was time-consuming and was gradually dwindling as supermarket shopping mounted.

Chapter 8 focuses on foodways in the family to examine how parents socialized gender roles and ideology in their children. It takes inspiration from Riddiough's (1981) reminder that the family is a critical agent of what Gramsci (1955a, 1955b) called "civil society," which includes social institutions such as schools, churches, and clubs that uphold "hegemony"—the worldview and interests of the ruling class.[10] The Florentine family played an important role in

inculcating compliant ideologies in children. Both mothers and fathers reproduced male privilege by socializing their daughters to serve and their sons to
expect service.

Chapter 9 explores the lives of the younger people in the study who were
just leaving the parental nest and forging new families in 1984. It looks at the
burdens and conflicts they faced around work inside and outside of the home
and at their changing food habits. It reveals the continuing conflicts between
men and women around the unequal management and value of production
and reproduction. It examines the meanings of modernity for Florentines by
describing culinary transformations and the continuing subordination of
women. Chapter 10 concludes the book by describing Florentines' attitudes
toward changing foodways in the 1980s and assessing further changes that occurred at the close of the twentieth century.

Florence

Settled at least by Roman times and renowned as the heart of the Italian Renaissance, Florence is the *capoluogo* or capital of the province of Florence and
of the central Italian region of Tuscany. Even while serving as destination for
countless foreign visitors over the centuries, Florence kept a distinct regional
Italian identity. *Mezzadria* sharecropping and small, artisanal industry predominated in the province prior to World War II. After the war, the economy
shifted away from the land and into the secondary and tertiary sectors. Between 1951 and 1961, there was a 40 percent diminution in agricultural
employment with a corresponding but not equal rise in industrial and commercial work in the main centers of Florence, Prato, and Empoli.[11]

When my middle-aged and older subjects were reaching their productive
years before and after World War II, craftwork and industry predominated in
the province of Florence and produced objects "of quality, precision and artistic character" (Camera di Commercio 1958, 27). The major industries have
been wool and textiles, especially in and around Prato, where forty-five-year-
old Rinaldo owned a dying factory;[12] clothing, especially the raincoat industry
in Empoli, where forty-eight-year-old Laura was a garment worker; woodwork
and furniture; food, especially olive oil and wine; and glass, ceramics, leather,
shoes, jewelry, minerals, and editorial production. Florence itself has always
been "a seat of classic Italian craftwork" and has excelled in *artigianato artistico*—artistic craftwork—typified by enameling, embroidery, artistic leather
work, ceramics, stone carving, mosaics, cabinet-making (practiced by Baldo's
father), inlaid wood, wrought iron, straw weaving (practiced by Baldo's
mother), goldsmithing, and silversmithing (once practiced by seventy-one-
year-old Marco). Commerce has always employed many Florentines, especially in retail stores, particularly grocery stores and bakeries, like the family
bakery that sixty-six-year-old Elena worked in for years (Camera di Commercio 1958, 32–33). Tourism has also contributed greatly to Florence's economy

as well as to its reputation as being an arrogant city, grudgingly admitted to by some of its natives.

Sixty-six-year-old Elena said, *Florence is a closed city. It is difficult to enter into certain environments where people feel—not where they* are *but where they* feel— *a little bit better than others. For heavens sake! They look down on everyone else from up on high. You know, I really don't like Florentines very much. Florence would be a beautiful city if it weren't for the Florentines. Look, as for character, we Florentines are nothing good. We would even make fun of Jesus Christ! We're argumentative and we think we're always right. We are the ones who do everything best. We criticize everything—we're* **criticoni.** *We're also arrogant. . . . Florentines are arrogant, precisely by nature—that's how Florentines are. If I have to throw a lance in our favor, I can say that we are lovers of beauty. Just so as not to say nothing but ill of us, let's say that we are lovers of beautiful things. We have a real appreciation for art, literature, all these things. Other than that, arrogance and nothing else.*

Some of my Florentine subjects displayed characteristics described by Elena, but they were also warm, generous, and fun-loving. Like many Italians, they had a sense of assurance about their food being best, their language being the purest Italian, their political views being the most reasonable. They were proud of Florence, a stunningly beautiful city with a rich creative history visible at every turn. Florentines vaunted their exquisite taste and their beautiful craftwork. Millions of tourists flock to pay homage to Florence, eight million per year by one account—"seventeen per year for every inhabitant" (Plattner n.d., 10).

The population of the province of Florence went from just over 906,000 in 1951 to 1.2 million in 1981 and dropped slightly in 2000. From 1951 to 1981, the population of the *comune* of Florence (the city and township) went from 375,000 to 448,000. Much of that growth of the city's population came from in-migration from the surrounding countryside such as that represented by my oldest subjects, the brothers Renzo and Massimo, and Massimo's wife, Berta. Although the population continued to be refreshed in the last two decades of the century by immigrants from all over the globe, especially from Asia, Eastern Europe, and North Africa, the overall population of Florence dropped to 376,662 in 2000.[13]

The subjects of this book are twenty-three diverse individuals whose lives have been interwoven in various links of parentage. They are articulate and informative, like many people in their community. They have worked, struggled, and made their way as best they could, and they have constructed lives like and unlike those of other Florentines. Their stories are valuable because ordinary people have so often been ignored in the literature. Many scholars have written about Florence's famous architects, artists, poets, philosophers, and ruling politicians over the centuries, but rarely have they described the people—and then usually only a quick glimpse of a landlord, a favorite baker, a village cook, or a wry peasant. Scholars have written extensively about Florence's past, but little about its present. Anthropologists have not only ignored Florence, but they have also given relatively little attention to Italy's urban culture, a lacuna in a country with an urban tradition extending back millennia, which this book seeks to rectify through a focus on food to discuss recent Florentine history, culture, and social life.[14]

One Florentine Family

My twenty-three subjects come from peasant, working-class, shopkeeper, and artisan backgrounds.[15] Seven (three male and four female) belong to what I call the older generation, born between 1908 and 1924. Eight belong to the middle generation (four male and four female), born between 1930 and 1945. Eight belong to the younger generation (three male and five female), born between 1956 and 1972. In total, ten of my subjects are male and thirteen are female. None of the older generation has had more than a ninth-grade education and most have reached only fifth or sixth grade. Three of the middle generation have attained higher education degrees: Sergia, Leonardo, and Giovanna, born successively during the war in 1943, 1944, and 1945. Of the younger generation, none were pursuing higher education in 1984, but by 2003, Piero had graduated from the University of Rome. My subjects range from working class to upper middle class, and are blue- and white-collar workers, artisans, clerks, retirees, and housewives. All live comfortably and with adequate income and housing, but none belong to the Florentine economic, social, or political elite.

The kinship chart shows the members of the family at the time of the study (see Figure 1). When I did the interviews, twenty-three Florentines were living.[16] My aim is to use their stories to bring readers into their lives. Their stories reveal what they ate and how they talked and thought about food, which is at the heart of their identities, their relationships, and their daily rhythms.

One key informant was my former father-in-law, Renzo, a self-described self-made man whose story presented a microcosm of changes in Florentine history and culture over the twentieth century. Nicknamed by his friends, "*il lungo*" ("the long one," "the tall one"), because of his height, he was born into a *mezzadria* peasant family in 1911 in Trespiano, in the township of Florence, on one of the many hills surrounding the city. His family sharecropped the land until Renzo was twenty-one, when he left the land like thousands of other peasants in the inter- and postwar years and went to work as a city policeman (*vigile urbano*). He held this job for thirty-seven years, at first on street patrol, then as a motorcycle policeman, and finally in an office regulating commercial automobile licenses. Right after the war, Renzo and his wife, Grazia, became entrepreneurs as so many other Italians did, and they started a small in-home artisanal handbag business. They made sufficient income in combination with Renzo's salary as a city policeman to buy and sell several apartments and row homes and to live a comfortable middle-class life.

Renzo's first wife, Grazia, was also from *mezzadria* peasant stock and grew up on another of the many hills surrounding Florence, in the ancient Etruscan and Roman town of Fiesole. She died of complications from surgery in 1973, and seven years later Renzo married again. His second wife, Marianna, was the only one of my informants who grew up as a member of the urban proletariat and was born and raised in public housing in the city of Florence. She was very poor because her father was disabled by disease and could not work, and her mother barely made ends meet running a newspaper kiosk on Via dei Neri. Marianna was unusual because she remained single and lived alone for much of her adult life. She supported herself by working for thirty-eight years in the marriage license department in Palazzo Vecchio, the Florence City Hall, until she married Renzo in 1980 at the age of fifty-seven and retired with a secure pension.

Renzo's brother, Massimo, was born two years before him in 1909. In 1933, Massimo married a peasant woman named Berta, who was born in 1908 in a mountain hamlet near Montorsoli. Like Renzo, Massimo and Berta also left the land and did a variety of jobs until they opened a flower shop in 1958 in Via dei Bardi, a stone's throw from the renowned Ponte Vecchio on the south side of the Arno River in the zone called Oltrarno, which they ran until they retired in 1974 (see Figure 1.3).

In 1984, Massimo and Berta lived in a three-bedroom apartment in a working-class public housing development in Florence called Isolotto that was later privatized and sold to residents. In 1984, Massimo and Berta lived with their daughter Valeria, her husband Baldo, and their unmarried twenty-one year old son Arturo. By 2003, Massimo, Berta, and Baldo had died, and Valeria lived alone in her apartment. Her daughter Caterina and family lived a few doors away in Isolotto, where they had purchased an apartment in 1995, and her son Arturo and his family lived nearby and visited often.

Valeria was born at home in the village of Trespiano on the hill just 5 kilometers northwest of Florence in 1934, and her sister Laura was born in 1936. They grew up in Trespiano and completed fifth grade. Then, right after the war, they both started to work at fancy dressmaker shops in Florence. Later, they got engaged to two best friends from Empoli, a provincial town 35 kilometers from Florence. Valeria stopped working outside the home after marrying Baldo in 1955, but for many years continued to sew pieces at home. Baldo's parents were former peasants who resided in Empoli, where his father was a cabinet-maker. Baldo was born in Empoli in 1930, and after completing eighth grade, he went into carpentry with his father for a few years. But he did not like it, and in 1958, he began to work as a sales representative for the same textile firm that later also employed his wife's younger cousin Leonardo. Baldo had an operation for spine cancer in 1979 and never walked again. He died in 1995.

Baldo and Valeria had their first child, Caterina, in 1958, and their second, Arturo, in 1963. Caterina had a nursery school teaching certificate but was unable to find a permanent job in this field that she loved, so she ended up working as a cashier at the COOP supermarket. She found her job boring, stressful,

Fig. 1.3 The flower shop in Via dei Bardi that belonged to Massimo and Berta until 1974, photographed in March 2003 with a "*Pace*" ("Peace") sign protesting the U.S. invasion of Iraq

and unrewarding, but was glad for the income and the escape from being at home all the time. She married Sandro in 1981. Originally from the neighboring town of Scandicci, Sandro had moved to Florence as a young boy and grew up a few blocks from Caterina in Isolotto. He finished the Dental Technical Institute (*Istituto Tecnico Ortodontico*) and eventually started his own dental workshop making crowns, bridges, and false teeth. He and Caterina lived in Scandicci right after their marriage, and in 1995 bought a third-floor apartment just one door down from Valeria's apartment in Isolotto. They spent several months having it fixed up and turning it into a stunning modern home. They knocked down a wall to make a large living room, then they lowered the ceiling and raised the roof so that they created a *mansarda* or attic space for their daughter with a second bathroom. In 2003, Caterina was still working part-time at the COOP, Sandro was still a dental technician, their seventeen-year-old daughter was in high school, and their twelve-year-old son was in middle school.

Caterina's younger brother Arturo completed middle school in 1976 and started accounting high school, but disliked it and quit. When I interviewed him in 1984, he had done a series of blue-collar jobs as a stockboy, plumber's helper, and construction worker, and was looking for a permanent position. He was engaged to Maria and they planned to marry once they were economically more secure, with permanent jobs and their own apartment. Maria was of working-class origins. Her mother was a household domestic and her father was a mason. She had graduated from secretarial school, but was unable to find a job as a secretary, so she had done a series of short-term factory jobs while she looked for a more secure job. In 2003, Arturo was driving a meat delivery truck, and Maria was working as a custodian in a school and was considering further schooling to get a better job. They had two children and were hoping to soon buy an apartment of their own.

Arturo's aunt Laura was born in Trespiano in 1936, two years after her sister Valeria. In 1958, Laura married Raffaele, who had grown up best friends with Valeria's husband Baldo in Empoli. The bond between their husbands helped tie the sisters together throughout their lives, even though Laura and Raffaele resided in Empoli and Valeria and Baldo lived in Florence. Laura sewed pieces at home until the children were in school, then got a job in a garment factory specializing in raincoats—an industry that developed in Empoli in the late 1950s and early 1960s and was still going strong in the 1980s. Raffaele was born in 1930 and grew up in dire poverty as the son of a glass-blower. He became a master glass-blower himself, but quit that job to spare his health, and got a much lower-paying job as a *magazziniere*—a warehouse supervisor—in a Catholic nursing home. He was a factotum there until he retired in 1983. By 2003, Laura was also retired.

Raffaele and Laura had two children, Piero and Piera. Piero went to the Science High School for a while, but then he quit and completed a vocational degree as a nurse. In 1984, he had a full-time job working for the Tuscan region, which he enjoyed and which only occupied his mornings (7:30 A.M. to 1:30 P.M. five days a week). In the afternoons, he worked as a disc jockey in a local radio station. By 2003, he had completed a university degree and was working as a supervisor of nursing for the Tuscan region in Empoli. He had one child. His sister Piera never liked school, but she stayed at it long enough to get a vocational degree in accounting. Piera secured a full-time job right after graduation. In 1984, she was engaged to Antonio, who was about to depart for his mandatory eighteen months of military service. Later they married, and in 2003, Piera was still working as an accountant. Her husband was working in a food export firm. They had a six-year-old boy and a two-year-old girl.

This first group of families were the living relatives of Leonardo's father, Renzo, and fill the left side of the kinship chart (see Figure 1). On the right side of the chart are the relatives of Leonardo's mother, Grazia. Several also had *mezzadria* peasant origins in mountain villages northwest of Florence. Grazia was born in 1913 and raised in the village of Fiesole just outside of Florence, where the family moved from Doccia. Grazia's older sister Margherita married Giovanni, who was the youngest of thirteen children from Santa Brígida. Giovanni left the land at age twelve and worked at several trades until he managed to acquire his own bakery in Piazza Donatello in Florence, an excellent location where he, his wife Margherita, and their daughters Elena and Tommasa worked for years. Elena was born in 1918 in Florence, and she helped in the family bakery with only brief interruptions from her teen years until they sold it in 1964. She married Giorgio in 1943, and he became a draftsman in an engineering firm in 1945, just a few weeks before their daughter Giovanna was born. Giovanna finished high school and became a tour guide in Florence. She met Joseph, an Italian-American, when he was touring Florence, and married him in 1967. She moved to the United States, but she regularly made extended visits to Florence on her summer vacations from her high school teaching job, and her mother Elena visited her in Massachusetts. Giovanna graduated Phi Beta Kappa from college in 1976 at age thirty-one and received an M.A. in international relations in 1985. She and Joseph had two daughters, Georgia and Susan. In 2003, Giovanna was still teaching languages part-time in a public high school in the northern suburbs of Boston, where she had been working for more than twenty years.

Giovanna's aunt Tommasa, her mother's younger sister, was born in 1920. She too worked in the family bakery before her marriage to Marco in 1942, whereupon she became a full-time housewife. Marco grew up in a comfortable artisan family and followed in his father's footsteps, becoming a silversmith. He started helping in Tommasa's family's bakery during the war, however, and took over the running of the business when Tommasa's and Elena's father Giovanni died in 1947. Marco and Tommasa had one daughter, Sergia, born in 1943. Sergia had a university teaching degree in physical education, and taught for three years at the Institute for the Blind in Fiesole, until she married

Rinaldo and became a full-time housewife in 1967. She had two daughters, Eugenia born in 1970 and Ondina born in 1972. They lived in a beautiful, completely modernized stone country farmhouse on several acres of rolling Tuscan countryside, just outside of Florence near the village of Pozzolatico. Rinaldo was born and raised in Prato. His parents were former peasants who became fruit and vegetable dealers after World War I. Rinaldo began in the fruit and vegetable business, then built a very successful dyeing factory with his brother-in-law. He sold that business, took several years of retirement, then returned to work and was running a uniform laundry business in 2003. Sergia and Rinaldo's two daughters lived in apartments bought by their parents in Florence. Thirty-three-year-old Eugenia had finished the university and was teaching in a high school; thirty-one-year-old Ondina was studying in the university and was also working part-time in a public institution.

In the summers of 1982 and 1984, I conducted from one to several interviews, each lasting an hour or two, with these twenty-three Florentines. They spoke freely and told wonderful stories about food in their lives. I have used their words to present a picture of food, family, and gender in Florence and the surrounding area. Their interviews covered the period from the second decade of the twentieth century, when my oldest subjects' memories started, through 1984. Descriptions of the period since 1984 come from the published literature and from data gathered during a visit to Florence in March 2003. I use these data to examine how changes in the production, distribution, and consumption of food in Florence over the twentieth century have affected people's lives, gender identity, and family relations.

2
Florentine Cuisine and Culture

In paradiso ci si canta e ci si suona   *In Paradise we play and sing*
e di mangiare non se ne ragiona.   *and think not about eating.*

Tuscan proverb, from Massimo[1]

Introduction

The Florentine proverb defined paradise as the place where *non se ne ragiona* about eating—a complicated expression that means the food is beyond reason, without need for thinking. It implies the inescapable fact of life for many Florentines throughout the first two-thirds of the twentieth century—that they always had to fret about eating. Through their ways of talking about food, people identified themselves as Florentines and Tuscans. Sixty-six-year-old Elena, who in Chapter 1 criticized her fellow Florentines for their arrogance, was happy to proclaim her pride in their food: *Oh, we eat well in Florence; we eat very well. Our cooking is not very refined, but it is delicious. It's not sophisticated because generally we just do our best and don't make fancy dishes like they do in many places, in the Italian Piemonte region, for example. There they cook French style and they make refined dishes that are beautiful to look at. But they are less flavorful than ours because they are cooked with lots of butter and have a delicate taste. But our cooking uses hot pepper and pepper, you know. We use olive oil— the really good kind—and garlic, onion, and hot peppers. Yes, yes, we Florentines care about eating.*

By acclaiming her food, Elena expressed pride in her Florentine identity and differentiated herself from other Italians and Europeans. Like many Italians, Florentines constantly reproduced their cuisine and its meanings through cooking, improvising dishes, exchanging recipes, eating with others, and talking about food. Their culinary narratives were a meaningful expression of culture, history, identity, family, and gender.

Florentine cuisine in the 1970s and 1980s was a loosely coherent system of rules applied with some regularity and logic as people combined foods and spices, constructed recipes, and consumed meals in their homes.[2] This cuisine evolved from a centuries-old tradition of human transformation of the Tuscan natural environment through the *mezzadria* sharecropping system to produce foods consistent with agrarian potential, economic realities, and taste preferences. There was a dietary core of Florentine cuisine that was crucial to Florentine identity, but it varied in content, quality, and elaboration across class,

Fig. 2.1 The Tuscan countryside near Cerreto Guidi in 1984, with olive, grape, and grain growing

urban-rural residence, and history. Although Florentine cuisine was always evolving, in the 1980s it began to show signs of significant alterations associated with the broader social and economic changes of modernity. In this chapter I present a panoramic overview of the most important issues that emerged as Florentines talked about food in the 1980s. In Chapter 4, I describe their diet in detail.

Florentines called their cuisine *il mangiare fiorentino*—"Florentine eating"—and *la cucina fiorentina,* meaning both "Florentine cooking" and "the Florentine kitchen." Their language emphasized what was important to them about food—its eating and cooking—both of which have traditionally taken place in the kitchen, the heart of family life and the domain of women. In this book I use *Florentine* and *Tuscan* to refer to the cuisine of Florence and the surrounding towns and countryside of central Tuscany (see Figure 2.1), whose produce fed the city and whose peasants swelled its ranks after World Wars I and II. Florentine cuisine had its roots in the longstanding *mezzadria* mode of production described in Chapter 3, which influenced city dwellers as well as peasants due to the close connections between city and country. In fact, the diet described by both poor and moderate-income city dwellers was similar to that of the peasants, differing in quality and abundance, but not in basic structure and ingredients.[3] Florentines argued endlessly during long convivial hours of shared meals about what precisely was the proper way to make any given dish, and they all thought their own way best. While they claimed affinity with the cooking of their ancestors, they also improvised constantly, and their meals and cuisine were always evolving, as they surely always have.

Florentine foodways shared much with those of other Italians in central Italy and across the nation. They were affected by similar economic imperatives, nutritional science precepts, political policies, and expert advice in nutrition, domestic science, and cuisine (Helstosky 1996, 2004). Yet because of Italy's extreme cultural diversity and historic provincialism or *campanalismo,* Florentines were also distinct. This detailed study of the foodways of former peasants, artisans, shopkeepers, clerks, and small businesspeople hopes to show how Florentines' cuisine reflected their cultural identity in central ways. It was never static, and it varied across time, place, and economic station.

Cuisine and Cultural Identity

Florentines used food to define an identity grounded in their illustrious history. In the following passage, fifty-four-year-old Raffaele from Empoli used a quintessential Florentine dish—*minestra di pane** (bread soup)—to express the connection between food, history, and identity: *Take bread soup—minestra di pane—the famous bread and bean soup. That is a dish that I make often, because we really love it. First you have to cook the white beans, and that takes hours. Then you have to prepare all the vegetables, and then you have to cook them all together, understand? We take advantage of the fact that there are all these fresh local vegetables at this time of year in early summer, and make a soup that is really good. We eat it willingly.*

*We eat this soup with leftover bread, for the **minestra di pane** was invented by poor people, no? When there was leftover bread in the old days, it was a waste to throw it away, so what happened? Well, someone must have invented this **minestra di pane** one hundred, two hundred, I don't know how many years ago, maybe even five hundred years ago, because even Dante ate it. Even Leonardo da Vinci ate **minestra di pane**. Why? Because bread was an essential food at that time. . . . So they created these condiments based on bean or vegetable broth and soaked the bread in it. The bread softened in the broth and took on the taste of the vegetables and the beans—it took on an exceptional taste; it is truly delicious.*

*In Tuscany especially, people adore it, everybody knows this **minestra di pane**. There's not a person who hasn't eaten it. That's the way it is; it's like spaghetti; everyone has eaten it. In Tuscany it's more popular than anywhere else because we have our special bread that is different from other places. You couldn't make a bread soup in the Emilia region because they have that delicate white bread. You have to have thick dark bread like we have, and it has to be old, hard, and dry.*

Raffaele's words emphasized how eating *minestra di pane* distinguished Tuscans from other Italians, linking them together and to their illustrious past filled with the likes of Dante and Leonardo da Vinci.[4] It was uniquely theirs, edible in different variants, but with a fundamental identity linked to the flavors, beans, and bread. Raffaele also expressed how his cuisine tied him to his own ancestors: *When my wife and I married and found ourselves on our own, what happened? What happened was my wife watched how her mother made things, and I observed my mother, understand? And the same way of cooking continued. After I got married, when I went to eat at my mother's house, I didn't find any differences between her cooking and mine, and neither did my children, because we cooked the same way. I am sure that the way I eat now is the same way*

*Recipes marked with an asterisk are included in Appendix D.

my grandfather and grandmother ate in 1800—the same way my great-grandfather ate. They made the same genuine foods that we are still making now.

Eating the same things in the same way expressed Florentine cultural and familial continuity across generations. Raffaele went on: *The basic menu that we regularly eat at home is how I ate in my mother's time. Practically speaking, I haven't invented anything in cooking. I took everything my mother made when I was little, and my mother must have taken it from her mother. . . . In short, spaghetti are always spaghetti, pomarola (tomato sauce) is always pomarola, meat sauce is always meat sauce. We don't invent anything, understand?* But although food and his discourse about it enabled Raffaele to claim an unchanging cultural identity, in fact Florentine cuisine and culture were inexorably changing under the impact of modernity, and *pomarola* was not always *pomarola*.

Florentines affirmed their identity by loving best of all their own home cooking, *la cucina casalinga*. Fifty-four-year-old Baldo from Empoli said: *There's little to throw away in Tuscan cooking. So many times, even when we go out to eat at a country restaurant, they bring us something new like perhaps wild boar cooked in some special way, and it is exquisite and we eat it willingly. In Tuscany we have this good fortune that all our food is delicious. In fact, we feel the blow when we travel elsewhere. My wife doesn't have any problems, but I do. These little soufflés, these little things in cream sauce—they don't appeal to me at all. I like home-style cooking—roba casalinga—especially my wife Valeria's cooking. For example, I like lasagna, but when she makes it, it is better than in restaurants. I eat it with more pleasure.*

Baldo put home cooking at the top of the culinary hierarchy, as many Florentines did. And like him, many expressed distaste for other cuisines— whether in Italy or abroad—as Elena complained above about the cuisine of the Piemonte region. Their food chauvinism was an overt expression of cultural identity, as Baldo made clear: *I don't like British cooking. I tried it at the hotel we stayed at in Palma di Mallorca. For us Tuscans it was a struggle to find something to eat to satisfy our hunger without feeling revolted. I don't like French cooking either. Fortunately, when I went to visit Marseilles, I stayed with my Italian relatives and ate with them. They have been there sixty years and they are retired now. They have always eaten Italian food. They make special trips into downtown Marseilles to buy Italian ingredients so they can cook Italian fare.* This stubborn habit of clinging to their own food wherever they went—even in France, a renowned center of gastronomy—was a legendary habit of Italians. Not only did Italian immigrants reproduce (and certainly modify) their cuisine in homes and restaurants all over the New World, but Italian tourists were famous for wanting to eat Italian pasta wherever they traveled (Corti 1998, Diner 2001, Levenstein 1985).

In the following story, Rinaldo, the forty-five-year-old owner of a cloth-dyeing factory in Prato, expressed his Tuscan culinary chauvinism: *I don't like a lot of sophisticated cooking, because we're not raised that way. But let me tell you this story about one time I went to Paris and had to eat duck in peach sauce. In Paris we work with French importers of our cloth and have a close relationship with them for everything to do with the colors and so on. So after years of working together, I went to Paris and the business colleagues took me to one of the best restaurants. One of them started raving about the specialty of the house—duck in peach sauce. He went on and on about how good this was. So I had to order it. Well, you know that French cooking is more sophisticated than ours, right? When the waiter brought it, I saw this duck in this thick peach syrup—this dense, rather sweet sauce. As soon as I tasted it, I was nauseated, truly revolted. However, this man kept saying, "Eh, how is it Rinaldo? How is it?" I absolutely could not tell him that I didn't like it. I found myself in the situation where I had to eat that duck in peach sauce even though it was completely disgusting to me. I could not refuse it. He was so content, so satisfied that he had enabled me to try this specialty that I would have eaten two of them so as not to offend him. He would have been really mortified because he had sung the praises of this dish so much beforehand. And he kept on saying at the table how good it was. Therefore I gave it all my effort.*

But I like simple foods. I don't go for sophisticated dishes—like soufflés, for example—I've tried them many times, but I just don't like them. They don't have any exact flavor but they have a strange taste. I never had them growing up. I don't like them. I don't like sophisticated foods and I try to avoid them. I had to eat that duck in peach sauce once, but I won't get caught again, eh. By now I have understood the kinds of foods that I like. If I go to a restaurant, I choose simple things, like **carpaccio**, *for example. It is a really thin slice of cured meat, not cooked, but steeped in olive oil, vinegar, and some other things. It's eaten with a light mayonnaise on top with other herbs and it is fabulous, really delicious, and very light too. I also like, for example, raw onions with tuna fish, or prosciutto.* In his next words, Rinaldo reiterated a central Tuscan value, rooted in a tradition of scarcity, *It's the quality not the quantity that counts for me.*

He also emphasized the basic foundation of Tuscan cuisine: *I'm happy if you make me a good* **pomarola***, *or a good meat sauce, or, I don't know, a risotto. I can dine with risotto—that's how I am. I can make a dinner out of it. I have two big plates full and that's enough. Or polenta. I love polenta. It's rare for me to stray from simple Tuscan cuisine.* For Rinaldo and many others, contented consumption of simple Tuscan cuisine enduring across families and generations was an important expression of cultural identity.

Cuisine and Gender

Florentines also expressed and enacted gender identity through foodways. Across the twentieth century, a rigid sexual division of labor prevailed, and men and women had clearly defined food roles: women to cook, serve, and clean up after food; men to produce and eat it. Their interdependent food roles mirrored and established interdependent gender roles, aptly expressed by sixty-six-year-old Elena, who said of her relationship with her husband Giorgio, *Forse ci si compensava a vicenda—maybe we counterbalanced each other.* Both a man and a woman were needed in a household to ensure the survival of the family. But since men's work was valued more highly, women had to contend with a societal and familial imbalance that disfavored them and privileged men. In Chapters 5, 6, 8, and 9 Florentines' food-centered narratives present the diverse, complex, and shifting workings of gender.

Cuisine and Class

Although Chapter 4 describes a basic Florentine cuisine, Florentines' diets varied according to their class as they have across many cultures and epochs.[5] In both urban and rural Tuscan families, socioeconomic differences in diet emerged principally through the greater consumption by the wealthy of meat, fats, and luxury foods such as coffee, wine, and sweets. That early–twentieth–century French chef Louis Monod's definition of *la cucina fiorentina* was steeped in the upper classes is revealed in the fact that his cookbook of 190 pages had 68 pages of meat recipes on beef, veal, pork, lamb, poultry, and game—foods that most Florentines rarely ate.[6]

Seventy-two-year-old Marco, raised in a family of silversmiths, said, *In the old days there was a class of workers who could not afford meat because they earned very little. They couldn't possibly eat meat every day. But there were other classes who could eat meat—artisans like we were, shopkeepers, and the true upper classes (i veri signori).*

Marco's sixty-four-year-old wife Tommasa confirmed her husband's view: *We were always pretty well off because my father had a store, no? He and my mother had a bakery. Because of that, we were relatively well off and could eat better than many. We ate meat every day, at least once a day.* Tommasa's sister, sixty-six-year-old Elena, agreed: *When my father was still alive, we had meat every day. Well, sometimes during the war no, because you couldn't find it then. But normally we had meat every day. Whether it was boiled with broth, or whether it was a roast, or whether it was chicken on Sunday, or little steaks flipped over and done, well in short, my father wanted meat every day. Very often we had meat at the evening meal too. And if not, at supper we ate prosciutto, salami, cheese, those kinds of things.*

Not only did the rich have more meat, but they also had more of other prized and expensive foods including cheese, fruit, sweets, wine, olive oil, butter, and fats in general. Children of the rich had white bread and meat for snacks (Helstosky 2004, chapter 4), while children of the poor ate brown bread with oil, wine, and sugar, or nothing at all. Marianna described her school days in the late 1920s and early 1930s: *Often when I went to school, all the other children had a snack to eat. Sometimes I had some bread; sometimes I didn't even have that. So the teacher called me over next to her. She said, "Marianna, come and sit here," because she knew I didn't have anything to eat.*

The diet of the poor lacked luxuries and was based on bread, cereals, legumes, and other vegetables. Marco described the diet of laborers: *Oh, people used to eat much more bread in the old days. Many masons and construction workers used to bring their lunch on their bicycles to work. When noon came, they sat there on the curb of the sidewalk and they took out these big chunks of bread. They had taken out the bread's soft inner part—the* **mollica**[7]*—and filled up the space with cooked white beans (***fagioli***), tomatoes, or eggs cooked at home the night before.*

Back then the workers didn't use butter, for it was too expensive. In the morning they had bread and surrogate coffee made of chicory or barley with milk—that was all. They didn't have anything else. But we did. We were in better conditions, and so I used to eat bread and cookies, or bread and butter.

There was so much poverty in the old days that instead of buying a flask of olive oil at a time, people went with a tiny little bottle to buy it. They bought a half a cup of olive oil at a time because they were so poor. You know, people earned very little. They worked so hard, but they earned nothing. There is a Tuscan saying that describes how they used olive oil to dress something in the old days: **fare il C**—*"to make a C." It was a way of describing how you made just a quick swirl with the olive oil and that was all, because it cost so much.*[8] None of my subjects remembered eating a lot of olive oil before the economic boom of the 1960s—a fact that was supported by Apergi and Bianco's (1991) study of mezzadria farmers and Lo Russo's (1999, 30) claim that it was only in the second half of the twentieth century that olive oil lost its "luxury character" and became widespread.

Sixty-one-year-old Marianna grew up extremely poor in urban Florence in the 1930s and 1940s. Her father was disabled and her mother earned barely enough to feed them by running a newspaper kiosk. Marianna's recollections of her childhood diet confirmed the differences in food consumption by class noted by Marco and Tommasa: *In the morning we all ate bread. My brothers took a big hunk of bread to work with them. They opened the bread and put the* **companatico** *(accompaniment) inside, and they closed it back up. Sometimes they put potatoes inside, sometimes cooked eggs—***frittata***—made by my mother. They also put in the refried leftover boiled meat, which we called* **lesso rifatto.*** *After boiling the meat to make a broth, we refried it with onions and potatoes. It had more substance that way. Even if there was just a little meat, we used to say,* "**lo stuffato di pelliccia, di molte patate e poca ciccia**"—*"the stew made of skin, with lots of potatoes and otherwise thin."*[9] *Sometimes we bought the cow's cheek—***la guancia***. It was good; we cut it into pieces; it cost much less than other meat. That's how we were. In my house, we tried to fill ourselves up even if we didn't have very much.*

In addition to eating little meat, Marianna's family lacked other expensive foods: *We hardly ever ate fruit, because how could we do it? We couldn't afford to buy it. But listen to what my mother sometimes did. She delivered newspapers along a route all over the center of Florence, around Piazza del Duomo, Santa*

Croce, all around there. There were some greengrocer shops and sometimes they kept some fruit for her. "Giulia, look, take this, bring it to your daughter." Oh, that was like Easter for me.

*In the old days we ate a lot of ricotta because it was very cheap. But butter—we only bought a little every once in a while because we couldn't afford it. . . . How could we afford it? We bought some every now and then to make a little **minest-rina*** or pasta with butter. I used to say, "When I grow up, I'm always going to make pasta with butter." I liked it so much, but we couldn't afford to eat it often. In those days it wasn't like today, eh; they sold butter in little 2-ounce pieces back then. Olive oil was the same; you could go and ask for a little tiny bit: "Give me one-half liter of oil."*

But while Marianna lacked luxury foods, during most of her childhood she ate plenty of vegetables, pasta, and bread, which staved off hunger. She said: *When I was little, I didn't go hungry. I was already used to the foods that we ate. You know, a few greens, and **minestra** every evening, maybe with a little olive oil. I had already gotten my mouth used to all the food we ate. Maybe we had, I don't know, a great big pan full of artichokes cut in pieces and cooked in sauce. Or maybe we had fried potatoes eaten with a little tomato sauce. Bread, bread, bread. Sometimes we even lacked bread, or it was the only thing that we had to eat. A woman said to me once, "Aren't you ashamed to tell all this?"*

I replied, "But excuse me, I really didn't do any harm to anybody, so why should I be ashamed?" Today I remember the foods we used to eat then and I eat them willingly. That means that I must have eaten them willingly as a child, because if not, I wouldn't eat them again happily.

Marianna's remark, *I had already gotten my mouth used to all the food we ate,* underscored the link between food consumption and culture. And for Marianna, the legumes, grains, and vegetables were a satisfying diet: *We ate, for example, **le bacelle**, dried fava beans, fresh fava beans. I ate them right after the war. Oh, we made some huge pans of them when I was living with my cousin. Last year I made **fave al pomodoro*** (fava beans in tomato sauce) for my husband Renzo. He said, "Make some for me. Go on." They were good and I ate them feeling satisfied and tranquil. I eat again willingly the foods I ate when I was young. All of it makes my mouth water.* Marianna's childhood foods followed the basic patterns of Tuscan cuisine, limited in meat and fats due to her family's poverty. Habit, hunger, freshness, flavorful cooking, and association with family made the foods beloved and important fifty years later when her economic situation permitted her a much richer diet.

Like Marianna, fifty-four-year-old Baldo grew up in the city, but in the smaller and more provincial Empoli, 35 kilometers from Florence. His parents grew up as peasants, but they moved to town where his father was a cabinet-maker, a *falegname,* and his mother ran the house and braided straw on Chianti flasks at home. Their diet also reflected their peasant roots and modest resources compounded by the limitations of city life. Baldo narrated: *I remem-*

ber that in my family when I was little we used to eat a lot of one-pot meals. We used to call those dishes the **tegamata**—the potful. You took a little meat and a lot of potatoes and you made a big pot full of that. Maybe another day we ate herring, or some other dried fish. Something I never thought I would get to eat when I was a child was a banana. I used to long for a banana when I went by the greengrocery. I looked at those bananas and I had such a desire to eat one, and I couldn't. How could I? With what a banana cost, we could buy dinner for all of us. There was no way we could afford to buy me a banana.[10]

Baldo's recollections underscored the widespread poverty: *In the old days we only ate things that cost little—things like anchovies, sardines, **salacchine**, **baccalà**, lard—those were things that had price controls and so were cheap. Chickpeas, beans, lettuce—these things were inexpensive. One of the cheapest things of all was chestnut flour—used for making **castagnaccio**—a sweet cake.*

Baldo had a vivid memory of bread, the most basic food: *I remember when I was little and going to school, we used to hear the doorbell ring at five or five-thirty in the morning. We lived on the fourth floor and my mother used to lower a basket down to the street for the bread-man—the **semelaio**.[11] This man went around every morning to his regular customers and knew how many rolls to deliver. Then my mother prepared them for us to take to school. She spread some marmalade on them that she had made after picking blackberries or other fruit out in the countryside. We took that with us to eat at school.* The scarcity of food for most Tuscans, like Baldo, meant that it was intensely consumed and vividly remembered.

Cuisine and Memory

Eating is recalling, Baldo said, *il mangiare è un richiamo*. That eating was a *richiamo* (*ri*, meaning "again," and *chiamare*, meaning "to call or name") suggests that it was a remembering, a calling back, and an attraction.[12] Because the consumption of foods caused physical sensations, often of great pleasure, sometimes of severe repugnance, meals lodged memories not only in people's minds but also in their bodies. Because foods were structured into dishes, meals, and daily and annual rhythms, their consumption had an order that assisted remembering. In the multiple sensory properties of food—sight, smell, texture, and taste—lay multiple ways of conveying meanings and memories.[13] Florentines repeatedly slipped into reminiscences as they recalled either wonderful or loathsome eating events. As Rinaldo's tale of the duck in peach sauce exemplified, a disgusting dinner left a strong memory as well as a bad taste. Moreover, unpleasant mealtime interactions could ruin good food. But when in good company a good meal filled the belly, corporeal contentment intensified recollection. Baldo's memory of the **semelaio** delivering fresh rolls in the morning linked him to his childhood, his past, and his mother's care.

Particularly desired foods became associated with particularly vivid memories. For example, seventy-three-year-old Renzo remembered ice cream: *Do you know what we did as kids to eat ice cream? There was one man who made it every Sunday in summer, two kinds, vanilla and chocolate. . . . He took a big container of wood like this, with ice inside it, and then he took a smaller copper container and put it inside this ice, and then we kids went "zum, zum, zum," and turned it and turned it until we turned it enough to make the ice cream. . . . And if by midnight he hadn't sold it all, well then we ate up the rest of it. Because it was impossible to keep it until the next day—there were no refrigerators then. So he sold it to us for very little, and we were there, all of us waiting. "Let's hope nobody else comes to buy ice cream." That was the scene every Sunday. When it got near midnight we said, "Only a little more to wait," and fortunately often there was plenty left, and for just a little money we bought it, all of us friends from up there in Trespiano.*

A strong memory of childhood and friendship was attached to the avid consumption of a rare and much-desired food—ice cream—which represented sumptuousness because it was made of high-fat cream rarely available to the poor, because it was sweet, and because it depended on the luxury of ice. Very often special rituals were celebrated with special foods with unique ingredients and flavors that reinforced the Florentines' memory. For example, Marianna remembered eating *finocchiona*—fennel-flavored salame—on her twenty-first birthday, because it was during the war and that was all she had.

Certain foods can become emblematic "objects of memory" (Sutton 2001), symbols of the past that are no longer regularly consumed because too difficult to prepare or no longer palatable or customary. Many such foods were emerging in Florence like the **minestra di pane** evoked by Raffaele above, and the bread, wine, and sugar snack recalled by forty-five-year-old factory owner Rinaldo from Prato:[14] *I don't remember much about what we used to eat back when I was a boy. I only remember one thing—the* **merende**—*the snacks, the delicious snacks that I haven't eaten since. Oh, I remember them—a slice of bread sprinkled with sugar and a little wine. Have you ever eaten that? I used to eat it every summer when my parents sent me out to the country to live with my aunt and uncle on their farm. Because my parents were very busy working and couldn't supervise me, they sent me out there to that farm, 6 or 7 kilometers from Prato. I loved it. I remember these delicious snacks made simply with bread, sugar and wine. The taste is stupendous. I've got to eat it again sometime soon—one of these days I'm going to have it. I'll have my daughters try it. I also used to eat bread, olive oil, and salt, but I remember best the bread with these layers of sugar. Maybe it's because in those days we felt a much greater desire for sugar because there was so much less.*

Today this farm is unrecognizable. It is unrecognizable. I went back there recently. Three years ago I stopped there in my car and I went on foot to look at the farm because I had been wanting to go for a long time. I walked in. There used to be this ditch of pure limpid water where we set traps to catch eels. I found the ditch and it was rotten, covered with dirty foam, and the water was a nauseating, sur-

real blue. When they built the highway, it cut the farm in half. Oh, it was better if I hadn't gone back there. At least this new image wouldn't have taken over my mind and I could have kept the old memories.

Recollection of a delicious traditional snack no longer eaten triggered Rinaldo's memory of a life and a countryside no longer extant. His memory moved from the beloved food he used to savor to the countryside where he ate it, to the degradation of that environment. Eating the traditional foods that they ate as children and that their parents and grandparents had eaten tied my subjects to their past. Even as they evoked and clung to that past in memory, it receded in reality as the environment suffered, local farming struggled, processed foods appeared, and cuisine changed. For my subjects, cooking and eating traditional Tuscan foods was a continual and powerful channel for memory as well as an enactment of class status and cultural identity. The growing replacement of their foods with more highly processed and quicker ones signified a transformation of their connection to their history, their traditional social life, and their memories.

Gola: Desire, Pleasure, and Moderation

A striking thing about Florentines' cuisine was how much they loved to eat yet how they also valued moderation.[15] They took their food seriously, prepared it thoughtfully, and ate it enthusiastically. Food was one of their main topics of conversation. At work, among relatives and friends, at meals, and while grocery shopping, Florentine women constantly discussed what they ate last night and planned to cook today, and bantered about the right way to prepare certain dishes. They believed their food was the best and they extolled its simplicity, freshness, variety, and rich flavor. Because food was so important to them, their attitudes toward eating revealed significant cultural beliefs about the self.

All of my subjects expressed enthusiasm for eating. As fifty-four-year-old Raffaele said, *I really love to eat—a me mi garba tanto mangiare.* Florentines called their love for food *gola,* which meant not gluttony as some dictionaries translate but "desire or longing for food." Gluttony implied an evil excess of desire that Florentines shunned, but they celebrated the sensual pleasure of eating delicious food. Many of my subjects described themselves or others as *golosa/o* or "avid, desirous, eager for" certain foods like pasta, sweets, or bread, as Baldo said, *Sono goloso di pane—I'm desirous for bread.* They might use the word *ghiotta/o*—"ravenous or gluttonous"—as Marianna called her mother *ghiotta della cioccolata—ravenous for chocolate.*

Love of food was a legitimate sensual pleasure for Florentine men and women. They felt that they had a right to enjoy food and that eating with gusto was a licit form of self-expression. *Gola* meant not only desire for food but also "throat," the passageway for speech and breath as well as food. These overlapping meanings linked taking pleasure in food to breathing and speech, to life

and self. Furthermore, because eating in Florence was inherently and unequiv-
ocally social, enjoying food was also a constant reaffirmation of family and
broader social relations.

Florentines' wholehearted approval of enjoying food had roots in their
peasant past. Peasants developed a visceral awareness of the need to fuel their
bodies to do their physically onerous work (Falassi 1980, 11–12). For peasants,
hunger was always knocking at the door, so pleasure in food was precarious
and valued. Distrust of excess consumption typified *mezzadria* peasants as
well as contemporary urban Florentines. Peasant proverbs encoded a sense of
measure: *Chi mangia troppo, la pancia li dole, e chi non mangia, lavorar non
pole*—"Who eats too much has his belly hurt; who does not eat, cannot work";
and *E' meglio alzarsi da tavola colla fame*—"It's better to get up from the table
feeling hungry" (Falassi 1980, 12).[16] Pecori (1980) reprinted the proverb: *Il
Fiorentino mangia sì poco e sì pulito, che sempre si conserva l'appetito*—"The
Florentine eats so neat and so small, that his appetite quits not at all."

Condemnation of excess consumption persisted among my subjects in the
1980s. For example, forty-five-year-old Rinaldo from Prato said, *I love to eat,
but I'm not a mangione*—*an excessively big eater.* Raffaele from Empoli said, *I
love to eat but non mi abbuffo*—*I don't pig out.* They distinguished between enjoying luscious food and eating to excess. As Rinaldo said above, *It's the quality,
not the quantity that counts for me.* Marianna's family imbibed her father's philosophy: "*Poco, ma buono*—*only a little, but let it be good.*" These values on taking pleasure in food and accepting parsimony were widespread among the
working and peasant classes in Italy due to decades of food scarcity and to
public political and scientific policies promoting measured food consumption
(Helstosky 2004).

Florentines valued the ability to control their eating. For example, twenty-
one-year-old Arturo said, *Look, as far as desire goes, I'm the type that until I'm
full, really full, I would keep eating. However, I try to brake myself (frenarmi) a
little.* Sixty-six-year-old Elena also used the word *frenarmi* in describing her
desire: *Yes, I'll tell you, I'm a little golosa. I'm golosa. I try to brake myself (frenarmi), but I'm golosa. Every now and then I feel the desire to eat something sweet.
So I go in the kitchen, and I look for, I don't know, the jam jar, a candy, something,
because it is clear that I need something sweet. If I don't have anything, I have to
put my shoes on and go out and buy myself something sweet. A couple of pastries
or something like that. Maybe I eat that and nothing else, but I feel the need to eat
it. Maybe my blood sugar falls or something. Sometimes I make a rice cake—torta
di riso*—which is delicious. It is just a simple home-style dish, but it is good. I
cook rice in milk, add eggs, sugar, a pinch of salt, and grated lemon peel. If I have
some, I add candied fruits or a little bit of rum or other liqueur or sometimes some
cocoa to vary the color and flavor.*

Elena respected the compulsion of desire, but also felt it had to be controlled. A baker's daughter, she recounted a story about pastries that revealed

the widely held belief that excess consumption destroyed desire and pleasure. *I remember that at one point my father decided to sell pastries as well as bread in our bakery. He hired a highly skilled confectioner—a **pasticciere**—who made exquisite pastries. Imagine, Sunday we had a line of cars in front of the bakery filled with people who came to buy our pastries because they were so good. I remember that on the first day that the pastry chef began with us, my father said to my sister Tommasa and me, "Girls, here are the sweet pastries. Eat as many of them as you want. Don't hold back. Go right ahead and eat as many as you want." And off we went, eating, eating, eating, eating—so much that the next day we could not even look at a pastry. And then we realized why he had urged us to dig in. Oh, we had such a nausea—we couldn't even look at those sweets. That was it; we had had enough, because after that, we could never eat another one.* Elena's words expressed a cultural belief in striking a balance between enjoying food greatly and consuming it moderately. Uncontrolled gluttony was bad because it destroyed delectation. But in the 1980s and even more at the turn of the millennium, Florentines were increasingly able to consume ever more abundantly.

Eating as Consolation

All Florentines recognized that eating brought satisfaction and pleasure, and for some it was an extremely important source of emotional comfort. Fifty-year-old Valeria said, *I have the kind of nervous system that I don't get mad, no, no, but I eat and eat in continuation until food comes out my ears. It's not hunger because I feel uncomfortably stuffed, but it's stronger than me. I can't help myself; I have to eat. It stems from my nerves—a doctor told me this. I need to treat my nerves. Do you know how many times I have said this? But the doctors always said, "Oh, no, just eat less." They told me this as if that was all there was to it. Instead, when I feel anxious, I feel that I have to eat. It doesn't matter what, as long as I eat. . . . Then maybe an hour later, I go back and I get something else. It's not like I eat huge sandwiches, but I snack (**sperluzzico**). I went through a period where I used to eat in the middle of the night—I had to eat. I am capable of eating four or five cookies in the middle of the night. In short, I eat things that I shouldn't eat, especially at that hour. I feel badly afterward because I feel stuffed and uncomfortable, but at the same time I always feel the craving for food, especially in these anxious periods. I don't know why, but when I'm in a state of anxiety, the need to put something in my mouth is overwhelming.*

Her daughter, twenty-six-year-old Caterina, expressed a similar relationship to food: *Look, when I am nervous, I would eat even an ox. For my nerves, understand? For release, I don't know, a kind of release. I don't understand it; it's just instinctive; it's stronger than me. I am like my mother. There's little to do about it. We vent ourselves by eating.*

The use of food to express and calm emotions was both dangerous and salutary.[17] It was dangerous because it could lead to excess weight gain that could threaten health and trigger diabetes. Caterina, for example, had been told by her gynecologist to lose weight to facilitate conceiving the child she wanted. She also feared developing adult-onset diabetes like her mother's mother Berta, who died from complications of the disease. Valeria weighed nearly 200 pounds and attributed her difficulty walking and her physical discomfort to her excess weight. But using food for consolation was salutary because it helped deal with difficult situations. Valeria had to bear Baldo's debilitating illness that left him bedridden for years. She had to manage the increased workload and bolster Baldo's spirits. His illness on top of her heavy caretaking role put Valeria under considerable stress. Eating helped her cope and assuaged her nerves because of its gratifying effect on both body and soul.

Health: Balance with Body and Nature

Although eating when anxious brought consolation to Valeria and Caterina, Florentines believed that excess eating not only ruined the pleasure of food but also destroyed the body's health that depended on measured consumption and balance between types of foods.[18] For example, Florentines eschewed extreme temperature differences between foods and the body, so they never drank ice cold drinks on hot days. Many avoided excessively spicy foods, and they ate meat moderately and in conjunction with vegetables, pasta, or bread. Most of my subjects drank wine at *pranzo* and *cena*—only at meals—and usually only a glass or two; never did I see any of them drunk.

Only my oldest subjects remembered using traditional folk healing techniques such as curing stomachaches with castor oil and applying the fat from pigs or sheep to treat colds or muscle aches.[19] Sixty-six-year-old Elena said that in her youth they used *sugna for pains. Sugna was a special kind of pig fat, aged, because if it was fresh it did nothing. It had to be aged for many years and stinking, and then they used it to cure their aches and pains. They rubbed it to make friction in the place of the pain.*

All my Florentine subjects advocated the traditional dietary treatment for illness—*mangiare in bianco*—literally, "to eat in white," meaning to eat bland foods.[20] When sick with stomach flu or fever, people ate rice or pasta with just a little butter or olive oil. They implicitly distinguished such "white" consumption from eating rice and pasta made with red tomato or brown meat sauces. Raffaele said, *If someone is sick, we'll cook rice with olive oil or rice with butter for the sick person and the rest of us will eat spaghetti with sauce.* White foods were believed easily digestible and restorative, allowing the body to regain its health. Seventy-six-year-old Berta said that when she was a peasant girl in the hills outside of Florence, *If someone was feeling sick and it wasn't too serious, they made her a little pap—una pappina—with a little bit of olive oil—or a little flour gruel—una farinata. They took flour ground from their own grain and mixed it up with water and boiled it. It had to be thin and soft to be restorative.*

Coffee was also defined as a treatment for illness. As seventy-five-year-old former peasant Massimo said, *We had coffee only when we were sick.* Marianna's father was sick all her life, first with bone tuberculosis and then with cancer. She remembered him getting special foods for strength: *Sometimes my father might have an egg, a raw egg beaten with sugar in the morning, because he was sick. No one begrudged it to him, truly. That egg did him good. We hardly ever had coffee, but if we did, it was for my father. In the old days, coffee was for sick people.* Seventy-three-year-old Renzo said, *When a woman went to buy coffee back then, they asked her, "Do you have someone sick at home?"* He added that when he contracted pneumonia right after World War II, he had to eat raw eggs and horsemeat as well as coffee to regain his strength.

Sixty-six-year-old Elena told of getting sick with worms from eating too many sweets that disturbed her body's equilibrium. Garlic and magic combined to make her well. *They told me when I was little I used to suffer from worms. I'll tell you how I got sick with worms. My father had his bakery in the piazza in Fiesole then, when I was really little, one or one and a half. I had just begun to walk, they told me. I used to wander around that piazza, which was always full of foreigners. Because I was a very sociable child, I went there and I talked with everyone, even though we couldn't understand each other. My mother recounted that I always came back to the bakery with my little apron full of candies, sweets, and pastries. My mother always said, "I had no idea how many they gave you. You brought some back home, but who knows how many you had eaten?" Oh, I ate them. Frankly, I admit I ate them. So because I ate so many sweets, I became infested with worms.*

*I have to tell you that I was near death from those worms. I really was. I grew up wearing a little necklace of garlic (**la collanina d'aglio**) until finally I rebelled and I said, "I won't wear it anymore." I wore it from the time of my birth. My grandmother burned some garlic, threaded a string through it, and hung it around my neck. They said that it made the worms go away, intestinal worms. My grandmother said, "You'll see, you'll see, with the little necklace of garlic they will flee." They say that they fled. Thank heavens I don't remember this because I have a terror of worms, a real terror.*

*I remember that there was an old woman in Fiesole, really, really old, who cast a spell to get rid of these worms (**segnava bachi**). I remember my mother telling me that I was like a little blob on the bed so sick was I with worms, but the doctor said it wasn't anything. So my mother called in this old woman, Tonina, who came and cast a spell on the worms, and I got well. They used to say that sometimes I vomited the worms out of my mouth.* Elena's graphic story described how an overindulgence of sweets made her sick, and a cure of magic and garlic restored her body's balance and health by causing her to vomit the worms that represented her immoderation back out of the mouth that had ingested them.

Florentines also believed that emotional distress could upset the body's psychosomatic balance, and special herbs or foods could restore it. In the following story, Elena told of how a severe fright threatened her body with illness and how her grandmother used an herb to make her well: *When I was young, there were many herbal cures. There was the famous "herb for fear"—l'erba da paura.*[21] *It is a plant that my grandmother Lisa used to gather in the forests, a special herb. My grandmother said that when a child got severely frightened, it was necessary to treat her with this herb for fear so that the child would not get sick.*

I remember one time when I was little and I was nearly run over by the tram in Via della Colonna. I was in first grade, and I used to go to school by myself because my mother and father were too busy in the bakery to accompany me. So one day when I came out of school, I saw my uncle in the distance, coming to get me with his bicycle. From the joy of seeing my uncle coming to pick me up—because I never had anyone come for me—I started to run towards him. I ran across the street in the exact moment that the tram was passing. Luckily, instead of running me over, it hit me and threw me a great distance. Then I lost consciousness and I didn't know what was happening. I remember vaguely that this uncle carried me home and then they took me to the doctor. The doctor checked me all over and I didn't have anything except a huge swollen ankle that I've always felt a little bit ever since. Then my grandmother immediately took off to Fiesole and searched in the woods for the herb for fear. I remember that my mother made an infusion from it and washed my legs with this black water to keep me from getting sick.

Florentine health beliefs mandated a psychosomatic corporeal balance dependent on proper eating with moderate consumption of complementary foods. They celebrated eating but disdained excess. Traditionally, they believed that a plump body reflected good health, emotional stability, and good care, and that a too thin body revealed poor health, emotional distress, and social neglect; Florentines especially loved fat babies.[22] Excessive thinness was problematical as the following story by sixty-six-year-old Elena revealed: *As a young girl I never ate. I would go even a week without eating. You see, I realized as an adult why I didn't eat—because in my house there was discord between my father and my mother. . . . I heard my parents arguing and my stomach closed and I couldn't eat. . . . So then my parents were extremely worried about me—not eating today, not eating tomorrow—it was bad. But I realized later that I didn't eat precisely because of my parents' disharmony. I am frighteningly emotional, so much so that from not eating—because I ate nothing—I found myself in bad shape. My health promised nothing good. I always had a fever. I was continually losing my voice. So they took me to the doctor, and he found that I had swollen glands that were of course due to my bad nutrition—to the fact that I didn't eat, in short. So my parents were really worried and they cried from desperation, even more so because in the family there was an uncle, my mother's brother, who had died from tuberculosis. So they had a terror of that illness, especially because I was so thin; I was like my little finger. I realized later, however, that it would have taken nothing to cure me—just having harmony in the family. For me, that was everything.*

Elena expressed a Florentine belief still widely held in the early 1980s that extreme thinness represented physical illness or emotional upset. Older Florentines did not think exclusively or primarily about the body as an aesthetic object but as a symbol of inner states—of mental and physical health. They derived this belief out of a past where hunger and infectious disease were chronic and where a thin body represented vulnerability. A common Florentine expression often uttered after lamenting something was, *"Basta la salute— health is enough,"* which meant that if you had health, you had everything essential. An excessively skinny body represented ill health and was considered ugly. As forty-five-year-old Rinaldo said, *Some people take thinness to absurd extremes. If a person tries to get thinner than his or her constitution permits, it interferes with the bodily equilibrium and health so much that it is difficult to recover. Getting that thin is not worth it.* A plump body signified both health and fertility. Their emphasis on health reduced Florentines' emphasis on appearance and made their standards for body appearance rather flexible. Under the increasing commodification of their economy, foods, and bodies, however, these beliefs were already eroding in the 1980s and giving way to an increasing cult of thinness in the new millennium (see Chapter 6).

Florentines also believed that bodily health depended on maintaining a balance with nature through their foodways, and they traditionally ate seasonal fresh fruits and vegetables.[23] Fifty-four-year-old Raffaele from Empoli, one of the few men I knew who regularly cooked, explicated, *Let me tell you something about our Tuscan cooking—it follows the seasons. It's the same old reason: poverty. When there was so much poverty, people ate what the earth gave them. If it was the period of tomatoes, they ate so many tomatoes. They ate them fried, they ate them stuffed, they ate them with eggs. Then when tomatoes were finished, there were string beans. So they ate those in sauce, boiled, or in a **frittata.*** They were always changing, but they were always string beans, understand? Then string beans finished and peas began, then asparagus, then artichokes.[24] In these parts there are so many artichokes. People invented spaghetti with artichokes, risotto with artichokes, fried artichokes, eggs with artichokes, stuffed artichokes. You can eat them a thousand ways, but they are always artichokes, for heavens sake. However, they take on a thousand different flavors. Understand?*

This is what the seasons mean for me, and this is important. You eat what the earth, what nature, gives you. Let's say that now is the time of artichokes, we should eat those. They do you good, because nature created this marvelous plant. It's the same when it is the time of grapes, of tomatoes, of potatoes, of peas, and of all these delicious vegetables that we have. Meat is different; meat is always available. But those vegetables also mark the end of winter, because in winter you don't have all these beautiful foods. You don't have tomatoes, you don't have string beans, you don't have peas, you don't have artichokes, you don't have any of these vegetables. Of course today they keep these vegetables in refrigerators and you can get them even in January, but nature didn't create refrigerators. It created peas, fava beans, each according to its own season. The fact is that the human body really needs to eat what matures in each season, because it is really good for you and it tastes good then. It would be laughable to eat a cold watermelon in January. Nature made them mature in August. Because watermelons are cool and thirst-quenching, they taste wonderful in the hot summer.

Raffaele expressed a traditional Florentine value on maintaining a balance with the earth through cuisine and consuming the seasonal round of fresh foods provided by nature. The freshness of the ingredients was one reason why their food was so delicious, and their enjoyment of food intensified its cultural significance. Their cuisine conveyed their identity as Florentines. They enjoyed eating as a channel for pleasure and self-expression, but were against unbridled desire. Implicit in their habits was the notion that unrestrained individual desires would decrease gustatory pleasure and lead to want. The next chapter examines the historical roots of Florentine cuisine in centuries of *mezzadria* farming inevitably altered by two world wars, twenty years of fascism, and the postwar economic recovery.

3
Historical Roots of Florentine Food, Family, and Gender

Introduction

My oldest informant, seventy-eight-year-old former peasant Berta, grew up in a poor sharecropping family in the Tuscan countryside far from Florence on mediocre hilly land: *We were* **mezzadria** *peasants up there in the hills beyond Trespiano, near Montorsoli. I had four younger brothers, my parents, my grandmother, and three aunts at home. We produced everything on our farm—wheat, corn, potatoes—everything, vegetables for the family, what fruit we could grow, but nothing to sell. We didn't have a big enough farm, and anyway, no one ever came up there to buy because we were way out in the country. We produced whatever could more or less grow up there: apples, plums, figs, rabbits, chickens, a pig.[1] We didn't have milk cows, but we raised a few oxen for work. We sent them out to graze in the woods.*

While Berta's family was not destitute, they had very limited resources, like most other **mezzadria** families: *We were more or less in the same conditions as the other peasants; we were all at the same level. What did we have to eat? Very little! Bread and onions many mornings. Bread and olive oil if we were out in the woods looking after the grazing animals. We gathered snails—oh, yes, as many as we wanted. For lunch, a little thin soup—**minestruccia**—made of water and herbs. We always ate lunch at home, just to have a little something hot. We always had **minestra**; you know, that's what they made in those days. Every now and then we had **pastasciutta**, but if not, soup made with a bouillon cube or with many greens. Oh, God, in those days that's how we always ate. We ate bread, bread, so much bread.*

*In the evening we ate a little gruel—**pappuccia, farinata**—just to have something in our stomachs, something light like that. And then we ate bread—oh, yes, plenty of bread. But with the bread—the **companatico**—was just a little something, some pork or bacon. We had that because we always slaughtered a pig, but we ate just a little, maybe one thin slice of raw bacon with our bread because there were so many of us. It wasn't like today. Today we may have little to eat, but then we had less. Oh, mother of mine, how things were in the old days! It's better not to think about it.*

This chapter uses food-centered memories like Berta's to describe the historical roots of Florentine foodways in the longstanding **mezzadria** peasant system, and in the social and economic transformations brought about by two world wars, fascism, and the post–World War II economic recovery.[2] For centuries, Florentine culture and diet were profoundly affected by *mezzadria*—"the dominant institution of the Tuscan countryside" until it was terminated by law in 1964 (Snowden 1989, 7).[3] Just before World War II, almost one-half of the Tuscan population was employed in agriculture, and over one-quarter was involved in *mezzadria* (Rossi 1986, 677). It was fundamental to gender, family, class relations, and foodways in both country and city, which were linked through a continuous flow of people, food, and other products. *Mezzadria* represented a premodern, "pre-capitalist economic formation" (Marx 1964), which still in the 1980s exerted an albeit waning influence on Florentine cuisine and culture. Of particular interest here is how the *mezzadria* system organized agricultural production, defined food, and reproduced family and gender relations; and how the apocalyptic events of the twentieth century caused inexorable changes in foodways and gender in Florence and the surrounding region. As many recent studies have noted, the overriding characteristic of Italian foodways for the majority of the population in the nineteenth and early twentieth centuries was constant scarcity and hunger. Tuscan peasants were no exception and many struggled for enough to eat.[4] Only in the last third of the twentieth century did Florentines and other Italians begin to reach an economic well-being that permitted consistent access to adequate food.

World War I affected Tuscan *mezzadria* peasants and led to the rise first of socialism and then fascism, which in turn led to Italy's entrance into World War II. Motivated by hunger and raised expectations, peasants and workers held food riots and labor strikes in Tuscany in the "Red Years" of 1919–20 and gained economic improvements. However, the Fascist reaction, backed solidly by landlords, took away the peasants' increased control over land and labor, and lessened their share of the crops. Mussolini's economic policy, especially the famous Battle of Grain, disrupted the multicrop agricultural system of Tuscany. Fascist legislation and propaganda exacerbated the imbalance between the sexes by dichotomizing production and reproduction. Fascist law undermined women's participation in paid work and propagated an ideology of maternity that institutionalized women's subordination in ways that have left an enduring mark on Italian gender relations. Springing from the ashes of World War I, fascism took Italy into World War II, which led to profound changes in Italian social, economic, and political life.

The *Mezzadria* System

Mezzadria was a peasant mode of production based on sharecropping.[5] Landlords owned one or more estates called *fattorie* that were divided into peasant farms called *poderi,* each with its own land, stone cottage, well, bread oven, and stable—everything necessary to support a family while its members labored to produce crops. Many landlords owned huge estates with numerous scattered peasant families working dozens of farms, and in 1946 over half the land in Tuscany consisted of plots of 100 hectares (247 acres) or more, the highest concentration of land ownership of all Italian regions.[6] While landlords owned the land and the means of production—land, most tools, seeds, wells, mills, houses, and work animals—peasants did all the work. Landlord and peasant theoretically split the costs of production and the harvest fifty-fifty—hence *mezzadria* from *mezzo,* meaning "half"—but in actuality, peasants bore more expenses than landlords, and by the time they finished paying off their debts, they had far less than half the crop. Their work was laborious and their subsistence was precarious (Snowden 1989, Clemente et al. 1980, Apergi and Bianco 1991).

Mezzadria peasants used human and animal labor and deep knowledge of the land to produce wheat, grapes, and olives for the market, and a variety of foods for consumption (see Figure 2.1). As seventy-five-year-old former peasant Massimo said, *We produced everything to eat. Rabbits, chickens, olive oil, wheat, wine, and fruit. We had a small vegetable garden for the family; we always had a vegetable garden. Pretty much everything we ate was of our own production.* Peasants were not, however, totally self-sufficient and always traded or sold some of their produce to buy necessary foods like sugar, pasta, and salt, as well as shoes and clothing (Apergi and Bianco 1991, chapter 3). Peasants worked hard and had big appetites, but very often did not have enough to eat, so they developed a deep appreciation for food. Their prevailing ideology toward consumption was encapsulated in Marianna's father's belief: *Poco ma buono*—*Only a little, but let it be good.*

The *mezzadria* system relied on peasants' knowledge and careful stewardship of the land. Almost the entire province of Florence is hilly or mountainous. To cultivate the land intensively necessitated constant attention to slight differences in soil, water, wind, sun, and exposure. *Mezzadria* peasants worked extremely hard and rarely made more than a marginal existence. By law, peasants not only had to work in the fields growing the main crops of wheat, corn, olives, and grapes, but they also had to do many other duties, including digging ditches, planting hedgerows, taking the landlord's harvest to market, providing wood and fowl for the landlord, and washing the laundry of the landlord's family.[7] Many landlords squeezed peasants continually, and when necessary, they could use force or eviction to get their way. Fifty-four-year-old Baldo described the onerous life of the peasants in the 1930s and 1940s: *Those unfortunate wretches had nothing left after the overseer and the landowner gobbled up their share. Thursday was market day in Empoli, and here's what the peasants did. They came in and sold maybe two or three chickens and a basket of eggs, and then what did they do? They went to the first grocery store they found and bought anchovies or **baccalà**—salted dried cod. They ate those things so they could save a little money—that was their only way to have any income.*

Peasants had to sell what they could of their gardens or courtyard animals or exchange them to pay their bills and purchase luxuries like sugar, shoes, and meat (Apergi and Bianco 1991, 17, 74). Renzo said that they paid their bills once a year after the harvest to all the artisans and tradespeople who served them throughout the year. Berta said of the 1920s and 1930s, *Eggs—when we needed money, we sold them. If we didn't need to earn those few pennies, we ate some eggs. . . . If my grandmother was going shopping, she took some of the eggs to Pratolino on Saturday and she sold the eggs so she could buy a little meat. Oh, yes, in those days things were very hard.* While *mezzadria* peasants did tend to have relative security on the land compared to other Italian peasants, they still worked very hard for little return and were at the mercy of the landlord from year to year. When landlords were rapacious, weather uncooperative, or pests rampant, peasants struggled for enough to eat. When everything went optimally, peasants ate a seasonally diverse diet centered on watery soups—*minestre*—with legumes, pasta, bread, greens, and limited animal products.

Mezzadria Family and Gender Relations

Mezzadria functioned by exploiting intensively the labor of the entire peasant family. The virilocal extended family—symbolically centered on commensality at the table—was the basic social and economic unit, responsible for production, distribution, and consumption. Big families—up to twenty or thirty members—were the norm, and they were so necessary to the mode of production that by law peasants had to gain the approval of the landlord for all moves and marriages (Coppi and Fineschi 1980, 191). In the early twentieth century, average *mezzadria* family size began to shrink until it reached seven members in 1930 (Snowden 1989, 28). The decline was due to the decrease in fertility and the decimation of male peasants in the First World War. Prior to Berta's marriage in 1933, for example, there were eleven members in her family, and three were spinster aunts, perhaps unmarried because of the shortage of males after the war ended in 1918. Berta's husband Massimo's family had only five members. His brother Renzo described their family, shrunken by the depredations of World War I: *We ourselves in the family were few. There was my grandmother (my father's mother), and four of us—my father, mother, Massimo, and myself—so that's five altogether. There had been all these other brothers of my father until they left for the First World War, and from then on I hardly ever saw them again. Three of them died during the war. One of them was off for eight or nine years as a soldier. He finally came back and married, and then we were five or six in the family.*

Small families had to employ hired hands or live-in *garzoni,*[8] who cost money and food and were never trusted the way family members were. Renzo said, *At certain times of the year, there were many people who worked for us, for a week or a month, so many, even a few for the whole year. They were called garzoni. Some came and slept at our house and ate with us too. There was so much work. There were all those workers to supervise, and, you know, they were always outsiders.* It was difficult to integrate nonfamily labor into the close cooperation necessary to run a farm, and the decline of *mezzadria* went hand in hand with the shrinking family size. The closed nature of the Tuscan family discussed in Chapter 7 was part and parcel of *mezzadria.*

Tuscan *mezzadria* depended on the coordinated labor of both men and women in a three-generation patrilineal stem family composed of a senior male and female, the *capoccia* and the *massaia,* who were usually husband and wife; their unmarried sons and daughters; and one or more married sons and their wives and children (Coppi and Fineschi 1980, 192). Married daughters moved out of their natal family and into their husbands' homes, where they came under the supervision of their mother-in-law. This postmarital virilocal residence pattern along with the greater value on men's productive work than on women's reproductive labor contributed to women's relatively weak position.[9] In the 1980s, an enduring Tuscan toast continued to reflect the value on boys, for people would lift their cups and exclaim, "*Figli maschi!*"—"To male children!"

Men continued the family name and lived with the parents when old. The *capoccia* regulated the work of all family members, represented the family to outsiders, kept the books, and controlled the money.[10] Seventy-three-year-old Renzo described his peasant father: *At the end of the year my father figured out the finances; he took our percentage. My father administered everything on the farm, everything, with real precision.* According to the *mezzadria* contracts, only the male head of household—the *capoccia*—had "juridical maturity; regardless of age, the other members of the family were locked in a permanent minority" (Snowden 1989, 18). An important way that the *capoccia* symbolically reinforced his authority was by sitting at the head of the table and serving the food cooked and placed before him by his wife. As Renzo said, *My father sat down at the head of this great big table and we all sat around it—we in the family and all those others who were with us. And "zac" my father would serve out the food.*

Although the father was the symbolic and juridical head of the household, his power according to Falassi (1980, 2) was largely in relations with the outside world. The *massaia*—the senior female—was important within the family, and she controlled "scrupulously all the activities of her daughters-in-law" and unmarried daughters (Coppi and Fineschi 1980, 196). Women carried out many essential tasks such as weaving cloth, sewing clothes, cleaning house, washing clothes, rearing children, and caring for the elderly. At the heart of women's activities were food production, preservation, and preparation. They "transformed raw materials into food products"—grain into bread, milk into cheese, toasted grain into surrogate coffee, and fruit and vegetables into dried or pickled forms that would last through the winter (Coppi and Fineschi 1980, 203). They took care of the vegetable garden and gathered wild foods. They tended, slaughtered, and cooked or sold the courtyard animals, including chickens, ducks, geese, turkeys, rabbits, pigeons, and even, according to fifty-year-old Valeria, guinea pigs. Women's roles involved not only the reproduction of the family but also the production of food.

Cooking was the *massaia*'s most important and prestigious activity, controlled by the senior female (Coppi and Fineschi 1980, 202). Seventy-six-year-old Berta described the 1920s and 1930s: *My grandmother, my father's mother, was the cook. She was one of these olden-day women who always did the cooking. The grandmothers were the cooks. As long as they wanted to do it, you could not take that job away from them. My mother worked in the fields and then she also helped in the house because my grandmother was getting old. But it was my grandmother who was in charge of the cooking and the shopping. In the olden-day families, that's how it was. There was no other way. . . . My grandmother made bread at home, and the other women helped her because there was so much work. They had to help her heat the wood oven, make the dough, put it in the oven, turn it—oh, there was plenty to do.* Similarly, Berta's brother-in-law Renzo remembered his grandmother as the cook, and emphasized her ability to give pleasure through her food role: *My grandmother was completely in charge of the kitchen. She was the food person—la vivandiera. My grandmother made bread once a week. We were all so happy when she made bread.*

Generally the *massaia* was in charge of the food work and the younger females—unmarried daughters and granddaughters, and resident daughters-in-law—helped in the fields, in the house, or in both. Fifty-four-year-old Baldo recounted memories of his peasant mother: *In those days the peasant families were large, with seven or eight children. So what did they do? One girl would say, "I was born to work in the fields." Another would say, "I was born to cook, to work in the house." That's what they did. My mother chose the fields because she felt free when she was cultivating the earth. But after she got married, she learned right away how to cook and do the housework.* Whether they did productive labor alongside men or not, women had to do housework, unless they lived in households where other women did it for them.

Women contributed fully to the household economy but were legally defined as dependents, and their contributions to the productive sphere were undervalued (Coppi and Fineschi 1980, 211). During both world wars, peasant men were drafted in high numbers, and women had to run many farms by themselves. Tuscan peasant women carried out many diverse tasks, including tending animals, gardening, working side by side with men at the harvests, and cooking life-sustaining food for their families with scarce food resources. They seem to have had recognized social value, especially if they produced sons, even though their productive contributions were underestimated.

Mezzadria Diet and Roots of Florentine Cuisine

Although peasants produced all the food, very often they ate only the least-valued items.[11] Their well-being depended on the quality of the land, the benevolence of the landlord, and their ability to benefit from trade by proximity to Florence or one of the urban centers like Empoli or Prato.[12] Many landlords were rapacious and squeezed the peasants continually. Most peasants struggled at the subsistence level with barely enough to eat and no luxuries. Snowden cites a report on *mezzadria* peasants conducted in 1922 that documented them working 300 days a year for an average of fourteen hours per day. They had little clothing and wore shoes only in winter. Their houses were humble, dark, crowded, and poorly furnished. The diet consisted of "ground meal prepared from wheat, corn, or chestnuts supplemented with potatoes, beans, and vegetable soup garnished with pigs' feet. Meat and eggs were saved for feasts, and wine was a luxury reserved for the harvest season" (Snowden 1989, 27).

Minestra and bread were the basis of the *mezzadria* diet. Most peasants slaughtered a pig and were skilled at making use of every bit of it, but a little meat had to go a long way.[13] Berta's family often relied on wild foods, not only snails but also mushrooms, radicchio and other greens, asparagus, strawberries, and chestnuts. Her husband Massimo and his brother Renzo had things a little easier because their landlord was relatively benevolent and their land was good. Renzo said, *Fortunately, when I was a youngster, for those days, you could say that we were pretty well off. We were better off than most peasants. I don't say it to give myself airs, but we never lacked anything. When we went to school, we always had a few pennies to buy chocolate. That was really a lot back then.*

In memories perhaps embellished by nostalgia, Renzo described his family's food: *While we were peasants at Santa Lucia di Trespiano, we always ate really well. Food wasn't abundant the same way it is today, but we ate well. First of all we had chickens and rabbits, all these kinds of things, as much as we wanted. I don't remember that we ever lacked anything. We had a garden with everything that there could possibly be. Everything. . . . So much. Beans, squashes, in season, out of season, always, everything there was that could be useful to a family. So many vegetables. Everything. Beans and chickpeas. We harvested our own legumes. We had so many artichokes. We had an artichoke bed—una carciofaia—as long as from here way down to there. We ate artichokes in every imaginable way—in sauce, fried, in frittate, in so many ways. And artichokes are something really special. We also had milk cows and as much milk as we wanted. Oh, that milk. Cheese, no.*

The peasants produced and ate little cheese—a fact recognized in the popular Florentine proverb recited by Renzo: "*Al contadino non lo fa sapere, quant'è buono il cascio con le pere*"—"*Do not let the peasant know, how well cheese and pears do go.*"[14] This well-known Florentine proverb implied the ignorance of the peasant, a persistent oppressive stereotype. The proverb also hinted at the age-old struggle between landlords and peasants over the allocation of resources, and the economic truth that peasants had access only to cheap foods that fueled their bodies for work, not high-fat foods like cheese, because they owed these to landlords or sold them.[15]

Seventy-six-year-old Berta also remembered consuming meat in scarce amounts and inexpensive cuts: *Only occasionally did we eat meat. It was difficult because there were so many of us. We bought the innards, which cost the least of all. Oh, my God, no, we couldn't eat meat every day, once a week at most. Sometimes they cooked up a rabbit or a chicken, but usually they sold them so we could earn a few pennies. Sometimes we had many, and sometimes they all died. Sometimes we had some sauce made with the rabbit, and we ate it with spaghetti, but that was rare. Because, you know, we were so many, we had to stretch the food because otherwise what was there to eat?*

The brothers Massimo and Renzo ate a bit more meat. Seventy-three-year-old Renzo remembered: *At the noon meal we ate rabbits, meat, but just a little, because there were so many of us, but we always had meat, at least twice a week for sure. In those days there was no butcher shop. They brought beef up to Trespiano on horseback. They came all the way from Careggi, imagine. By the time they arrived up in Trespiano in the summer, there was such a stink from that meat. We had our own rabbits, so many of them. We slaughtered a pig every year, one or two. We had hams hanging and everything that you could make from a pig: sausages, bacon, prosciutto, salame. We had all this because there were so many people at the table.* Renzo's brother Massimo recalled meat consumption: *We ate our rabbits, and we sold them. Every now and then, we ate one. We ate one when it was a holiday. We ate only a little piece because there were so many of us.*

Massimo and Renzo were relatively well-off because their 5-hectare farm was near enough to Florence to sell their produce in the city and they grew a lot of fruit for which there was a good market. Renzo recounted: *We had land in Trespiano. . . . The owner . . . had just a little land, very little. It was mainly planted with fruit and olive trees, grapes, and just a little wheat. We earned most from the fruit and the olive oil. We sold the products and divided the income in half with the landlord. One thing my father did was he chose the best fruit, wrapped each piece carefully, packed it in beautiful baskets, took it to the Campo di Marte train station, and sent it off to Germany. He also took fruit to the Grand Hotel in Florence. We took another part of our produce, the ripest fruits, to the Sant'Ambrogio market in Florence, really early in the morning. At 4 A.M., my father rode his horse with these baskets that were masterpieces. Oh, they were arranged carefully, not like today. My father wove these baskets; with a piece of hay he worked them to make sure that they stayed tied on to the horse. It was a wonderful thing to see. There could be no tricks; underneath the fruit had to be as good as that on the top, not like today, eh. That's the way my father was.*

Oh, he took so much fruit to the market. As kids, we went with him sometimes. I went every Sunday morning on horseback. We left at 4 A.M. We stayed only a little while in the market, because at that time, the Sant'Ambrogio market was like it is today, eh. It is not a market where the producers sell directly to the consumer—no, they sell to dealers who buy the produce from the peasants and then they take care of selling it. In the market there was a bench where we used to play while the dealers bargained with the peasants.

Although trade and good land made Renzo and Massimo's family relatively well-off, even they had little to squander. Massimo said, *In the summer we* *didn't wear our shoes. We used to say in those days, "**Io mi alzo, chi non ha scarpe, vada scalzo**"—"I get up, who doesn't have shoes, barefoot he goes."*[16] They lived among other peasants whose conditions were dire. Massimo commented, *We were among the better-off peasants, but I remember that one time I went to visit another peasant family. There were five people and there was just a little pot of minestra. And there was one little plate of wild radicchio, but not much, just a little. In that family the calories came in the summer when the sun shone!* Renzo remembered sharing food with neighbors: *Eating with us were also friends who had nothing to eat; we fed them as a good deed. These poor friends of ours—two brothers and their mother—were always in our house; they were always there to eat with us. There were always people sharing our meals, always.*

Under *mezzadria,* most peasants worked extremely hard and nonetheless lived at the margins of sufficiency. They valued food highly because of its always threatening scarcity, and they developed a sharp appreciation for fresh ingredients and tasty cooking. However, even as they were living as peasants in the 1920s, history was taking an inexorable course that led to the weakening and eventual termination of the *mezzadria* system.

Mezzadria Peasants, World War I, and the Red Years

World War I profoundly affected Italian peasants. It developed their "collective consciousness" because as soldiers they encountered men and ideas from all over Italy (Snowden 1989, 33). Peasants composed over half the Italian army, and their numbers were even higher among combat troops. They preponderated among the dead, wounded, and disabled, while landlords avoided service and reaped war profits (Snowden 1989, 37). Excluding children and the elderly, almost one out of every two men in Tuscany was "involved in the war army and the war experience." In the First World War, 450,595 Tuscans fought and 46,911 died (Soldani 1986, 353). The war stimulated expectations for a better life in repayment for laying their bodies on the line and increased resentment against landlords because so many shirked conscription.[17]

Seventy-five-year-old Massimo recalled the impact of the war on his peasant family: *In 1915, the war began, the First World War—la guerra quindici-diciotto. My father and all the men departed. I was left to do everything. At that time in 1915, even a young boy like I was had to try to work because there wasn't a single man at home. There was only my mother, my grandmother, and my younger brother Renzo. So I tried to work even though I was only six years old. I did what I could. In the summer there was a lot of fruit, so I helped pick it and get it ready. We had some workers at home who took it to market. Eventually my father returned home on an agricultural furlough, because there was a real need for the country to grow food. The men who worked in agriculture as he did came back home to farm in spring 1918, before the war ended. My father was one of six brothers. Five went off to war and one stayed home. In one year, in thirteen months, three of his brothers were killed and then only three were left.*

World War I not only took many peasant men's lives but also involved a "systematic draining of resources from agriculture to the cities and the front" through requisitioning of grain and livestock and the fixing of food prices (Snowden 1989, 34). During the war, food was scarce and expensive. Renzo remembers his mother making and selling butter from their home in Trespiano, 5 kilometers from Florence, to help them get by while his father was off at the front: *My poor mother, with that milk, in the other war, World War I, with those cows and that milk. We used it ourselves and my mother sold what was extra. We took it almost all the way to Florence, with a little horse, with my mother—I'll always remember that. Butter, my mother made butter during the war, I'll always remember it. Do you know how she made butter? She milked the cow in the evening and by morning the milk had this high layer of cream. She collected all this cream and she put it all together into a canister and she shook it up and down until the butter came.*

With men at the front, women worked the farms, but agricultural production went down to 90 percent of prewar production, and black markets and profiteering thrived, increasing prices and augmenting resentment among the poor. In Florence, indexing 1914 prices at 100, by 1918 meat had risen to 500, milk to 250, and bread to 180. The overall cost of living in Florence doubled from 1914 to 1917, tripled by 1918, quadrupled by 1920, and more than quintupled by 1921 (Soldani 1986, 373–374). Between 1915 and the end of World War I, there were periodic food riots all over Italy, usually centered on the rising price of grain and bread (Helstosky 1996, 50–80). In 1915, there were riots in Florence in February and again in summer, which resulted in a *calmiere* or price control on bread.[18] There was a charitably run soup kitchen or *cucina economica* in Florence during the war to combat hunger. Yet because of full employment and government intervention, particularly in subsidizing the price of bread, average food consumption actually rose during the war (Helstosky 1996, 80–99).

When the Italian front collapsed in 1917, there were mass uprisings all over Italy. There were riots in Florence in the fall of 1917 and again in the winter of 1918 protesting rising food prices. Seventy-two-year-old Marco remembered: *After the war there was this movement of rebellion. The workers wanted to take over the government. It was bolshevism, but in Florence they called it the bosci-bosci. . . . It was a Bolshevik movement, inspired of course by the 1917 revolution in Russia during the First World War. They wanted to control everything and they began to sack the stores. The first thing they did was to loot all the stores, beginning with the general food stores, dry good stores—everything that they could break into, they did. The police were impotent to stop them. There was wine and olive oil everywhere in the streets. My father-in-law had a store in Fiesole, and they broke into his store and all the olive oil, all the wine, everything was smashed, broken, everything completely ruined. That's the way it was.*

The food riots that Marco remembered occurred in Florence on July 3–4, 1919, as part of nationwide food riots that spread across Italy between June 30 and July 13 (Salvemini 1973). They started in Forlí in Romagna and spread to scores of cities including Florence, Turin, Brescia, Pisa, Palermo, Milan, Genoa, Rome, and Naples. The riots began in protest against rapidly rising prices of important foodstuffs such as eggs, vegetables, fruit, and fish, and they were directed at retailers who were perceived as price-gougers. Of all the cities that participated, Florence had far and away the "the most extensive damage and . . . the highest number of citizens arrested for looting," with an estimated 6.5 million lire in damages, 404 business looted, and 725 persons arrested— eight times the amount of damages and twice the number of arrests as Milan (Helstosky 1996, 101, 465).

Marco linked the food riots to the rise of fascism: *After the food riots came a certain movement by some veterans of the First World War, who said, "What's this? We fought the war, and we finally come back home and we find this chaos?" And they began to slap around and beat up the Socialists, and from this came a movement that developed into fascism. Look, the birth of fascism came out of that chaos. In 1921–1922, fascism came out. It came somewhat in consequence of those actions that really were not good, because to break in and loot, well, the majority of the population said, "If God wills it, something has come to put these bad people, these Socialists, under control." That's what they thought. But instead, slowly fascism transformed itself into a dictatorship. That's what happened, and it took us into the Second World War.*[19]

Fascism's promise of law and order had appeal in the tumultuous Red Years. Collusion of landlords and owners of the small Tuscan food, quarrying, textile, ceramics, and brickmaking industries was instrumental in the Fascist rise to power (Snowden 1989, 105). The *fasci di combattimento* (fascist squads) drew members from the young junior officers recently demobilized from the army who became "political secretaries, squad commanders and office holders in branches throughout the region," especially in Florence (Snowden 1989, 159).

The association between Fascists and veterans led to trouble for Renzo's father, who joined the veterans' association after fighting in World War I. Renzo said, *Look, here's why I don't like communism or any kind of political fanaticism. There was this difficult period in 1919 when the communists were talking about revolution and all these other things. The communists came to our house while we were still peasants in Trespiano and they took everything they could find. Luckily my poor father had hidden the olive oil. He made a big hole in the ground—I can still see it now. It was deep and he put a big terra-cotta urn there full of oil and covered it all up with dirt. My father had hidden the chickens and rabbits in a field, but they found them and took them all away. They beat him up also. It was the time of the* **bosci-bosci,** *when all these Italians were talking about bolshevism, in 1919–1920, right before fascism came in. The communists said that my father*

was a veteran and there was this association of veterans, many of whom sup-
ported fascism. My father had joined this association and they didn't like it, and
they beat him up. But my father didn't do anything wrong and he never paid any
attention to politics, never. That's why I don't like fanaticism of any kind.

While some peasants joined the ex-combatants' association, others joined
the burgeoning Socialist movement. The uprisings of the Red Years in 1919–20
were fueled by the peasants' demands that the government fulfill the promises
of more control over land and a higher standard of living. The *mezzadria*
movement began in the spring of 1919 with spontaneous local strikes all over
Tuscany, which became a massive movement in autumn 1919 and spring 1920,
involving over 500,000 out of a total of 711,000 *mezzadria* peasants. It was
"the largest agricultural strike in Italian history" (Snowden 1989, 52).

Landlords gave in to many peasant demands in July 1920, but they soon
used their alliance with fascists to revoke the concessions that threatened their
political and economic privilege. They regained the power of eviction, the
right to the labor of the entire peasant family, a favorable division of costs with
peasants, and the right to be arbiters of all disputes. Landlords supported the
local fascist groups (*fasci*) that launched "a tidal wave of murder, assault, and
intimidation" (Snowden 1989, 56). By repressing the peasant struggles for land
and contract reform, fascists blocked not only improvement in the material
well-being of thousands of poor peasants, but also hindered agricultural development and contributed to the demise of *mezzadria.* Although Mussolini
conducted propaganda campaigns to keep Italians on the land by extolling the
virtues of the peasant life (Sorcinelli 1998, 488–489), his economic policies, especially the "battle for grain," destroyed the multicrop basis of the peasant
economy and increased poverty in the countryside, which contributed to the
massive exodus of peasants to the cities.

Fascist Food Policy

Mussolini's definitive rise to power occurred after the march of thousands of
fascists on Rome on October 28–30, 1922, when King Vittorio Emmanuele III
appointed Mussolini head of state. The "culinary policy of fascism" (Sacchetti
1999) fit in with Mussolini's bigger goals of imperialist expansion, national autarky, and traditional patriarchal family values.[20] Fascist propaganda extolled
peasant dishes high in carbohydrates and low in meat, and praised the virtues
of domestic products, modest consumption, and creative use of leftovers. Yet
in the early years of fascism (1922–24), the government ended wartime price
controls and food prices rose steadily along with public anger against retailers.
Bread prices rose 25 percent in 1925 and led to the government initiative on
grain (Helstosky 1996, 143–146).

The so-called Battle for Grain—*la battaglia del grano*—exemplified Mussolini's culinary politics.[21] Inaugurated in 1925, it aimed to raise Italian wheat

production and reduce imports to conserve scarce Italian foreign exchange and raise self-sufficiency in preparation for war and imperial expansion. The government passed wheat tariffs in 1925, 1928, and 1929 to protect home production and encouraged farmers to switch to grain from other crops and to bring marginally arable areas under grain cultivation, discouraging more diverse land use. While wheat production rose to meet the nation's consumption needs, production of other grains and vegetables declined, as did export of cash crops.[22]

Mussolini declared *la battaglia del grano* a success in 1935, but it was economically deleterious to *mezzadria* peasants, especially those like Berta from the marginal agricultural areas in the foothills of the Tuscan Apennines where grain was not an easily cultivable crop (Preti 1986, 628). Many peasants in these regions had to buy grain, and its price rose steadily due to Mussolini's protectionist grain policies, while prices for crops traditionally produced in Tuscany's hilly regions dropped precipitously. Indexing the prices of 1922–24 as 100, by 1931–32 the price for chestnuts had dropped to 56, charcoal to 69, lambs to 53, wool to 26, and cheese to 25, while the price of grain had risen to 116 (Preti 1986, 628). This alteration in the balance of prices contributed to the steady emigration of peasants from Tuscany's rural mountain zones to the cities. Furthermore, misery continued for many. During the 1930s, "on Italian tables, consumption diminished of legumes, tomatoes, vegetables, fruit, pork, mutton, animal fats, wine and coffee and—contrary to what one would expect from the particular policy adopted by fascism in this sector—also of cereals" (Sorcinelli 1998, 485).

Fascism and Gender

In the areas of food and reproductive policy, Fascist law and propaganda sank deeply into Italian culture and affected gender and family relations in myriad ways that still reverberated in my subjects' narratives in the 1980s. Fascism exalted a sharp division of labor with women as homemakers catering to husbands and children, and men as breadwinners ruling the family.[23] Mussolini's campaign for alimentary autarky and parsimony put the burden on housewives to use local products, recycle leftovers, and limit waste (Helstosky 2004, chapter 4).

Fascist policy encouraged early marriage and big families, and discouraged women from working outside the home, where they earned on average only half what men earned. Many women, including several of my subjects, did piecework at home to earn a few lire, but they were "unprotected, underemployed and ill-paid" (De Grazia 1992, 168). Berta did embroidery—*ricamo antico*—in Montorsoli in the 1920s *to earn a few pennies*. Grazia crocheted doilies and handbags in Florence from the 1940s through the 1960s. Both Valeria and Laura sewed pants and elegant women's clothes from precut pieces at home from the 1950s through the 1970s. In Empoli in the 1930s, 1940s, and

1950s, Raffaele's mother sewed buttons and finished buttonholes, while Baldo's mother braided straw onto Chianti flasks—work practiced in 1930 by an estimated 40,000 female straw-braiders (*trecciaiole*).[24] Baldo described his mother's work: *Like so many women in Empoli, my mother wove straw onto the wine bottles we call fiaschi. . . . The straw grew in the swamps near Empoli. They harvested this plant called sala from the swamp and put the stalks in warehouses to dry and whiten. Then at a certain point they burned sulfur continuously in the warehouses, and that made the straw completely white. Then the women worked the straw around the bottles. All the women in Empoli used to do this work at home. My mother could cover a barrelful of wine flasks in a day.*

Fascist policy marginalized women in the workforce, so most had to marry because they could not survive without a man's income.[25] Fascist policy valued women's work in the fields at 60 percent of men's labor. Yet a study of Tuscan *mezzadria* peasants in the 1930s estimated that women consistently worked longer and harder than their husbands—over 1,000 hours more per year in one household. Peasant women "were at once artisans, domestic servants, tenders of animals, and seasonal field hands as well; their labor in the home alone easily took up 1500 hours a year" (De Grazia 1992, 182). Nevertheless, fascist agricultural laws gave men both juridical and economic superiority over women.

Fascist educational policy under Giovanni Gentile, Mussolini's first minister of public instruction (1922–24), discouraged women from education.[26] Elena, born in 1918, reflected this educational tracking: *The only thing I wanted to be when I grew up was a veterinarian. But in those days, imagine, it was impossible. I wanted to do that because I've always been a great lover of animals. . . . I would have really liked to be an animal doctor. But I never even told anybody because imagine! I cherished the idea for a while, but then it passed. First of all, I couldn't do it because we didn't have the financial possibilities. It was something only for upper-class people. Furthermore, it wasn't something that a woman could do. I would have had to study medicine and then specialize in veterinary medicine. Women just didn't do that in those days.* Unable to overcome class and gender barriers, Elena progressed through three typically female professions as a dressmaker, secretary, and finally sales clerk in the family bakery, where she worked for thirty years without formal wages or benefits.

Fascism exalted marriage and the family, and relied heavily on the unpaid labor of women to provide care for the elderly and children. Propaganda equated spinsterhood with selfishness, inadequacy, unattractiveness, and probable poverty—notions that lingered in my subjects' gender ideology in the 1980s. In spite of Mussolini's pro-natalist policies, Italy's birthrate per thousand dropped steadily under fascism—from 29.9 in 1921–25 to 19.9 in 1941–45 (De Grazia 1992, 46).[27] The regime's exaltation of maternity and domestic work for women echoed in my female subjects' belief that they had total responsibility for home and children, no matter what else they did.

Premarital virginity was essential for women who both before and after marriage were symbols of male virility and honor (De Grazia 1992, 116–140). Baldo, born in 1930, said, *In the old days, if a girl made love with someone, she was already damaged goods; she was half a whore already. . . . Oh, people talk about Sicily and all, but here too the woman's virginity was a big deal, for God's sake.* Seventy-three-year-old Renzo concurred: *A man wanted the woman to be a virgin. Oh, it was a big deal. Imagine. Porca miseria! Jealousy was strong then, for everybody, eh.* He also described at length the many houses of prostitution—*casotti*—in Florence that presumably existed to facilitate the coexistence of female virginity and male virility, both exalted by fascism.[28]

Fascist propaganda legitimated men's right to define and judge female beauty and underscored women's duty to please men (De Grazia 1992, 212). The legacy of such propaganda was still evident in my subjects' discussions of gender in the 1980s (see Chapter 6). Fascist literature and visual imagery extolled "women as optimally round and robust" (Caldwell 1986, 113), and Mussolini personally propagandized against extreme thinness in women. In the 1980s older Florentine women were relatively comfortable with large bodies but younger ones were increasingly concerned with thinness.

Fascism's enduring effects on women's status were encapsulated by a female peasant who said in 1939, "In our homes, we are at once everything and nothing"[29]—totally indispensable, but totally taken for granted. Fascism exalted women as guardians of the home and procreators, discouraged them from education and work outside the home, legitimated a lower pay scale, earmarked plum jobs for men, and promoted female dependence by defining their role as giving service. Many of these trends were deeply rooted in Italy's past, however, fascism solidified traditions subordinating women that Italians were still struggling to overcome in the 1980s.[30] Fascism also contributed to the demise of the *mezzadria* peasantry in Italy by blocking reforms that would have ensured peasants a more equitable share of profits and by forcing excessive production of grain to the detriment of the traditional multicrop economy.

Food and Hunger in Florence in World War II

Mussolini's imperialism and megalomania led to war and fascism's demise.[31] Many Italians opposed Mussolini's alliance with Germany and grew increasingly discontent with the privations of the war and the vast losses of men. Among the peasants, "as crop requisitions for Mussolini's military adventures had increased, so had the spirit of rebellion" (Wilhelm 1988, 218). Severe food shortages and high prices plagued Italy while rationing led to a flourishing black market that was insufficient to satisfy hunger (Helstosky 2004, chapter 4). Although trafficking in black market foods was illegal and punishable by two years in prison, a great number of Italians produced, sold, and/or consumed them even though they commanded prices many times higher than official ones. For example, sugar sold for nine times its official price—230 versus

25 lire/kilogram—and butter for twelve times as much—600 versus 47.50 lire/kilogram (Helstosky 2004, chapter 4). Several of my subjects hinted that Marco had used the family bakery to make millions on the black market during the war and expressed some distaste for this fact—perhaps more because he took all the profits for himself than because he did what many others were doing.

In spite of the active black market, many Florentines—like many Italians—suffered hunger during the war. The government instituted rationing in an effort to ensure some nutrition to all. Meat sale was restricted nine months before Italy entered the war in June 1940. By early 1941, the government rationed coffee, sugar, olive oil, lard, wheat, pasta, and rice. In October 1941, it rationed bread, allowing only 200 grams per day, which was reduced to 150 by the beginning of 1942 (Sorcinelli 1998, 490). During the Nazi occupation of Florence in summer 1944, food was increasingly scarce, and Elena remembered that the state gave each bakery 100 grams of grain per person per day. By the last days of the war, Elena said that they no longer had sufficient wheat flour and used flour made from corn and later from dried peas.

A 1946 League of Nations study of food rationing and hunger during World War II showed that Italy was one of the worst countries. On a national basis, Italy rationed only cereals, fats, coffee, and sugar, but local communities rationed potatoes, eggs, cheese, and milk according to supply. The total average rations of normal consumers in Italy dropped from 1,160 calories in 1941 to 930 in 1943 and rose slightly to 990 in 1944. Total rations in Germany, by contrast, hovered around 2,000 calories per consumer for the entire war.[32] Oral histories have confirmed the dire nutritional level of most Italians during the war (Helstosky 2004, chapter 4).

Because Italy was still highly agricultural in the 1940s, many people had more to eat than their rations, especially peasants and landowners in rural areas. Although peasants had to deliver a certain amount of their produce to government stores called *ammassi*, approximately 12 million rural cultivators were allowed to keep enough food for their own consumption. Furthermore, peasants had access to wild foods unavailable to city dwellers. Seventy-five-year-old Massimo recalled: *During the war we had ration cards, and you had to make do as best you could. The ones who had only ration cards and no other food were the ones who suffered hunger, the ones who didn't have any other help. But we had our garden with vegetables, grapes, and fruit. We went out into the woods to gather chestnuts. I used to go to Gagliano on my bicycle. Who knows how many times I went up there on my bicycle, 21 miles. I brought back 20, 30, 40 pounds of chestnuts, depending, and you know 40 pounds of chestnuts in those days were really appreciated. We always had food in the war; we always managed to eat. Sometimes we went into the countryside, often to Cercina or to Guaglio, places where they made bread. They had bakeries and there was always a little extra, and sometimes they gave us a loaf of bread. At that time, a loaf of bread was so much.*

Gathering wild foods, foraging for bread in the countryside, and eating foods customarily shunned were important ways that Florentines survived hunger during the war. Massimo also described how he exchanged labor for food: *I continued to work in the Trespiano cemetery, but not a lot, because of the war. There were three or four of us who worked on maintenance of the tombs based on directives from the families. We watered the plants, and in the summer we cleaned up around the graves. We got a monthly sum from each of these private families. And among these families there was one who was a butcher, in Via Gioberti in Florence. When I came to Florence during the war, I always went to visit him and he always gave me a little meat, a few little pieces. Then there was a woman whose family graves I looked after who had a banana warehouse, and she supplied me with bananas instead of paying me for the work I had done. And that's how it went.* Networks and labor exchanges for food enabled many Florentines to gain access to more than rations.

But many urban workers suffered hunger, and food became increasingly scarce for all Italians as the war wore on, especially after Italy broke with Germany in 1943. Marco and others called this *the* **rigirata**—*the turnaround, the flip-flop. It came in September 1943. We made peace with the Allies and suddenly were on the opposite side from the Germans.* Although a young child at the time, Rinaldo remembered vividly the German occupation: *During the war, I stayed with my aunt and uncle on their farm. I remember perfectly so many things. I remember exactly when the Germans occupied my aunt and uncle's farmhouse. I remember the shooting when the Allies came through. There was a group of SS soldiers who stayed at our farm and they requisitioned everything. They stayed a couple of weeks and they helped themselves to everything there.*[33] *I remember all this perfectly—I was almost five years old because it was the summer of 1944.*

Born in 1930, Baldo was ten when Italy entered the war. He said that his family always managed to get enough to eat because his father made furniture and could trade it with peasants for food, but others in the city of Empoli, where he lived, did not fare as well: *I was in fifth grade when the war came. . . . During the war there was terrible suffering as people tried to save their lives. Oh, I saw the whole war and I was old enough to remember a lot—the bombardments, fleeing here and there—it got so we didn't know where to hide. Fortunately, I never suffered hunger during the war. Maybe we had to sell my father's bedroom suites cheap just to eat—once we even sold one for two sacks of wheat flour and one sack of corn flour. We raised a pig inside the warehouse. My father said, "Let's just focus on surviving. Let's just get through this war. It has to end, and when it ends, then we'll decide what to do next." There were some young boys who went out from Empoli into the countryside seeking bread—we used to say, "andavano a far pane." They went all over the countryside to all the peasants saying, "Please give me a piece of bread." Nobody could refuse them. Then these boys returned home and brought this food to their parents. There was no other way for them to eat.*

Marianna, born in 1923, came from a poor urban family. During the war they had little more than their official daily rations of less than 1,000 calories per person. The situation in Florence became particularly dire during and right after the German occupation, from September 11, 1943, through August 31, 1944: *I really suffered from hunger during the war. We used to go to bed very early in the evening so we wouldn't feel the hunger. I'm telling the truth. All we had to eat was maybe a spoonful of sugar. We used to scrape together some sugar because we had a deathly hunger—una fame da morire. I remember when I had my twenty-first birthday, on September 17, 1944, all I had to eat was a little piece of dry bread with a piece of finocchiona (fennel-flavored salame) that I found in the house, and that was all.*

To survive, Marianna and her family ate the cheapest foods: *During the war we often used to eat the cow's udder, cooked with tomato sauce. Nobody eats that stuff anymore. . . . We used to buy the cow's lungs to make into stew, eh. It cost almost nothing; it's like the cow's cheek. At other times we ate a different cheap cut of meat, boiled to make broth. There across the street from my mother's newspaper kiosk lived a woman who had a butcher shop on the ground floor. My mother went every day to ask her if she would like the pleasure of my mother straightening up her apartment. So then my mother went to clean, poor thing, after already going all over the center of town delivering newspapers. Then the butcher's wife gave her some meat to boil or something else for us. She returned and she said, "Well, at least for today I've brought something to eat." During the war we used to eat lentils, dried lentils, because we couldn't get beans (fagioli) during wartime. We also ate split peas during the war, and I haven't eaten them since. We ate them occasionally during the war, but what do you want, we had such a hunger that we ate whatever we could get. I remember that we used to go nearby to a house in a little alley where we could buy pattona. Do you know what pattona is? It's like polenta, but it is made out of chestnut flour instead of corn flour. When it is used for fritters, we call it migliaccio, but when it's boiled with water and salt, we call it pattona in Florence.*

During the war, many combated hunger by resorting to foods they did not usually eat. Marianna remembered: *I started work in City Hall in 1944, and we used to eat in the office in those days in a little room they had for us. I remember one time towards the end of the war, one of my colleagues arrived. "I brought a rabbit for us to eat," she said.*

"Oh, great. Let's go everybody, a little piece for each of us."

After we finished, my colleague asked, "Did you like the rabbit?"

Another colleague answered, "Rabbit, no way. It wasn't rabbit; it was cat. It was cat, and give me another piece, because it was really good!" Renzo said you could not find cats to save your life in Florence in the last years of the war for they were all eaten. People usually cooked them *in umido*—in a tomato sauce made with onion and the *odori* or with garlic and rosemary—and they really did taste like rabbit, he said.

Marianna suffered significant hunger, but unlike many Italians who lost weight during the war (Helstosky 2004, chapter 4), she reported a surprising weight gain: *Before the war I didn't even weigh 100 pounds, but then during the war I went up to 175 pounds. I don't know why; maybe because during the war we used to eat so many starchy things. The state gave us flour and we used to make these gruels with water called* **farinate***. We ate* **pattona***. Who knows—maybe it was this kind of food that did it? But all of a sudden I got really fat, with a huge belly. After the war ended, little by little I lost the weight, and now I'm back to 140 pounds.* Marianna's weight gain may have been what Bruch (1973, 126) called "*Kummerspeck*"—"the fat of sorrow"—a form of "reactive obesity" that develops in response to emotional trauma, an understandable response to war.

Massimo, Berta, and their young daughters lived with his parents outside of Florence in Trespiano and sold flowers at the cemetery during the war until they moved in with his brother: *During the siege of Florence in 1944, we moved into the city and stayed with Renzo and Grazia six or seven months. I, my wife, and the girls, like gypsies, we hid there in their house. We left Trespiano just in time, because after we left, the Germans began to take people away.*[34] *I remember that we brought with us a pushcart full of food, a big sack of flour, geese for slaughter, a lot of fruit. We always had bread, because there in Florence, Renzo's sister-in-law Margherita had a bakery. Every day Renzo's mother-in-law Lisa would go from where we all were living in Via Sercambi across the railroad crossing at Le Cure to Margherita's bakery in Piazza Donatello. That railroad crossing was the front line.*[35] *On our side were the Germans, and on the other side the Americans. They let her cross, and she went to Piazza Donatello and she brought us back bread and a newspaper. . . . However, one day they wouldn't let her go across and then we were left without bread. So we began again to make* **migliacciole** *with flour, and we ate those. We never suffered hunger.*

During the German occupation, Florentines from the five major anti-Fascist parties founded the CTLN (Tuscan Committee of National Liberation; see Rotelli 1980) to direct the resistance. During the occupation, food became even scarcer, and men went into hiding to avoid being sent off to work camps in Germany, leaving the women to forage for food as grandmother Lisa did. Florence was finally liberated in August 1944, and Massimo described the bounty that came with the U.S. Army: *My wife Berta's family were still peasants, and I went to help them up there on their farm near Montorsoli. After the front passed through, there were American soldiers staying with them, and they had a room full of all kinds of things to eat. Pasta, sugar, precooked soup, precooked pasta, so much coffee, chocolate, every imaginable thing. I ate so much, so much, so much. They had canned food—at that time it tasted really good. It was good. However, you've got to understand that at that time anything to eat was good.*

When we finally returned back up there to Trespiano after the front had passed through—me, my wife, my father, and the girls—nothing was the same. . . . The first time we went back up there, I went with my father to our house, near the cemetery. Then later I went down to see some friends at another house. They had been away in hiding too. I was with these friends and there were peaches; it was September and the trees were full of peaches. Now listen, before the war, I never could stand peaches; I couldn't even touch them. But I went with these friends and we began to gather peaches and to peel them, and we ate so many. Massimo's memory of the end of the war was linked to eating peaches, delicious and sweet. Florentines survived hunger in the war by relying on family networks, gathering wild foods, and stretching what they had. This probably strengthened their deep appreciation for food and their aversion for excess consumption and waste.

Postwar Italy

At the end of World War II, Italy was in terrible shape. Bombardments and fighting had devastated cities and the countryside, destroying crops and leaving many thousands homeless, injured, and dead. Food was in short supply, inflation was rampant, and jobs were scarce. The cost of living rose twice as fast as wages between 1938 and 1945, and demobilized soldiers flooded the job market, leading to conflicts with women who had worked during the war and were expected to cede their jobs to men. In 1947, 1.6 million Italians were out of work (Ginsborg 1990, 80).

The fact that the Italian people provided essential help to the Allies enabled Italy to get a quite favorable peace treaty, and American Marshall Plan funds poured into Italy to influence the economic and political recovery in ways favorable to U.S. goals. Between 1943 and 1947, $2 billion in Marshall Plan funds were expended (Helstosky 2004, chapter 5); between 1948 and 1952, over $1.4 billion in Marshall Plan funds went to Italy, approximately 11 percent of total funds sent to Europe and 2 percent of Italy's gross national product in this period (Ginsborg 1990, 158). These funds helped launch the economic recovery of Italy and pave the way for the Italian economic miracle of the late 1950s and early 1960s that led to Italy's ascendance as one of the seven richest nations in the world.

Over 2.5 million Italians left rural areas for the cities between 1951 and 1967, and the number of Italians employed in agriculture dropped from 8.6 million in 1945 to 2.5 million in 1990 (Helstosky 2004, chapter 5). In Tuscany, peasants continued to flee *mezzadria* after World War II, when there were numerous work opportunities, from playing mandolin for the troops to starting small businesses. Massimo, Berta, and Renzo were part of a massive exodus of Florentines from agriculture to industry and service, and from the countryside to the city in the inter- and postwar years. The relentless and heavy workload was one reason why peasants left the land in the 1930s, '40s, and '50s. As Massimo said, *Every day we worked. We got tired of working the land. Oh, there was a lot to do; there was a lot of work. There was too much toil. There was always work, even on Sunday, for we had to clean the stalls, feed and milk the cows. We were always working.*

Not only did the work never end, but it was also poorly remunerated, habitations were rudimentary, peasants were subservient to the landlord, and they were looked down upon (Sabbatucci Severini 1990, 805). As Renzo put it, *Everybody in those days was trying to get off the land, everybody. Cultivating the land was so many hours of work, so many hours. There was also the social stigma of being a peasant. I was a youth in fine fettle (in gamba) and I had a chance to talk with girls, but there was always this little thing about being a peasant. In those days people were already leaving the land and we were all trying to set ourselves up as best we could.* Thousands of former Tuscan peasants ended up in the cities, where the men worked outside the home as laborers and entrepreneurs, and the women worked inside the homes, doing the domestic chores and often contributing to production as well, though usually for little or no wages.[36]

After the war, the government, the United Nations, and the Catholic Church provided public food assistance through school lunches, subsidized factory and workplace cafeterias, soup kitchens, and food giveaways (Helstosky 2004, chapter 5). Marianna remembered fondly the *mensa* for city workers in the Palazzo Vecchio in Florence that opened soon after the war's end: *A cafeteria opened at work, and so I ate there, in City Hall. It was really inexpensive. Later on, in 1966, the flood came and ruined it all, and they never rebuilt it. That was too bad, because we always went there to eat.*[37] Public canteens fed an estimated 2 to 3 million Italian workers daily in the early postwar years and contributed greatly to public health and nutrition (Helstosky 2004, chapter 5).

A parliamentary inquest in 1951 found that food consumption for most Italians was still confined to basic foodstuffs with scant consumption of the luxuries of meat, sugar, and wine. The average household expenditure on food was 62 percent of the family budget. Total caloric intake had risen radically compared to the war years, and *impiegati* (white-collar workers) had doubled their consumption to an average of 3,000 calories per day. Eating better was an important way in which Italians participated in the postwar economic recovery, and there were gradual increases in packaged foods and restaurant and snack bar dining (Helstosky 2004). The food, however, changed more in quantity than in composition, and people still consumed a largely vegetarian diet based on pasta, vegetables, legumes, and bread.

The *mezzadria* mode of production profoundly shaped Florentine economy, culture, and foodways. It was a premodern form of social, economic, and ideological organization that was changing throughout the century toward modernity, marked by entrepreneurial capitalism, industrialism, urbanization, and the demise of the peasant mode of production. Three things were particularly important in the transition to modernity: (1) The primary focus of most people's production was no longer food but goods and services for wages in an increasingly industrialized economy. (2) The male-headed family remained the central social unit of consumption but was no longer the locus of production. (3) Conspicuous consumption was becoming normative, and foods were increasingly standardized, processed, and preserved. Yet as we shall see in the next chapter, the traditional Florentine diet and cuisine grounded in the *mezzadria* system persisted in the 1980s but with increases in processed foods, animal products, fats, and calories.

4
Florentine Diet and Culture

Quel che non ammazza ingrassa.   *What does not kill, fattens.*
                                           Tuscan proverb (Raddi 2001, 223)

Introduction

Forty-eight-year-old Laura encapsulated her culinary culture: *Food is important for the pleasure of eating. We eat more for pleasure than necessity in my family. Our diet is very varied—we like to change all the time. We like to get up in the morning and talk about what we're going to eat that day. For the first course we always eat spaghetti. We all love it. And then we eat roast beef, or roast chicken, or meat cooked in tomato sauce, potatoes—more than anything, potatoes—tomatoes, salad greens, zucchini, beans, lots of variety. Look, a little of everything, that's what we eat.*

This chapter uses Florentines' words to describe their cuisine in the early 1980s compared to that of their more scanty childhoods and their evolving present. Their descriptions accorded well with published sources.[1] Their diet and culinary attitudes were rooted in the *mezzadria* system and the gender and family relations it spawned (see Chapter 3); but as the economy and culture changed, so did their diet and culinary attitudes. In the 1980s, older Florentines still reflected their history of hunger by appreciating abundance, taking pleasure in eating, and insisting on variety—"*a little of everything.*" They also repeatedly stressed that their cuisine has so much variety—*tanta varietà.* Marianna said, *When I cook, I try never to cook something so often to reach the point where I can't stand it. Instead, I try to cook something so that the next time I have it, I eat it willingly.* Raffaele and Laura claimed proudly that in a month they ate thirty different dinners. As the proverb implies, anything that did not kill you was fine fare and would do you good.

Over and over, Florentines said that theirs was a simple cuisine—*una cucina semplice.* Sixty-four-year-old Tommasa said, *The most simple cuisine is the most valid, especially for us Tuscans.* Crucial to its simplicity and variety was the fact that their food was composed of fresh, in-season, predominantly vegetarian ingredients. Florentine cuisine was based on constant improvisation around certain key elements that in addition to fresh vegetables consisted of pasta, legumes, tomatoes, various cuts of meat and fowl, and the *odori* or seasonings. Starches—bread, pasta, rice, polenta, potatoes, and legumes, especially the white beans called *fagioli*—formed the bulk of the dietary calories.

Many meals combined grains and legumes, which enhanced the protein content. For the poor who were the majority of the population, meat, cheese, olive oil, and other fats were scarce until the economic upswing after World War II. In 1984, older people still gathered wild plant foods, but as a diversion rather than a necessity, especially chestnuts, snails, blackberries, strawberries, porcini mushrooms, radicchio, and other greens.[2] Several kinds of preserved fish—herring, anchovies, and especially dried cod called *baccalà*—had been integral to the diet, especially of the poor, but were fast becoming nostalgic memories in the 1980s, and by 2003 had become precious exemplars of a nostalgically remembered past (see Figure 4.1).

Meals

In the 1980s, Florentine meals were dependable, regular, and central to family and social life, giving order to the days, weeks, and seasons. Florentines almost never ate alone or in between meals. In the morning they had *colazione* (breakfast) composed of espresso coffee, caffelatte, or cappuccino at home or in a local bar, usually with cookies, pastry, toast, or bread. *Colazione* was invariably light and served to tide people over until the main noon meal of the day, *pranzo*. But peasants in the first half of the twentieth century ate a large *colazione* based on grain products, as seventy-five-year-old Massimo remembered: *We got up at dawn and didn't eat anything until 8, 8:30 when we had breakfast. We ate bread with a little raw bacon or that kind of thing. And of course we ate so many of the famous* **migliacciole**. *Flour, eggs, and water, shaped with a twist and fried in olive oil. Oh, they were great, with a piece of bread.*[3]

Pranzo (dinner or lunch) was the most important meal of the day for most people who returned home to eat if they could. It took place between twelve-thirty and one-thirty, with *il tocco*—one o'clock—the preferred time in the 1980s. While there was a growing trend to shorter lunch breaks in northern cities like Milan, in Florence in the early 1980s most people still took a long lunch break to eat at home, and in the mid-1990s, according to Vercelloni (1998), eight out of ten Italians still ate *pranzo* at home. The main meal had a *primo* or first course, a *secondo* or second course, and *frutta,* a fruit course. This complex lunchtime meal meant that someone had to be home to cook and clean up after it, and that someone was almost always a woman. In families where members could not return home for lunch, *cena* (supper or dinner) was the main meal. By 2003, many Florentines reported increasing consumption of *pranzo* away from home.

In the 1980s as well as in 2003, on special occasions—holidays, dinners out, weddings, and the like—the *pranzo* or *cena* had an *antipasto* ("before the meal," appetizer course) preceding the *primo,* and a *dolce* or sweet dessert course before the fruit. The most common antipasto was *crostini** ("crusts")—either the traditional Tuscan *crostini*—chicken liver pâté made with onion, anchovies, and capers on bread—or a version made of butter

Fig. 4.1 Menu board in elegant restaurant, with *baccalà,* which used to be "the cheapest food of all," featured as one of the most expensive items, March 2003

creamed with anchovies or tuna on bread. Antipasto could consist of many other foods such as *sott'aceti* (pickled vegetables) and preserved meats like salame or prosciutto, often presented with fresh sliced cantaloupe—the renowned *prosciutto e melone*—or with fresh figs.

Most people loved the *primo* course best, and it was the most filling. It almost always consisted of either *minestra*—soup, usually with pasta or bread—or *pastasciutta*—pasta with sauce. *Pastasciutta* literally means "dry" pasta and is opposed to pasta in soup, which is implicitly wet. In the old days, different kinds of *minestra* (or *zuppa*)—like the *minestra di pane* discussed in Chapter 2—were the main foods of the peasants and urban poor. They were watery to soak up lots of bread. As Marianna said, *Some kind of soup, minestra or minestrina, every day, every day, lunch and dinner. We had to eat soup, because if not, we didn't get as filled up.* There could also be *minestrone**—"big soup" with vegetables, or *minestrina**—"little soup" of just broth with some kind of tiny pasta or semolina cooked into it. The very poor ate *acqua cotta*—"*cooked water.*" Marianna described it: *There was a minestrina made of broth, but it wasn't broth. It was made with a little bit of butter, or made with a little oil, cooked in the water. We used a little cheese if there was any, and if there wasn't, we didn't use it. Just a drop of oil. Oh, yes, so many times at my house we ate exactly this soup with oil.*[4]

But for my subjects in the 1980s, *acqua cotta* was only a memory, and richer soups filled their bowls. People also ate other foods for the primo, like *polenta* (cornmeal mush), eaten plain, fried, or cooked with tomato sauce. Fifty-year-old Valeria remembered: *Today if we make polenta, we do it because we desire it; if not, we don't make it. I might make it once or twice a year. But in the old days, we ate polenta because there was nothing else.* On occasion people made *gnocchi* or dumplings of potatoes, pasta, or cornmeal and ate them with sauce. Leonardo remembered: *My mother made cornmeal gnocchi, with meat sauce and cheese. The sauce was often made with mushrooms or sausage. This was a winter dish, and it certainly wouldn't be made in summer because it was too heavy.* In the 1980s, *pastasciutta* was the most favorite *primo,* with rice a distant second, eaten as risotto in as many ways as pasta. Rice, however, was less important than wheat and mainly grown in southwestern Tuscany in the Maremma zone. Wheat eaten as pasta and bread was the most important grain.

In the 1980s, the *secondo* was invariably meat, fish, or fowl, with a *contorno* or vegetable. The vegetable and meat sometimes had a traditional connection—for example, pork went with cooked greens—spinach, Swiss chard, or beet greens—which were often sautéed with or without garlic in the pork fat. Roasts went with roast potatoes. *Bistecca alla milanese*—breaded beef cutlet— went with fried potatoes. Meat had traditionally played a relatively minor role in Florentine cuisine, and many people found it more boring or less tasty than the ever-varied procession of flavorful vegetables, legumes, and pasta that they loved. Especially in my older subjects' childhood, meat, poultry, and fish were flavorings for potatoes, pasta, cornmeal, and vegetables, rather than substances that stood alone. In the old days, the *secondo* was often just vegetables, lots of them. As Valeria said, *Today we eat vegetables as a side dish (contorno), but then we ate them to eat. They were the meal.* They were cooked in tomato sauce (*in umido*) or into a *frittata* made of beaten eggs, fried in a frying pan and cooked on both sides. Every imaginable vegetable could appear in a *frittata,* and some of the favorites were artichokes, zucchini, spinach, and peas. Although my Florentine subjects ate much more meat in the 1980s than in the past, it still had not surpassed nonmeat foods in dietary or gustatory centrality.[5]

The evening meal called *cena* was eaten at seven-thirty (winter) or eight (summer). It was a smaller or simpler version of *pranzo* except in homes where it was the main meal (or a second big meal). Older folks especially preferred to eat a lighter evening meal, so they often had a *piatto unico* or one-course meal such as *frittata* or leftovers from *pranzo*.

Some Florentines, especially younger, hungrier ones, ate a *merenda* or afternoon snack. They ate this at around four or five o'clock to tide them over until *cena*. *Merenda* always used to be *pane e companatico*—bread and "that which goes with bread." In the old days, the *companatico* might be olive oil, wine and sugar, homemade marmalade, or occasionally a sliver of butter, ricotta, cold cuts, or *pecorino* cheese. The relatively well-off former peasant Massimo remembered: *Our snacks were always bread with olive oil, or bread with wine and sugar.* His brother Renzo said, *We ate butter on bread. We also loved bread with wine and sugar sprinkled on it, and also bread with olive oil. So much bread—we ate so much bread in the old days. Nothing like today.* When Renzo's son, forty-year-old Leonardo, was growing up in the 1950s and 1960s, he too ate *pane e companatico: I remember as a child always eating bread, bread with olive oil, and bread with wine and sugar.* But by the 1980s, the *merenda* often consisted of pastry, cookies, fruit, or bread and Nutella, the commercially processed gooey sweet chocolate-hazelnut spread whose traces were visible on so many young Italian faces across the nation every afternoon (Padovani 2000). At the end of the twentieth century, snacks outside meals were increasing (Vercelloni 1998, 985). Sugar consumption in Italy doubled between 1951 and 1971, from 14.5 kg per capita to 29.4, but by 1992 it had dropped slightly to 26.9 (Zamagni 1998, 189).

Sweets were rare in informants' childhoods except for dried figs or homemade jam. Florentines observed a strict separation between sweet and salt or savory. Their food was not sweet at all unless it was "a sweet," eaten with coffee in the mornings, at afternoon snack, or as dessert on special occasions. In the 1980s, families had sweet desserts only for celebrations, and there were many delicious Florentine desserts like *schiacciata alla fiorentina* (a sheet cake), *crème caramel* (flan), *crostate* (fruit tarts), *fritelle di riso* (rice fritters), *zuppa inglese* ("English soup," a trifle), or *cenci*—"rags"—fried dough made from flour, butter, salt, and eggs, rolled out thin and cut into irregular shapes like rags, fried in olive oil, and sprinkled with sugar.[6]

Fruit in season concluded every *pranzo* and *cena* in most of my subjects' homes in the 1980s, and continued to be widely consumed at the turn of the millennium. As Marco said, *If I don't have fruit, I don't feel like I've eaten.* But in the old days, fruit was expensive and unavailable to peasants and the urban poor except on special occasions, as Baldo and Marianna said in Chapter 2.

Holidays

Massimo spoke for all Florentines when he said, *Sundays and holidays we ate special foods.*[7] Sunday was the most common holiday or *festa,* and was always marked with an abundant noon meal capped by some extraordinary dish. Before World War II, this was most notably meat or **pastasciutta.** Fifty-year-old Valeria spoke of her childhood: *Sunday was a little bit different. Without fail, we ate meat on Sunday, even if we hadn't eaten any all week. Maybe roast chicken or rabbit.* Sixty-one-year-old Marianna said, *On Sunday we had fried minute steaks—braciole—with fried potatoes. And* **pastasciutta.** Seventy-three-year-old former peasant Renzo said, *Sunday was the main holiday. We ate better on holidays, meat, steak, something unusual. Macaroni, something better because it was a holiday.* His sister-in-law, seventy-six-year-old Berta who grew up in a family of more modest means, celebrated *feste,* but not with the steak that Renzo's family occasionally had: *On Sundays, we had a special meal. We ate* **pastasciutta** *at midday. Or if not, do you know what those old women did? They went and bought some beef innards and they cooked up a huge pot with potatoes, and we ate it at midday. Or they made broth with the entrails, or they made spaghetti sauce with celery, onion, and entrails.*

In the past, eating roast chicken was a popular way to celebrate Sundays and holidays. Seventy-five-year-old Massimo said: *We ate chicken for Christmas and New Year's, and we ate a hen at Easter.* Sixty-one-year-old Marianna, of poor, working-class origins, recounted: *I remember this. When I had my confirmation, we had to evacuate our apartment, and we were in a warehouse. So what happened? There were all these boxes, and we set our table on one of these boxes. We all sat around it on little chairs, and we began to eat the special meal of roast chicken. So then my brother said, "Too bad every day is not a holiday so we could always eat chicken." Eating chicken was rare and truly special.*

My subjects also told of celebrating holidays by having some extra wine, or a sweet dessert—things that they could not eat on a daily basis. On Christmas many ate **panforte,** a fruitcake traditionally made in Siena. Fifty-four-year-old Baldo from Empoli remembered: *In the old days we tried to save up a little money so we could have a special meal for the holidays, for Christmas and Easter. At the midday meal we ate chicken. Chicken was really special. For Christmas in Empoli something everybody knew was the fruitcake called* **panforte di Siena,** *because we were near to Siena. A week before the holiday the Sienese vendors came with their stands to sell it in the town squares. There was certainly no* **spumante**—*no champagne, no, no, no. If we had a* **fiasco** *of wine, that was already a lot. That was enough.* Massimo said, *For Christmas in those days, there was great feasting, not at all like today. So much food,* **panforte.** *There had to be* **panforte,** . . . *and other things as well.* When Marianna was growing up, they always had a capon for Christmas, and, *For the New Year's Day holiday, my mother always made tortellini, to have them with meat sauce.* Leonardo remembered in the 1950s always having Christmas with his paternal grandparents in Trespiano: *I remember well the zuppa inglese at the end. I loved it. And I remember crostini at the beginning.*

Easter was a special holiday for Florentines because of its place in the Catholic liturgy and its traditional association with spring. Leonardo recounted an important Easter ritual: *I remember Easter with my parents and the story of the eggs of my mother. She went the morning of Easter, I think at eight in the morning, to church with her hard-boiled eggs, and the priest blessed the eggs in the church. Each person went with her own plate, I remember it perfectly, with the eggs tied up in a napkin. It was something that the woman did, the mother of the family. She took one egg for each member of the family. I remember she put them on this large table placed under the altar and the eggs were blessed during the mass. Then she brought them home and we had to eat them on an empty stomach. It bothered me. I didn't like it. I didn't understand the sense of these things. . . . But if you think about it, it is a beautiful thing, a sort of communion.* Renzo's cousin Valeria and her extended family took hard-boiled eggs to mass to be blessed for Easter and ate them together right before the Easter meal, *a piece for each person,* said Valeria. But she wondered if her children would continue this ritual after the old people were gone. In the 1980s, the main holidays were Sundays, Christmas, New Year's Day, *La Beffana* (January 6), Easter, and Carnival; however, none of these holidays were extraordinary anymore, because, as several people said, *every day is a holiday.*

Flavors and Spices

Tuscan cuisine was *saporoso*—rich in seasoning—and based on a clear separation of savory and sweet. The key tastes came from *gli odori*—"the flavors." *Gli odori* consisted of carrot, celery, basil, and parsley. So basic were these to Florentine cuisine in the 1980s that greengrocers always gave shoppers *gli odori* for free with any purchase. In 2003, some greengrocers gave the odori for free to long-standing clients, but others gave only a small bunch of parsley or basil to clients, and supermarkets sold the odori (Lo Russo 2003). The first step in many recipes was to take a *mezzaluna*—a half-moon–shaped knife—and make a *battuto*—a finely chopped mass—out of the *odori.* The second step was to sauté them in olive oil to release the flavors. Onion and garlic were also essential flavors in Florentine cuisine, and one or the other was usually sautéed with the *odori.* Raffaele said that they did not use onion and garlic together because the onion sweetens (*radolceva*) the food, so it should be kept separate from garlic, which is not sweet but pungent. Only in a classic meat sauce for spaghetti—*sugo* or *ragù*—or in some meat dishes, did people regularly use both onion and garlic.

While the *odori* were the main spices, Florentines also used thyme, pepper, oregano, hot pepper, sage, ginger, nutmeg, rosemary, cloves, cinnamon, lemon, and anise. Cooks used other spices on occasion, but those were the principal ones.[8] Raffaele and Laura's family loved *spaghetti aglio, olio e pepperoncino,** pasta dressed with olive oil in which hot pepper, garlic, and parsley were sautéed. But other Florentines were less enthusiastic about red pepper, which in one family became a symbol of the differences between a sophisticated northern Italian city girl and her isolated peasant in-laws (see Chapter 7). Black pepper was essential in the famous *bistecca alla fiorentina**—charcoal-grilled T-bone steak—and in the beloved *pinzimonio** dip for raw vegetables, consisting of extra-virgin olive oil with lots of salt and pepper.

Bread

Bread has always been the most important food in Florentine cuisine, and it was an essential component of every meal. As Taddei (1998, 31) said, "The entire history of mezzadria foodways is the history of bread and grains." Florentine bread was thick and dense and was most commonly sold in the form of a *filone*—a long, flat loaf of a *mezzo kilo, kilo,* or *due kili*—approximately 1 or 2 or 4.5 pounds—of either white or whole-wheat flour. When fresh, the bread was spongy and flavorful; as it aged, it got hard and even denser, less appealing by itself but of a perfect consistency to go into soups. Many Florentine dishes soaked the old bread in broth or other liquid, like the *minestra di pane* described by Raffaele in Chapter 2. Other characteristic Florentine dishes using old bread were *ribollita**—day-old bread steeped in day-old soup, *pappa al pomodoro**—tomato pap, and the summer salad *panzanella.** Seventy-five-year-old former peasant Massimo said, *We ate a huge amount of **panzanella** in the summer. It is a salad of old bread soaked in water, squeezed dry, crumbled, and tossed with tomatoes, onions, basil, olive oil, and vinegar. We ate **pappa al pomodoro***—you know, old bread soaked with fresh tomatoes and olive oil.*[9]

Older informants all agreed with fifty-year-old Valeria, who said, *We used to eat so much bread in the old days—tanto pane.* Older subjects recounted that when they were young they were always admonished, *"Eat with bread—mangia col pane."* Bread was filling and nutritious; its consumption made the other, more expensive foods—oil, meat, vegetables—stretch farther. As long as there was bread, people kept hunger at bay. They often ate bread with *companatico*—"that which goes with bread"—which played a minor dietary role compared to the major role of the bread.[10] As fifty-year-old Valeria recalled: *In the old days I brought a slice of bread to work with me to eat during the morning. On the bread I had maybe a little olive oil, cream skimmed from the milk with a little sugar, a little wine and sugar, or a little marmalade if there was any. We didn't have much at all to eat with the bread.* Bread was the critical food, the sine qua non, the last bastion against hunger. As seventy-six-year-old former peasant Berta said, *We never suffered hunger because we always had as much bread as we wanted. Maybe we ate it with olive oil, or we ate it with an onion, or we ate it with whatever there was, but we always had bread.*

Although in the 1980s my subjects ate much less bread than they used to, there were still many like Baldo who said, *I would not be able to eat without bread. Even just a little, for we really don't even eat very much bread anymore, but there has to be some, because without bread I just could not eat.* In fact, Italians never sat down to a meal without bread, a habit marked in restaurants by the inevitable *pane e coperto*—the bread and cover charge. Bread's importance was not only dietary and economic but symbolic as well.[11] Florentines hated to see bread turned upside down and would always turn it right side up, a habit also noted by Console (1993), who reported proverbs, habits, and a children's poem (*filastrocca*) that aimed to inculcate "respect and veneration for bread," which had an important cultural value. People admonished against wasting bread or dropping crumbs on the ground. The Florentine saying, "*Far cascare il pan di mano*," ("to cause bread to fall from the hand"), means to discourage or demoralize someone (Raddi 2001, 110). In Florence, *essere a pane*—"to be at bread" with someone—was to be close and friendly (Cantagalli 1981, 25; Raddi 2001, 96). When Florentines said a man was "*un pezzo di pane*," ("a piece of bread"), they meant he was dependable and solid—like bread.

Peoples all over the Mediterranean shared Florentines' love of bread;[12] however, Florentine bread was unusual because it had no salt. Florentines loved salty food and they even had a disparaging word for food that lacked salt—*sciocco*. As well as meaning "lacking adequate salt," *sciocco* meant unintelligent and insipid. As the etymology suggests, for food to lack salt was a serious failing. To cook pasta, Florentines salted the water heavily so that the pasta would absorb the salt while cooking. The announcement by a family member that "*la pasta è sciocca*"—"the pasta lacks salt" always brought woe to the cook. Tuscan foods were either salted in cooking or they were salted in processing like the traditional *salame toscano* or *pecorino* cheese. Unsalted bread worked in Florence because other foods were salty, as Codacci (1981, 10) explained: "Tuscan bread has the characteristic of being without salt because in centuries past the excessive price of salt prohibited its use. Then it became tradition to make the bread insipid and we realized that having it thus exalts the tastes of the viands with which it is united."

Legumes and *Minestre*

Legumes have always been a mainstay of the Tuscan diet, including chickpeas, lentils, favas, and many other varieties of beans, especially *fagioli*, white beans similar to those in the United States known as *cannellini* or Great Northern beans. In describing the past, Massimo said, *What did we eat? Beans. One year my grandfather, my father, Renzo, and I ate a hundred and ten pounds of beans— in not even a year, in six or seven months.*[13] Seventy-six-year-old Berta remarked about her childhood: *You ask if we ate beans? Chickpeas? Oh, yes, don't doubt that. Those took away our hunger.* A well-known proverb encapsulates the long-lasting importance of beans to Florentine diet and culture: *"Fiorentin mangia fagioli, lecca piatti e romaioli"*—"Bean eater is the Florentine, licks the plates and ladles clean" (Cantagalli 1981, 129).[14] Many Florentine dishes were built around *fagioli,* especially the renowned *minestra di pane* discussed in Chapter 2, *fagioli all'uccelletto** cooked with tomatoes and sage, and *fagioli conditi**—boiled and dressed with olive oil and pepper. Raddi (2001, 176) said, "Florentines, it is well-known . . . are renowned consumers of this delicious legume," which explains their saying, *"Mi va a fagiolo,"* meaning "That suits me to a bean," or "That's perfect for me." In fact, Cantagalli (1981, 129) wondered why "in the coat of arms of Florence there is a lily and not a bean."

Traditionally Florentines ate most of their legumes in *minestre*—soups centered on legumes and pasta or bread, flavored with herbs and vegetables cooked in abundant water. Renzo commented about his childhood in the 1920s and 1930s: *In those days there had to be minestra day and night, one way or another, because that filled you up, you know. With some bread in it, always bread.* His brother Massimo's thoughts of *minestre* reminded him of a childhood memory: *In the winter we ate a pot full of minestra made of beans or vegetables, and bread. We ate minestra di pane—bread soup. Two big bowls of that soup, or three, depending. There was enough for all of us. I always remember one time—I don't know if I was sick or what—and I didn't go to work in the fields. My grandmother had prepared everything for making minestra di pane: the greens, the Tuscan kale—cavolo nero. Well, I called out to ask my grandmother whether I should put the cavolo nero in the soup whole or whether I should cut it. I still remember this. She answered, "Cut it! How can you put it in the pot without cutting it?" We ate so much Tuscan kale—tanto, ma tanto cavolo nero.* This member of the cabbage family was integral to Florentine cuisine and it grew well just about anywhere.[15]

Massimo described other soups: *We ate pap, gruel—pappa, farinata. . . . I still like zuppa lombarda*—Lombard soup.*[16] *We ate soup made of rice and cabbage—riso col cavolo.* We also ate chickpeas, cabbage, and cauliflower in the winter. Sometimes . . . we ate a couple of bowls of minestra with bread. Sometimes we had pasta made at home in the soup; other times we bought those little kinds of pasta, Ave Maria (Hail Mary), the Pater Nostre (Our Father), and ate them in the soup. We put the herbs and the tomatoes in the minestra and made it very watery so we could put lots of bread in it.*

Massimo's fifty-year-old daughter Valeria also remembered legumes being a mainstay of her childhood diet in the thirties and forties, in contrast to her diet in the eighties, when they had become an infrequent delicacy: *We ate so many legumes then, but now we just eat a little, when we have the desire, to vary our diet. But then we ate them to eat. We ate white beans—fagioli all'uccelletto—because in that way they filled us up more and tasted better—with two or three sausages in the winter—a little piece for each of us just to have the flavor. We ate white beans, chickpeas, and fava beans just a little, although I've always liked them.*[17]

Pasta and Other Grains

The habit of pasta consumption was rooted in the peasant past where pasta in soup in poorer homes and with sauce in better-off ones was common.[18] Seventy-three-year-old Renzo reported on his childhood in the 1920s: *We always ate pasta. Almost every day it was the **sfoglia** (pastry sheet) made by hand. The **sfoglia** is made with eggs and flour, rolled out flat, and cut into strips of spaghetti or macaroni—you know, big strips, called **nastroni**.*[19] *We ate that almost every day. We always had pasta made at home, day and night. Sometimes we ate it with sauce, sometimes cooked with beans, like **pasta e fagioli**, or sometimes **pastasciutta** with sauce. We ate it with tomato sauce or with meat sauce or with so many things. We rarely had store-bought pasta. There were very few kinds, you know; there was that kind called the **Ave Maria** (Hail Mary), the **stelline** (little stars), the ones you use for **pasta e fagioli***—pasta and bean soup. And then . . . there were **penne, lasagne,** three or four things. But it cost money; you had to buy that kind of pasta. At home it was just flour, egg, and oil—so with very little expense, you had your pasta. It was all like that.*

Renzo's peasant family's relatively comfortable status was reflected in their ability to eat egg pasta with sauce, whereas the poorer people reported eating plain pasta mainly in soup and *pastasciutta* only on special occasions. But by the 1980s, not only was pasta regularly eaten in sauce, but also the kinds of sauces were expanding to include richer substances unheard of in the past. As fifty-four-year-old Raffaele, the rare male family cook, said, *In my opinion, pasta is the most basic food—l'alimento base. In my family, we always eat it, always, at both lunch and supper. We never get tired of pasta. I always make the spaghetti sauce on the spot, always, almost always. We make simple sauces that take very little time. While the pasta is boiling, I can make the sauce. I make it with tuna, with tomato, with garlic and hot pepper, with fish, with cream, with four cheeses—there are many varieties, and all of them take only ten or fifteen minutes.* Pasta was valued because it was delicious, filling, cheap, varied, quick, and flexible.

In the 1980s, people loved pasta and experimented with it constantly. As Raffaele's twenty-year-old daughter Piera said, *I can eat pasta any way at any time of the day or night.* She described some of the ways her father cooked pasta: *Often he makes spaghetti with tomato sauce—**pomarola**. He makes pasta with anchovies, with clams, with fish. He makes it all kinds of ways. He makes **spaghetti aglio, olio e pepperoncino***—with garlic and hot pepper—I love that. He makes **spaghetti alla carbonara** with parmesan, eggs, and bacon, which I like a little less.* Florentines ate pasta in a variety of shapes and sauces: spaghetti, tagliatelle, linguine, bavette, pappardelle, penne, spaghettini, tortellini, ravioli, lasagne, and so on. Each sauce had its own most appropriate form of pasta. For example, *pappardelle*—broad lasagna-like noodles—were eaten with hare or rabbit sauce,[20] and *tagliatelle*—flat, long noodles—were eaten with *sugo* (meat sauce).

In the 1980s, wheat as pasta and bread was the main grain consumed by Florentines; however, they also ate rice, sometimes in soup instead of pasta, or at other times as *risotto,* cooked with vegetables or meat, as the *primo*—for example, *risotto alla milanese** with onion and saffron; *alla finanziera* with chicken livers, onions, and nutmeg; *al pomodoro* with tomato sauce; or with shellfish, mushrooms, asparagus, artichokes, and many other vegetables. Codacci (1981, 48) reported recipes for *risotto* with *ortica* (nettles) and *risotto alla fiorentina* cooked with all the *odori,* onion, and ground beef. In the first half of the century, Florentines ate a broader variety of grains in more diverse forms. Depending on where they lived and what their economic conditions were, they also ate less prized grains like rye, barley, or cornmeal cooked as polenta, gnocchi, or fritters. In Italy as a whole, wheat consumption stayed fairly stable across the second half of the twentieth century at 165 kilograms per capita in 1951 and 160 in 1992, as did rice at 9 and 8 kilograms per capita in those years; corn, however, dropped from 22.2 kilograms per capita in 1951 to 7.5 in 1971 to a negligible amount in 1992 (Zamagni 1998, 189).

In the old days, peasants drank boiled toasted grains rather than coffee. Renzo said, *There was only surrogate coffee in those days. We drank very, very little real coffee. It was expensive and we didn't have the custom of drinking it. Instead there was this surrogate, this chicory. We made a huge pot of it and mixed it with milk. Oh, we drank some glasses, some big glasses like this, full of milk. We also grew barley and we toasted it ourselves to make coffee out of, to have with milk. Yes, it was good; it was good because there was nothing else!* But by the 1980s, coffee was an integral part of the Italian diet and some people drank it several times a day—for breakfast, for a midmorning or midafternoon coffee break, after lunch, and after supper.

Vegetables

Many of the older people reported that their childhood diets were heavily vegetarian. Berta said, *Potatoes, those were what we ate most, those and perhaps beans and chickpeas in soup. We had greens in our garden—Swiss chard, beet greens, cabbage, whatever peasants could grow. We ate wild radicchio; we ate so much of that.* Peasants grew vegetables of all kinds in the countryside around Florence and used them abundantly in cooking. Vegetables were cooked in pasta sauces, in *minestre, in umido* (in a tomato sauce), in *frittate,* and were also eaten deep-fried, or raw with the oil-pepper-salt *pinzimonio* dip. Florentines regularly consumed artichokes, asparagus, beets, cabbage, carrots, cauliflower, celery, eggplant, fennel, garlic, kale, Tuscan kale, leeks, mushrooms, onions, peas, peppers, potatoes, spinach, Swiss chard, string beans, tomatoes, and zucchini, all in several varieties.

Marianna said that after the war she lived with her cousins in central Florence: *We used to eat lots of vegetables there because my aunt worked at the Sant'Ambrogio farmers' market. She would return home for lunch at two o'clock with this thing, or that other thing—for example, fava beans, fresh or dried. Oh, yes, we ate a lot of vegetables there, and I was already used to eating just vegetables, without any meat, because we couldn't always afford meat when I was a child. I remember what we ate there at my cousin's, right after the war ended. Peas, maybe; she would make a huge pan full of peas. We were ten or twelve people eating, eh. My cousin cooked a pot as big as this, full of peas with bacon, and we all dug in, we all ate it. . . . Then, I don't know, one day she would make asparagus for everyone. And there would be that. Bread, and always soup, yes, yes.*

Fifty-year-old Valeria remembered her diet growing up in the 1940s and 1950s: *We made **pastasciutta,** but we had it without meat. There was very little meat then, and we made the sauce with just tomato and the **odori.** I still make it that way sometimes. I whip up a quick little tomato sauce—**sugo scappato***— "escaped sauce" we call it, without meat, but today I do it for variety, because I don't know what to cook. But in the old days we made it precisely to eat. That was all we had. In the old days, maybe we had spaghetti with that kind of sauce and then followed it with some fried potatoes, without meat, understand?* Although meat consumption was rising in the 1980s and vegetable consumption was declining among younger folks (Turrini et al. 2001), Florentines still loved and ate a lot of diverse fresh vegetables.[21]

Fruits and Nuts

Many fruits and nuts grew well in the Tuscan climate, including almonds, apples, apricots, chestnuts, figs, grapes, hazelnuts, olives, peaches, pears, plums, and walnuts. These played an important part in the diet and contributed fats, proteins, carbohydrates, vitamins, minerals, variety, and sweetness. Sugar was quite scarce until after the Second World War, as seventy-five-year-old Massimo recalled: *Sweets? Who made sweets? Every now and then in the winter we could buy a few cookies. And we made so many dried figs in the month of September, and we ate them during the winter with bread—dried figs, and dried olives with bread. We had walnuts and almonds; we had so many almonds. After the **minestra** we ate dried figs or walnuts.*

We had those round figs, the totally round ones. You took a fig and you cut it in half and you put it on a cane mat in the sun to dry, and then when it was completely dry, you put anise inside it and you closed the two sides back up. Then you put it in the middle of laurel leaves to dry some more and it took on the fragrance of the laurel. They came out great and we ate them. We made many sacks of them. We also took other dried figs and put them in empty flour sacks and the leftover flour stuck to them; it turned them white and kept them very soft.[22] When the grapes were ripe, we hung them up on racks all over the bedrooms of the house, and they got more and more dried out and sweet. In the bedrooms on top of all the dressers and hanging all around were pears. We ate a lot of dried fruit and nuts.

Massimo's wife, seventy-six-year-old Berta, had similar, though somewhat more cynical, memories: *On our farm we had a few almond trees, and several fig and walnut trees. We dried the fruit and nuts, and they were enough for the family. We had three or four walnut trees right there in front of the house, as far as you are from me. I liked to eat the walnuts green too. We harvested grapes and hung them up for the winter, there in the house, I don't know if you've ever seen them. Two bunches of grapes and a piece of the vine and we hung them from the rafters. The bedrooms were full of this greenery. The grapes dried out and were good—if they didn't rot. But, oh, God, in truth a few went bad.*

Berta and Massimo's daughter Valeria also remembered in her childhood eating fruit in modest amounts with great pleasure: *We had a garden with a few fruit trees and vegetables. But we certainly didn't eat fruit every day then the way we do now. We ate just a little. We made marmalade out of blackberries—it is really good, I still love that—and out of figs and quince-apples (**mele cotogne**) that grew in the garden. My grandfather also dried the figs on cane mats in the sun. We also dried olives to eat in the winter.*

Chestnuts (*castagne*) and chestnut flour (*farina dolce*) were important foods, particularly in staving off hunger. In Chapter 3, Massimo told of bicycling 21 miles to Gagliano during the war to gather chestnuts and he remembered eating them regularly as a child, sometimes as a second course after the **minestra.** They ate chestnuts boiled as **ballocche** or roasted over coals as **bruciate.** They ground them into flour, which they boiled into a polenta-like substance called **pattona,** baked into a brownie-like cake with raisins and pine nuts called **migliaccio** or **castagnaccio,** or fried into fritters called **migliacciole.** Seventy-three-year-old former peasant Renzo remembered: *In the summer we ate a big meal in the morning because we began to work at 5 A.M. At around 8 or 9, my grandmother made a huge tray full of fritters—either fried wheat flour— **pasta fritta**—or fried chestnut flour—**migliacciole**—we used to call them, mountains of them, so many of them. **Migliacciole** are fritters made out of water and chestnut flour. You needed a lot of oil to fry them, but we had plenty of olive oil. Those fritters really stuck to your ribs because they were dripping with olive oil, and we ate so many of them.* In the 1980s none of my subjects cooked chestnut flour products nor did they preserve nuts and figs. Very rarely they might eat a piece of **castagnaccio** purchased at a bakery or rustic **trattoria,** but they ate a lot more fresh fruit than they had even dreamed about in their childhoods. Between 1951 and 1992, fruit consumption in Italy more than tripled, increasing from 56 to 170 kilograms per capita (Zamagni 1998, 189).

Meat, Milk, and Cheese

Before the impact of the Italian economic miracle, meat was not a major part of most people's diet in and around Florence, even though a famous Florentine dish was *bistecca alla fiorentina**—a thick, charcoal grilled T-bone steak.[23] In the 1980s, meat was still relatively expensive, prized, and eaten in small quantities. Florentines stretched meat by cooking it with broth, sauce, or vegetables. In the old days, people of poor or modest incomes ate very little muscle meat, which went to the wealthy, and consumed more devalued cuts and organ meats like lungs, brains, kidneys, liver, tongue, heart, tripe, cheek, blood, and so on.[24] For example, a favorite Florentine dish was *roventini,* pig's blood fried with a little flour, salt, pepper, and grated cheese (Raddi 2001, 238; Codacci 1981, 69). But in the 1980s, organ meats were almost never eaten and then only by the older people.

A favorite way older people like meat is boiled into broth (*brodo*) with onions, celery, parsley, basil, and carrot. Meat cooked this way was called *lesso*—"boiled." Older folks liked the broth made not just with a cheap cut of tasty muscle meat (*spicchio di petto* or *costoline*) but also with tongue (*lingua*), tail (*coda*), and foot (*zampa*), which flavored the broth richly at little expense (Codacci 1981). Leftover *lesso* was eaten as *lesso rifatto**—refried in olive oil with onions and perhaps potatoes. Baldo commented: *I like the traditional foods. Even today, if there is a little boiled meat left over, fry it up for me with onions and I'll eat it with pleasure. It's a habit; that's the way I like it.* *Trippa alla fiorentina*—tripe Florentine style—was a famous dish made from cleaned, boiled tripe cooked with tomatoes and *odori.* In the 1980s, you could still buy fresh boiled tripe from a *trippaio* or street vendor in Florence, which people ate in sandwiches or took home and cooked into *trippa alla fiorentina.*[25]

Berta reflected on meat consumption in her youth and in the 1980s: *Meat is better today, more expensive, but better. Today at least you can eat a little steak, but in the old days we never ate that kind of meat. We didn't even know it existed. Steak—mother of mine what are you saying? We were many, we were a big family; so what do you want, if we had wanted steak, we would have had to buy how many, four or five steaks, to have a little piece for each of us. We could not possibly do that. We never ate steak.*

Berta's older daughter Valeria, born in 1934, also remembered relatively little meat when she worked in Florence in the early 1950s: *For lunch I used to take a little pot (tegamino) to work. Maybe inside were an egg and a piece of bread. Every now and then I took a little piece of meat with my bread if some was left over from supper. At supper we ate whatever there was—an egg, or some vegetables. Maybe we ate a little meat, but it was always an inexpensive cut. It wasn't like today where we eat costly little steaks without any fat on them. Then we ate the cheap cuts in stew with a lot of potatoes—you know, the famous* **stuffato di pelliccia, di molte patate e poca ciccia**—*"the stew of skin with a lot of potatoes but otherwise thin."*

We lived in the country, so we raised rabbits, chickens, ducks, geese, and turkeys. We raised them on this little bit of land that we rented there in Trespiano—not to sell but to eat ourselves. We ate them and we ate the eggs. We ate so much bad stuff, stuff that I would never eat now. For example—guinea pigs—we used to eat them.[26] *I remember that my grandfather raised them when we lived in Trespiano. We had a chicken coop and we had a cage for these guinea pigs. I wouldn't eat them today; I'd rather have a piece of bread dipped in olive oil or wine. We also used to eat hedgehogs—you know, those animals that they run over in the roads sometimes? The men went out in the woods to catch them and I don't have any idea how they cleaned them, but we ate those too. Now I would never eat them.*

Sometimes we ate chicken, but it wasn't like today. Today, if I cook a chicken and all of us are at the table, we eat the whole thing in one meal. In the old days, you made a chicken last for two or three meals and you only ate a little bit each time. We ate rabbits sometimes and we ate so many vegetables. So many potatoes, so much bread. Instead, today we eat meat, lots of meat, whereas before we ate only a little tiny piece.

Depending on where they lived and the availability of game, Tuscans ate more or less of it. Romer (1984) reported that people still ate lots of game in the 1980s on the Tuscan border with Umbria, and my subjects ate game sometimes when they went on an outing to a country restaurant. But game played a minor part in both their diet and their recollections. Apergi and Bianco (1991, 59) pointed out that *mezzadria* peasants had little free time in which to hunt and hence ate little game in their traditional diet.

While peasants consumed little meat and then mostly less-prized organ meats, *padroni* and more well-off city dwellers, like artisans and shopkeepers, ate more. But in the years following World War II and the Italian economic miracle of the 1960s and beyond, the consumption of meat increased rapidly for all of the population, and much of it was produced in factory farms. People ate roast pork, fried pork chops, chicken breasts in white wine, and so on, and meat grew in its share of the Italian diet from just under 18 kilograms per capita in 1951, to 75 in 1981, to almost 86 in 1992 (Zamagni 1998, 189).

Meat and cheese were marginal in the diet of most people in the first half of the twentieth century. Cheese consumption rose steadily throughout the century and reached 56 kilograms per capita in the 1950s and 102 kilograms per capita in 1992. In the old days, some peasants kept a cow or some sheep to milk. Most people consumed only *pecorino* and ricotta, and *parmigiano* was extremely expensive. Fifty-year-old Valeria said of her youth: *Maybe we ate a little cheese, but not like today when we have all these different kinds of cheeses from Germany, France, and all over Italy. In the old days, all we had was a little pecorino—sheep's milk cheese—just a little.* Codacci (1981, 133) says, "The characteristic Tuscan cheese is *pecorino*." The importance of and value on cheese were signified in Tuscan sayings, for example, *"Quest'è il cacio sui maccheroni"* (Raddi 2001, 224)—"This is the cheese on the macaroni," meaning "this is just what is needed."

Eggs

Eggs played an important part of the diet of peasants and city folk throughout the twentieth century, moving from 7 kg per capita in 1952 to almost 13 in 1992 in Italy as a whole (Zamagni 1998, 189). Florentines ate eggs in *frittate* and in many other ways.[27] Seventy-six-year-old former peasant Berta said, *We ate frittate because the eggs stretched farther; maybe we had two frittate so everybody had at least a piece. Oh, yes, in those days things were very hard.* Frittate were made with eggs and vegetables, including onions, potatoes, zucchini, spinach, artichokes, asparagus, peas, Swiss chard, leeks, wild radicchio, nettles, and mushrooms. To make *frittate,* the vegetables were sautéed in olive oil, and the eggs were beaten vigorously and poured over the vegetables in the hot oil and cooked until set, then flipped over and cooked on the other side. *Frittate* were very common, even too much so, according to seventy-three-year-old Renzo: *We ate frittate. In the evenings my grandmother might make four huge frittate, as big as a dinner plate. Sometimes she made them with bacon, all kinds of things like that. Wholesome food. Oh, she made so many frittate, in fact, I've eaten enough frittate to last a lifetime.*

Another favorite way to eat eggs was *uova al pomodoro**—eggs cooked in tomato sauce. Florentines ate fried or scrambled eggs, *uova in tegamino* or *uova strapazzate.* They ate soft-, medium-, or hard-boiled eggs called *uova alla cocca, uova barzotte,* and *uova sode.* They ate *uova in camicia*—"eggs in the shirt"—by breaking raw eggs into boiling water and cooking them for a couple of minutes. They ate *uova frullate*—raw eggs beaten in a cup with a little sugar, which was considered a restorative food, good for the sick, as Marianna mentioned in Chapter 2. They often used the eggs to make a batter for fried vegetables and occasionally used them to make pasta or sweets.

Dried Fish

Baccalà, dried salted codfish, and other kinds of dried fish, especially herring and another cheap dried fish called *salacche* or *salacchine,* made extremely important contributions to Florentines' diet in the first half of the twentieth century, especially for peasants and others of modest means (Apergi and Bianco 1991, 59–61). *Baccalà* was, as sixty-six-year-old Elena said, *the cheapest food of all.* Peasants sold their chickens, eggs, and rabbits, and bought the cheap dried cod, using the money left over to buy necessities like sugar, kerosene, and shoes. Seventy-three-year-old former peasant Renzo said, *In the winter we ate baccalà—dried codfish—and lots of other foods in sauces with potatoes. We ate so much baccalà, eh. The peasants went and sold their chickens and bought baccalà to earn a little money, understand? Baccalà cost least of all. And herring. If you only knew how many herrings I have eaten, not just one or two, you know. And then there were salacchine, relatives of the herring. We ate mountains of them.* Berta evoked the famous image immortalized in

Bertolucci's film *1900*: *Oh, yes, we ate herring, and* **baccalà**. *We made polenta and we rubbed it alongside the dried herring so it would take up the flavor of the herring.*

Louis Monod, the French-Swiss chef who spent several years in Florence at the turn of the twentieth century and wrote a cookbook on Florentine cuisine, commented, *"I fiorentini sono estremamente golosi del baccalà"*—"Florentines really love **baccalà**," and he offered ten different recipes (Lo Russo and Pratesi 1999, 70–71).[28] To cook **baccalà**, the dried cod had to be soaked in running water for a long time to *farlo rinvenire*—"make it return to itself"—and be purged of its excessive saltiness. In the 1980s, all over Florence on Fridays outside of stores were water tables trickling water over the soaking **baccalà**. Florentines invented many delicious ways to cook it. Elena loved it. *It's superlative!* she said. She cooked **baccalà alla livornese*** with tomato, garlic, parsley, and hot pepper, a recipe that others made without hot pepper. People also fried **baccalà** or cooked it with chickpeas, with leeks and tomatoes, or with polenta (Codacci 1981, 108–109). It was declining in popularity in the 1980s, and by 2003, had attained a nostalgic status but was rarely eaten.

Olives, Olive Oil, Lard, and Other Fats

The production of olives was a mainstay of the Tuscan economy for hundreds of years, and the Renaissance paintings for which Florence is so renowned showed the Tuscan landscape dotted with olive trees already in the 1200s. Olive culture grew significantly between the early 1800s and the mid-1900s, causing tension between landlords who grew olives for profit and peasants who wanted to grow subsistence crops, especially grains, which were less lucrative for landlords (Lo Russo and Pratesi 1999). Olive oil was expensive and precious, but olives were relatively cheap and were eaten often with bread as *companatico* by my older subjects after curing them in salt to remove their extreme bitterness.

Olive oil has always been a key element in Tuscan cooking, although it was consumed sparingly until the 1960s and 1970s, when its consumption rose with prosperity.[29] Codacci (1981, 11) described the ideal Tuscan olive oil:

> I am speaking of the true olive oil, that obtained from the pressing of olives gathered before their complete maturation, when they are still violet and not completely black. They must be picked and not knocked nor fallen to the ground. I repeat, they must be picked at the exact right moment. This is the olive oil that after pressing has that natural effervescence that is "out of this world," to quote the old peasant Rosa at the olive mill in Valigondoli.

This olive oil was thick, gold-green, fragrant, delicious, and free of toxins, even when fried at high temperatures.[30] In the past, my subjects' consumption of olive oil varied directly with their economic status, with the poorest consuming tiny amounts. Seventy-six-year-old Berta said, *We had olive oil, enough for our own consumption, but, oh, they just put a little olive oil, nothing like today. Today we make a lake, but then they just put a drop or two into the pan for all to share.*

In the 1980s, Florentines were serious about olive oil and used it generously for everything including sauces and the famous *fritto,* which the early twentieth century French-Swiss chef Monod defined as "the characteristic and fundamental base of the flavorful Tuscan cuisine" (Lo Russo and Pratesi 1999, 85). A *fritto* was any dish of food that was fried, often with some kind of batter. Common fried foods were fish, chicken, rabbit, artichokes, polenta, potatoes, zucchini, and zucchini flowers, called *pesci di campo*—"fish of the field." *Fritto misto* was a dish of mixed fried foods consisting of fish, shellfish, vegetables, or meats.

In the 1980s, to ensure the best possible quality of their olive oil, my subjects obtained it in bulk from the producers in large 50- or 100-kilogram (100- or 200-pound) jugs called *damigiane,* which they bottled at home. Raffaele reported: *A basic element of Tuscan cuisine is olive oil. It is essential. In our house, we use only and exclusively virgin olive oil that I buy directly from the producer. I go to the mill and buy 50 liters a year. In Emilia they cook with margarine, in Milan with butter, but we're not used to those tastes. We don't like the taste of those fats, and they are worse for your health. Olive oil is truly natural and good for you, but it has to be extra-virgin olive oil. It's even good to fry with. Lots of people think that it's better to fry with vegetable oils, but it's not true. Olive oil is less harmful than all of them. In fact, I use it to make a* **fritto**—*a fried dish, just like the olden-day peasants used to do. Oh, you could eat an exquisite* **fritto** *at a peasant's house because they made it with their own homemade olive oil. . . . In my house we like butter on* **pastasciutta,** *but that's all. We only use olive oil for cooking, even if the recipe calls for butter.*

Raffaele shared a widespread misconception that olden-day peasants used olive oil for *fritto,* when, in fact, many used lard. But his report on the spare use of butter was correct. As his mother-in-law Berta said, *Butter? For heavens sake! If someone was sick and needed a doctor who told them to eat "*in bianco*"— bland foods—then they ate a little butter, but if not, it was always olive oil, just a little.* Still in the 1980s, butter use was marginal in Tuscan cuisine.[31]

In the 1980s, my Florentine subjects rarely used lard, but in the first half of the century they used it more widely than olive oil because it was cheaper (Apergi and Bianco 1991, 60–61). Fifty-five-year-old Baldo, who grew up in an artisan family of modest means in the city of Empoli, recalled: *In the old days we didn't use much olive oil; we used lard made from pigs. They boiled up the pig fat, put it in terra-cotta containers, covered it up, and kept it for years. When we wanted to fry something, that's what we used, certainly not olive oil; we only used that to make sauces. But to make a* **fritto** *of artichokes, or a couple of zucchini flowers, lard was good. Even today it would still be delicious, but nobody in the city uses it anymore; only in the countryside do they still use it a little.*

In the old days, peasants and the urban poor spread lard on bread, used it for *fritto,* and sautéed vegetables in it. Seventy-five-year-old Massimo remembered fondly: *We began to slaughter a pig toward the end of our time as* **mezzadria** *peasants. Before that, we couldn't afford it. We ate everything—the fat, the lard, everything. We always ate bacon and that white lard; we ate all of the pig. We used the lard for frying and we sold some. Later, across the street from us in Trespiano, the fellow who had the bakery also had a small restaurant, a* **trattoria,** *with a room where you could go and eat. He brought huge trays full of pork to roast in our oven together with our bread. When it was cooked, he took the pork and left us the fat. We would pour it into jars and let it cool. We ate it with bread. Oh, it was really tasty. Otherwise, we would cook the greens or the cabbage in that fat.*

Wine

A final important element of Tuscan cuisine was wine—especially *vino rosso*—red wine, also called *vino nero*—black wine. *Mezzadria* peasants made wine but often drank little because most went to the landlord. In the 1980s, wine was cheap enough to be drunk by all, and many older people bought it in bulk from producers and bottled it at home. They continued this practice in 2003. Men and women both drank it at meals in Tuscany.[32] Even the poor in the old days drank a little wine, as sixty-one-year-old Marianna remembered: *We always drank wine, maybe just a little, but we always drank it.* Poor people's wine was sometimes mixed with lots of water, or was a wine by-product called **acquarello.** Seventy-six-year-old Berta from a peasant family in the Tuscan foothills said, *We had wine, enough for our own consumption. We had wine at lunch. Do you know what the peasants in the old days made? L'acquarello. They took the wine and put a lot of water in it and they called it l'acquarello or l'acqua pazza—crazy water. It was water barely colored with wine—watered way down.*[33]

Tuscan proverbs emphasized the importance and salubriousness of wine— for example, *"Il vino è il latte dei vecchi"*—"Wine is the old people's milk"; *"Buon vino fa buon sangue"*—"Good wine makes good blood"; and *"Chi ha pane e vino sta me' che il suo vicino"*—"Who has wine and bread, better than his neighbor is fed" (Falassi 1980, 210, my translations). Seventy-three-year-old Renzo remembered the wine of his *mezzadria* family in Trespiano: *We made our wine at home. That wine was special, because the wine up there was like Chianti, eh. That wine was good. It was sufficient for us and there was some left over. We drank so much wine, so much. For all those people we had at the table, we needed wine, also for working. That wine was good.*

My subjects drank wine with moderation and pleasure, almost exclusively at meals.[34] This practice alleviated wine's toxic effects by slowing absorption, stabilizing blood sugar levels, increasing alcohol's oxidation, and promoting heart function (Lolli 1958, 73).[35] Furthermore, drinking wine with meals reinforced the sociability of both the alcohol consumption and the meal.

Between 1950 and 1992, Italian per capita food consumption increased not only in quantity but also in quality, marked particularly by the dramatic increase in meat consumption. Yet Florentines still ate a classic Mediterranean diet composed of pasta, fresh vegetables, legumes, olive oil, bread, and a little meat or fish, all cooked simply and with the rich flavors of garlic, onion, parsley, basil, pepper, sage, rosemary, thyme, hot pepper, and tomatoes, and washed down with moderate amounts of red wine. It was a balanced diet that fit recommendations for optimal nutrition closely.[36] Florentines ate varied and highly seasoned simple food with gusto, seriousness, and sociability. Their foods emerged out of the *mezzadria* peasant economic system practiced for centuries in close proximity to Florence, which made fresh foods available daily to country and city dwellers alike. The following chapters move beyond diet to how Florentines constructed gender and family through producing, cooking, and consuming food.

5
Food Production, Reproduction, and Gender

Production, Reproduction, and Gender Power

Cooking was an essential part of women's reproductive labor, identity, and power, especially if domestic work was their main occupation. As forty-one-year-old Sergia put it, *Listen, I'm a housewife. If I don't know how to cook, you tell me, what else is there? At least if I worked, understand? It's important for a housewife to know how to cook, to know how to do other things too, but cooking is the essential thing.* Her words recalled the legacy of *mezzadria,* where the *massaia* did the cooking and *"there was no other way."*

This chapter uses Florentines' food-centered narratives to portray how the transition to modernity affected men's and women's allocation of production and reproduction, which many feminists have deemed critical to gender status and power. On the *mezzadria* peasant farms, as we saw in Chapter 3, women's work involved both reproduction in the home and production in the courtyard, garden, and fields. But when peasants left the countryside, they experienced a process typical of capitalism and urbanization: the splitting of reproduction and production, the former into the domestic, private sphere of unpaid labor for the family, and the latter into the public sphere of paid work. Production was associated with men and socially valued, while reproduction was viewed as women's "natural" duty, isolated in the home, and taken for granted. The transformation of women's "socially necessary labor into a private service" severely undermined their social status (Leacock 1972, 41).

Early second-wave feminists focused on the parallel dichotomies: male/female, production/reproduction, public/private, dominance/subordination (Rosaldo 1974). Later feminists have emphasized the permeability and complementarity of production and reproduction and the many ways women in different historical moments and social locations have managed them (Lamphere 2000). Here I focus specifically on food as an example of Florentines' handling of production and reproduction. Food is a useful lens because it is a central part of reproductive labor and can stand for all reproductive labor symbolically, but it is also a primary object of production, whether directly as under *mezzadria,* or indirectly, as a major expense for those who work for wages.[1] Thus food-centered life histories provide a fruitful window into the cultural construction of the production/reproduction relationship, people's feelings about it, and gender power.[2]

Florentine women's roles in production and reproduction varied over the twentieth century and among diverse individuals. However, most of my female subjects had near-total responsibility for domestic chores unless they lived in extended families where they could share this work with other women (none had paid household help). In Chapter 3, we saw how the extended *mezzadria* families usually included several women who cooperated in multiple productive and reproductive chores, enabling some to work more outside the house and others more inside. In this chapter, I explore how Florentine women and men who lived in the city in the 1980s managed and felt about production and reproduction. Women's domestic chores were fewer than on the farms, but they had fewer women to help them. Most of my female subjects did paid work as well—mainly, however, "black work" (*lavoro nero*), outside the formal economy and relatively poorly paid, usually piecework in the home.

Men, in contrast, had full-time jobs outside the home in the formal economy and had little or no responsibility for domestic labor. In the 1980s, Florentines were beginning to discuss the possibility of men taking on more household chores, but most still did little or nothing in the home, even among the younger generations, as Chapter 9 describes.

Women, Reproductive Labor, and Cooking

In the 1980s, Florentine women were struggling to manage the claims of family and the need and desire to work for wages. Whereas the men reported a relatively clear identity defined principally in terms of work and providing materially for the family, the women described their lives as a complex and evolving balance between productive work for wages and unpaid reproductive work. They maintained this balance in a variety of ways, but, except for Marianna, they all defined themselves primarily through their family roles and reproductive labor and secondarily through their productive work. Florentine women reported differing levels of satisfaction with this balance. Their economic contribution and status were low, but their daily workload was high. Because Italian standards for neatness and meal complexity were demanding, household chores took a lot of time. In addition to all food preparation and cleanup, women reared children, did piles of laundry, ironed everything down to the underwear, swept and dusted every day, washed the bathroom and kitchen floor every day, and often mended clothes and darned socks as well. This practice continued into the 1990s, when, as Whitaker (2000, 281) said, "Even women who work[ed] outside the home [were] responsible for housework and child care, almost to the complete exclusion of men."

Many women, like fifty-year-old housewife Valeria, took great pleasure in cooking: *I sincerely love to cook and see that people are eating with pleasure, even if they are only my family members—le persone mie di casa. I love to see them eat with satisfaction and enjoy something made well, even if it's just something ordi-*

nary. And I like to change and not always make the same things. Sixty-four-year-old Elena reported that after she retired at age forty-six from thirty years of working in the family bakery, she threw herself into the culinary arts: *Look, for me, cooking was my greatest satisfaction. I loved to invent new dishes, to re–elaborate all the . . . foods I knew how to make, and to make new things. I found great satisfaction this way for me and for the family. I saw how much they appreciated all that I did for them. And so I invented; I tried to make new little things, to vary my cooking, and that too was a beautiful thing.*

Elena's sister Tommasa did not work outside the home, and cooking was the major source of her identity and status as the following exchange with her husband Marco revealed:

Tommasa: *Carole, ask Marco if he likes my cooking. Go ahead and ask him.*

Carole: *Marco, do you like Tommasa's cooking?*

Marco: *Of course. If not, I never would have married her. I already tried her out first. Before marrying her, I looked carefully at how she cooked, and then I said, "Yes, it's fine." I married her willingly because she is a good cook. Look, the young women of today like to pass the time doing other things—I don't know, playing cards, going around to all the boutiques. But not Tommasa, you know, because as I said before, I married her willingly because she cooks well.*

Tommasa: *[jokingly] I'll leave you. After forty years of marriage I'll leave! You married me only for that? In the kitchen, I'm in charge.*

Marco: *Look out. She's in charge in some other place too—in some other place too. But when it comes to paying, I pay.*

Tommasa: *When it comes to paying, he pays.*

Marco and Tommasa explicitly stated the balance of power in their home that reflected the central production/reproduction gender dichotomy: he paid, she cooked. He claimed economic control and she concurred; she asserted power in the kitchen and he affirmed her power there and *in some other place too.* He was perhaps alluding to her sexual power and associating it with her food power, a common linkage in Italy. Cooking was a central part of Tommasa's work, self-expression, and status as the continuation of her conversation with Marco revealed:

Tommasa: *I learned how to cook a little bit from my mother and a little bit from our clients when I worked in the bakery. I used to ask them how they made certain dishes. I learned a valid cuisine. I tease Marco that that's why he married me; everybody jokes about this. They say to me, "He married you because you are such a good cook."*

Marco: *Sometimes someone might say joking, only joking, he might say, "Maybe you will break up some day."*

And I always answer, "No way, forget it. Where could I find a woman who is a better cook than she is?" It wouldn't be in the least bit advantageous for me to break up.

Tommasa: *It's not at all true—I'm certainly not the only woman in the world who cooks well. There are unquestionably other women who are excellent cooks.*

But I do have a valid cuisine. It's mostly in my head. Only on very rare occasions do I consult a cookbook. It's truly in my head.

That Tommasa's cuisine was in her head was an apt allusion to the fact that her identity was wrapped up in cooking. Her cooking clearly gave her power in the relationship with her husband Marco, known for his dominating personality; it was an important reason why it would not be *"advantageous"* for him to break up with her. Whereas under the *mezzadria* system women could garner a little cash from their reproductive work by selling chickens, eggs, or rabbits, with the transition to a capitalist economy women's food work was privatized and demonetized, leaving women with even less economic power unless their husbands chose to give it to them. That cooking was Tommasa's only power because she did not work and had no money of her own may have led to her guarding her cooking skill, even from her daughter Sergia.

For forty-one-year-old Sergia, cooking was a source of anxiety because she did not learn how to do it growing up, yet felt it was an essential female task. Perhaps because of jealousy of this important household domain, her mother Tommasa was reluctant to teach her to cook and never acknowledged that Sergia had any skill. Sergia recounted: *Oh, there was no way I could learn to cook with my mother. I got married on the late side, at twenty-four years old, so there was all the time in the world to learn. But never—there was no way to do it the way she does—even now, you know. When she used to come to visit me here, I always let her cook, because never has she said that I could make anything well.* But Sergia learned to cook in spite of her mother's resistance.[3] She described her strategy: *The day of my marriage approached and I didn't know what to do because my mother was not a good teacher. So every day that she cooked I asked her, "Mom, what is that?" I wrote what she did in a notebook. Little by little I wrote down the ingredients as she added them, because if I had asked her just to dictate the recipe, she would have forgotten something for sure. I have a notebook full of basic recipes: roast chicken,* **pomarola** *sauce, beans—all the things that are central to Tuscan cuisine. I had to write them down because my cookbooks did not have the home-cooking recipes that I had always eaten.*[4]

Sergia was terribly insecure about her cooking: *I said to myself, okay, if Rinaldo wants to marry me, he'll take me as I am. Oh, I threw away a lot of those dishes—so many, believe me. Oh, huge pots full of minestrone. Oh, dear, it was crazy. Let me tell you this story. One of the first days after my marriage, I invited my brother-in-law to dinner while my sister-in-law was on vacation at the beach. I made him a salad with cucumbers. Cucumbers—I thought you didn't have to peel them, because they're like zucchini, and you don't peel zucchini. So I cut them all in little slices with the skin on them. I saw this man begin to slice all around the outside of the cucumber slices with his knife and fork. The shame I felt!*

Not knowing how to cook caused her to feel inadequate and ashamed, so Sergia desperately tried to learn by copying her mother as closely as possible. But nonetheless her mother never acknowledged that she could cook anything well: *In my house there was no way to stand at the stove because I would always be criticized. My mother always said, "You don't know how to do anything." What could I do—will you tell me? How could I learn? When she had a kidney operation, she stayed a week in the hospital. I made a **pomarola*** sauce. I'd never made it before, and I made **pomarola**. When I didn't have her in the house, I managed to make something. But with her, there was no way ever to do anything.*

Sergia told a story about rice fritters, which are traditional in Florence and Tuscany for the Feast of St. Joseph on March 19:[5] *Let me tell you the story of* **le frittelle*** *(rice fritters). Listen to this. Well, one year for the Feast of St. Joseph, my mother made fritters, and, because it is a custom here in Florence to make rice fritters for St. Joseph, I made them too. So on the day of St. Joseph, my mother invited me to her house. I replied, "Mom, I can't come because I too made fritters. This evening Rinaldo will be coming home, and then some friends are coming over."*

"But you can't make fritters as well as I can," she retorted. The recipe is the same, identical, because I copied it exactly from the one they gave to her! So now, can you believe it? She even made me have a complex about my fritters. Sergia's story revealed not only how important cooking was to women's identity and confidence but also how other women's support was crucial to their acquisition of domestic skills. In Sergia's tiny nuclear family increasingly typical of postwar Italy, she did not have other women to teach her. Her mother's unwillingness to share her knowledge with Sergia seriously hampered her ability to fulfill her culturally mandated responsibilities and undermined her self-confidence.

Even a career woman like Marianna, who spent most of her adult life unmarried as a full-time employee in the marriage bureau of the Florence city hall, felt insecure about her lack of cooking skill: *I have learned to make many things since I married Renzo—but, of course, I didn't know how to make anything. However, I live always with the fear that it won't come out right. Will it be ruined? But look what I've made. Will it be good?* It is not surprising that women worried about their cooking skills and competence in domestic chores, for they were judged by rigorous standards of domestic proficiency, whether they had paying jobs or not.

Cooking stood for all nurturance, including psychological nurturance. In most couples, the wife nurtured the husband and children through feeding them but not vice versa. Women's responsibility for nurturance was both a burden and a source of gratification. Giovanna was bicultural—she lived in Florence until age twenty-one, then she moved to the United States and married an Italian-American. She visited Florence regularly and made astute observations of social mores: *I think women take on the nurturing role. In fact, I was discussing this the other night at dinner with Sergia and Rinaldo. Rinaldo asked, "Why are my daughters more attached to their mother?"*

Sergia replied, "It's because I'm always at home; it's me who is always there." *The father goes off to work and many times he's not there. So the women take on* *this psychological nurturance (**nutrimento psicologico**) that is more implicit than explicit for both children and husband. When you get right down to it, Italian men in certain situations are children. So I think that Italian men seek an image of the mother in their wife. They grew up with a mother who spooned them out their soup. I visit my married friends here and I see many of the wives continuing to spoon out the soup for their husbands.*

By using the metaphor of spooning the soup, Giovanna encapsulated the servile aspects of women's reproductive roles. They waited on others and defined altruism as pleasure. As fifty-year-old stay-at-home wife and mother Valeria put it, *I love to cook . . . not only for the pleasure and the taste but also for the satisfaction of making things for other people, whether guests or just the family. When the children come home for the midday dinner, I always like to vary the meals and make them something good. For me the satisfaction is to see if I made something that other people like, something that came out well.* Through cooking, Valeria expressed herself and her love in an ever-changing array of delicious meals. Through feeding, she gained some status and appreciation from family members, even though they also took for granted her unwavering nurturance and rarely reciprocated it. Cooking often gave Florentine women satisfaction, but because they "had" to do it, it reinforced the naturalness of their deference to others through feeding (cf. DeVault 1991).

The imbalance in expectations for and rewards to men and women for doing reproductive work emerged clearly in the relationship between the middle-aged couple Laura and Raffaele, the only couple I knew where the man regularly cooked. Laura was clear that cooking was more gratifying than other household chores because it involved variation, creativity, pleasure, and acclaim. Yet to be able to work outside the home, she gave up cooking because it was the one chore that her husband would do. Raffaele had the male privilege to spurn most domestic chores but to choose to cook, for which he received a great deal of praise. Even though Laura would have rather given Raffaele other chores, she was grateful for his help, even if in relinquishing cooking she gave up some of her identity and felt regret at its loss: *We try to work together. Raffaele has been helping with the cooking for many years. He started more or less right after we got married in 1958. He inherited cooking, and he likes it. I do too. But Raffaele, he especially loves cooking, so he started right away. Then after we moved back to Empoli, there was a need for him to cook, because we had our son Piero and I had to work. Raffaele worked in the glass factory; however, he was on either the morning or the afternoon shift, so he had more time than I did. So he helped me; he helped me with the cooking and it gave him satisfaction. But with the other domestic chores no, you can be sure of that!*

It didn't bother me. I like to cook too; however, if there is someone who will do it for me, I don't mind. I would rather get the other chores done—there's the cleaning, washing, ironing, mending. If he wants to help me do something, for me

that's already a lot.... He does the shopping too.... He likes many little special-
ties, and so he really prefers to do the shopping. It's just something that evolved.

    I have mixed feelings about Raffaele's cooking. On the one hand, it's good, be-
cause I come home from work and I find everything ready. On the other hand, it's
a little—how can I say it? I feel a little bit excluded from doing the shopping and
cooking. For the convenience I like him cooking, but for other reasons, I'd rather
do it. If you shop, you know the prices. Now since I never shop, I have no idea how
much things cost. Going shopping, doing it all yourself, you feel like more of a
woman. You feel more up on things; you see people. But it's convenient to have
him do it, because the food is ready when I return from work, and moreover, shop-
ping takes a lot of time. So does cooking. Because I work, my time is precious.

    If I could have chosen a chore to give to Raffaele, I would have given him the
ironing. It's a sacrifice. I have always disliked ironing—it takes so much time and
it is so hot. For me, ironing is exactly the thing that I would love to give away to
anyone else.

    I would have enjoyed cooking. It's something—oh, God, I'm not one of those
who are passionate about cooking, no; I don't adore cooking. I'm not one of those;
however, I would have done it with pleasure. I too would cook willingly, and when
it falls to me, I do it, of course. Cooking is pleasurable maybe because it is more
varied than other household jobs. What can I tell you? You make one thing one
day, something else another day. You can vary the work. But cleaning and ironing
and washing are always the same. Cooking, you can vary it as you choose. There's
more imagination involved, more satisfaction, and then you make something that
everybody eats and that too gives you fulfillment. If they like it, they say it's good.
When you cook for people, you give them something; it seems like you're giving
them everything. You worked hard, you did well, you made something good. If you
iron a shirt, well, they don't even look at it because it is something that has to be
done and they take it for granted. But eating is something else, and if you make
something new, it is really appreciated. Men could choose to help with the reproductive labor or not. When they helped, it was usually with the cooking, the
most creative and appreciated task. Women accepted men's help willingly, because any help was better than none.

    Women's support of each other was critical in enabling them to manage
work outside the home in addition to all the household chores. Laura explained: *When my mother-in-law Angela was alive, going to work didn't involve a*
sacrifice for me because I found everything ready, everything done at home, even
though she was quite old. She did all the housework. She did the washing, the
ironing, the cooking, the shopping, and she took the initiative to do whatever
needed to be done. So when I returned home at six, I was free. I didn't have any-
thing to do. Raffaele could make the supper or do some errands or do the shop-
ping—things that now he doesn't have time to do. Laura's comments underscore
the benefits for women of living in an extended family household. With the

decline of peasant farming and the urbanization of the population, families shrunk. In the 1980s, several of my informants lived in slightly extended families, but by 2003, none did.

Sixty-four-year-old Elena shared the household chores and the work in the family bakery with her mother and her sister until her sister started a new household at marriage: *My mother had to work in the shop night and day. My father made the bread at night, and many times my mother also had to get up at night to help him, because they couldn't afford to hire a worker. They had to do it all by themselves. Then my mother went into the shop in the morning to sell bread from morning until night, and so she had little time for cooking. She might take a chicken and put it in the oven—on Sundays, eh, because, you know, chicken was something really special. Or she might make some broth. She would put the pot on the fire when there was nobody in the shop, and, oh, she made a dash to go and see if it boiled, and then we would have that. Then when my sister and I got older, we began to cook too, at a very early age, oh, yes, because we were needed. And we began to develop enthusiasm for cooking. We made the spaghetti sauce; we made sweets; we did what we could. We cooked the roast in the bread oven, you know. What with the fact that the oven was always hot, we cooked everything in there.*

Later, when my sister and I began to work in the shop, my mother sometimes made lasagna. She had a little more time now that we were working in the bakery, and she went back to the apartment and cooked. She made lasagna; she made **saltimbocca alla romana****—with* **prosciutto** *inside.* Elena's mother worked both in the home and in the bakery, while her father was exempt from the domestic chores. These were a major burden on Elena's mother until she and her sister were old enough to help, whereupon the three of them shared the productive work in the bakery and the reproductive work in the home. After Tommasa married and moved out, Elena and her mother continued to live together and share chores: *In my household, my mother and I took turns—either she did the household chores and I worked in the bakery, or else she worked in the bakery and I did the things in the house. But today the situation is tragic when a woman works outside the home and doesn't have another woman in the house to help her.*

That cooperation between women in an extended family household lightened each one's individual load was also evident in Valeria's extended family. She and her husband Baldo lived with their unmarried son Arturo, and Valeria's parents Massimo and Berta. Massimo and Berta ran a flower shop near the Ponte Vecchio and worked all day, so Valeria shouldered the major domestic responsibilities and cooked not only for resident family members but also for her married daughter Caterina and her husband Sandro. Valeria did everyone's laundry, kept the house tidy, shopped for food, planned meals, and managed all the other miscellaneous tasks: *I was in charge of the household because Baldo went off to work and so did my parents. Sometimes my mother stayed home in the afternoon if there was a lot of housework to do. She was younger then and she spent an occasional afternoon at home helping out. She did ironing and other things, but there was so much to do, shopping, cooking—everything, in short.* Having the support of other women was crucial in enabling some women to hold down jobs outside the home, and not having other women to do the reproductive labor made it very difficult for women to do productive work, which in the 1980s was becoming increasingly important to their attainment of social value.

Women and Production

Women had a complex relationship to wage work. None of my female subjects came from wealthy homes, so all began wage work at an early age, usually in typically female handcraft industries for low and inconsistent pay. But at marriage, all took primary responsibility for the household for a number of years while their children were small, and at most continued earning through part-time piecework. Valeria reflected on the conflicts between productive and reproductive work faced by women: *I would have loved to have a good job. To tell you the truth, I would have loved to have had a woman come in and do the housework— cooking no, but one who cleaned the whole house for me really well, even just once a week—if I had had a good job. But when my children were little, I didn't want to work outside the house. I didn't feel like leaving them. However, now they are already grown and more independent, and I would love to have a good job.* Valeria wanted to stay home with her children when they were young. That, however, greatly reduced her chances of getting a good job when her children were older, for the only work she had done was sewing fancy clothes at home from precut pieces.

Valeria continued, *Oh, yes, I did the famous **lavoro nero**—"black work"— without insurance, without retirement contributions, without anything. We worked so much under the table like that. My work didn't pay badly compared to many other jobs because it was delicate work, skilled work, and who knew how much the owner sold each dress for? But it had to be done perfectly. If there was any little thing, she sent it back to you, eh, if a stitch was crooked or a seam wasn't perfectly smooth. It's hard to work with knitted silk and all that really delicate cloth. But anyway, I don't remember how much they paid me, but it wasn't bad compared to other sewing jobs I did at home. I didn't dislike it.*

Although she "*didn't dislike*" her sewing, Valeria recognized that there were many drawbacks to it: *Doing piecework at home you don't earn much. You work and work and you can't get anything done because you're at home and you have all the housework to do, and if the phone rings, you have to get up; if the doorbell rings, you have to get up; if someone comes over, you have to give them some coffee. The end of the day comes and you've accomplished nothing. But if you go off to work, you're more at ease, you do your eight hours, and you're done, and then you go home and do the other things.*

Valeria underscored the benefits of separating productive and reproductive work and the conflicts when productive work took place in the home where many other responsibilities inevitably demanded women's attention. Yet her "black work" did have its rewards: *My sewing work gave me a certain satisfaction because there are so many needs when you have two children, understand? There are so many things to do and to buy that it is hard to cover it all with one salary. I guess the satisfaction is knowing that you have a little money. It's not that I had a husband who told me, "You have to do this; you cannot do that." No, no, Baldo is not like that. However, if we had some extra money, we were better off, even if it wasn't very much. It seemed to me that it enabled me to do some things and make some purchases that maybe weren't really necessary but that gave pleasure. I took the money and I did these things and it seemed like so much. I got my pay and said, "Let's go, I'm going to do this thing," maybe buy something for one of the children or a gift for someone, whatever I wanted in short. . . . If I had the money, it's not that Baldo ever said to me, "You cannot buy this." I always did what I wanted because he valued me.* Valeria equated her husband's valuing her with his granting her economic control. One way around economic dependence was being given power of the purse the way Valeria was.

Sixty-one-year-old Marianna took another, much less common route to economic independence, which was not to marry but rather to be a full-time worker at the Florence city hall, Palazzo Vecchio, until she married Renzo in 1981 at the age of fifty-eight. After three years of marriage, she gave her thoughts: *I worked my whole life. I always liked working. Even aside from the fact that I was alone and had to work, I really enjoyed it. First of all, it gave me the wherewithal to survive. . . . If I hadn't married Renzo, maybe I'd still be working. I would have finished this year forty-one years of service. I started when I was nineteen and a half and I stopped after thirty-eight years. Frankly, I have really good memories of work.*

Work was important to Marianna, for it gave her independence, and until she married, her reproductive chores were minimal: *Even with keeping the house in order, things are different now that I'm married. Sure, I used to keep my house in order, but when I used to live with my cousin, I had only one room, and I'd make my bed in the morning and then do the big cleaning on Saturday. And anyway, nobody ever came into that apartment. But now with a whole house, it's really different. But anyway, I hope I do a good job. Here I find myself at home, cleaning the house, cooking, getting things ready. Oh, I like it well enough.*

But Marianna missed work: *I was used to working with the public. Oh, I'm content now; things are fine because I've always felt good here. I'm fine, because I go out with Renzo. We always go out together. But it was too many years that I was always among lots of people, always, always, always. It's a big change. I find myself feeling alone, especially in the winter. Renzo says, "I'm here"—yes, but . . . it's completely different.* For Marianna, quitting her job and becoming a wife meant social isolation, which was especially acute because she had no children.

Because Marianna quit her job before she took on major domestic chores, she did not endure the heavy workload suffered by many women who did both at once. Laura was a full-time garment worker, wife, and mother of two children. Laura valued the social connectedness and economic independence gained at work just as Marianna did, but she complained of overwork and women's double day: *If I had to choose again, I don't know if I would choose work or being a housewife. Because going off to work, you are always in contact with people, and you are cognizant of so many things—for example, union affairs. Staying at home I wouldn't be so aware—I would watch television, but it's not the same. So if you think about it, what you lose by going to work, you find by staying home, but what you lose by staying at home, you find at work. If you stay at home, you're always doing the same things, always the same this and that. But at work there are always new things happening; maybe there are strikes to discuss, or like now, we're all talking about the continuous workday.[6] In short, at work there is always something going on and you are more informed than if you stay at home.*

I tried staying at home and I didn't do well. I didn't like it. A woman who stays home is more dull and backward. And if there are strikes and a woman is at home, what does she do? She works; there's no way out. But if I'm working at the factory and there are strikes, I have to go on strike. There are meetings, and so many things that don't happen when you're at home. So each choice has advantages and disadvantages. Laura articulated the no-win situation faced by women due to the dichotomization of production and reproduction and their responsibility for the latter, whether they worked outside the home or not. She summed up women's difficult situation: *But listen, we women are all **sacrificate**—we're all sacrificed, we're all overburdened. The housewife is sacrificed because she's a housewife and doesn't want to be. The woman who works is sacrificed because she goes to work and then she has to do all the housework, so she longs for more time at home. Understand? It's never just one thing; you never find the woman who is content. There is always so much work.*

But ultimately, Laura concluded, it was worth it to hold a job in spite of the sacrifices: *A housewife never gets the recognition that a working woman gets. It is much more likely that people will understand the sacrifices a working woman makes. A woman who stays home, well, of course, she's home, so she has to do the housework. It is rare that her sacrifices are recognized even though she has to do everything around the house. Her work is taken for granted because it is perceived as an obligation and not a sacrifice. She has to do it; it is her work; she has to do it.*

In Florence, housework was women's work, whether they worked outside the home or not. But when women did not work outside the home, they suffered because they lacked their own money, were isolated, and were taken for granted. Even if they did paid work at home, it was tainted by its location in the reproductive sphere and was poorly paid and undervalued. Men, in contrast, usually earned more money than women and were more valued because their work was public and paid. They were freer at home because they had no cultural mandate to do reproductive work. Hence Laura's conclusion that *le donne sono sempre sacrificate*— *"women are always sacrificed."*

Men: Freedom from Reproductive Labor

In the 1980s, men did not complain of being *sacrificati* as women did, though the older men remembered excessive toil in their youth, but it was toil outside the home. They had no responsibility for reproductive work and benefited in many ways from the definition of that work as "women's." As sixty-six-year-old Elena said, *Most men in Italy only do the men's chores; they don't do women's chores.* At best, men "helped" women, and they received approbation from friends and family if they "helped," and no condemnation if they did nothing. Elena encapsulated men's ignorance of cooking in the following anecdote about her father:

My father was the negation for cooking and doing anything around the house. He didn't even know how to fry an egg. One time we were at the beach—my mother, my sister, and I. My father stayed in Florence because he couldn't leave the bakery. By that time my parents had hired a worker to help. One night, he and our worker were making bread together and they wanted some coffee. My father asked, "How do you make coffee? Do you know how to do it?"

The worker answered, "No, I don't. Do you know how to make it?"

"No," my father responded. "I don't know how to make it either."

"So what shall we do?"

My father said, "Here's what we'll do. We'll call the telephone operator and we'll get her to teach us."

"But it's four in the morning."

"Oh, they're there even in the middle of the night," my father answered. "Let's give it a try." In fact, they telephoned the operator.

The operator answered, "Yes, I can teach you, but how much coffee do you want to make?"

*My father answered, "Tell us how to make a wine jug (**fiasco**) full."*

*"A jug full of coffee?" answered the young woman. "I have no idea how to do that. I can tell you how to make an espresso maker full (**una macchinetta**[7])."*

*My father said, "But a **macchinetta** will only last us for a little while. We wanted to make enough coffee to last us several nights."*

She replied, "But the next night, you just make it again." Imagine!

In the prevailing Tuscan gender division of labor, most men like Elena's father were ignorant of the mysteries of the kitchen. Seventy-three-year-old Renzo said, *Growing up, I had no responsibilities to do with food, nothing, except to eat. "**Mangiare e ringraziare Dio**"— "Eat and thank God," we say in Florence. My brother Massimo and I did nothing in the kitchen. We just ate our meals, and that was all.* Men defined themselves through work and through the characteristics they felt necessary to be effective workers and providers.

Renzo's first wife, Grazia, quit her job outside the home at marriage, though continued to work hard at the family at-home business, doing unpaid and unregistered "black work" crocheting and sewing handbags, and she did all the domestic chores and cooking. After Grazia died in 1973, Renzo just put on an apron and tackled the household chores. He learned how to cook for himself, which he did with quite a bit of success and pride. He said, *When Grazia died, I knew nothing about cooking. I learned, like this, with the will to try, out of my own head. I made something once; maybe one time it came out badly, so I made it again. I didn't ever know anything about cooking, only how to grill chicken on the barbecue, and that was all. And steak, how to grill a steak,* **bistecca alla fiorentina.*** *I never got into cooking, because first of all, I didn't have time. I was always running, always running. I never paid any attention to the kitchen business. But after Grazia died, with willing effort, I learned.* His comments on the ease of learning to cook served in some sense to belittle its importance and the importance of the women who did it day in and day out. Furthermore, after he married again at age seventy, Renzo passed to his second wife Marianna most of the domestic chores that he had learned so well in his seven years of being a widower—chores that ironically she had never had to do for anyone but herself. Marianna shouldered them willingly, and felt that it was right and proper that she do so, even though she lacked experience and confidence in the kitchen.

Florentine men and women concurred that housework was not men's work. As forty-five-year-old Rinaldo said, *For me to sweep or mop the floor, I just can't see it. It's stronger than me (**è più forte di me**). Sure, at home with just the family, I could sweep if I really had to, but I just couldn't mop the floor. I wouldn't be able to do it—not physically—but I don't know; it would really bother me. I just don't have the inclination to do it (**non me la sento proprio**). I don't know—doing the laundry—come on, it is not men's work. Traditionally, it is just not men's work. Maybe in the United States the men iron, but for me to iron, Sergia would have to be sick—no, not even then would I iron. I would send my clothes out.*

Although he felt that he could not possibly do housework, Rinaldo did have some sensitivity to the dilemma of men lacking responsibility for the home and women being overburdened: *I don't think it is right that when they both work outside the home that the husband does nothing in the home. Many times I feel guilty on Saturday or Sunday if I'm home and don't help out, even if I do have many things to see to on our farm. So I usually try to clear the table—not because Sergia asks me to but because I feel it is my duty. It bothers me to see her working while I'm doing nothing. It is true that women make many sacrifices and are heavily burdened at home.* Rinaldo, however, explained that his habits were ingrained from childhood: *You see, I come from a family in which if the women were overburdened, it had no importance, understand? That was the woman's job. I never saw my father sweep or even clear the table. Instead, I do that.* He made small steps toward helping in the reproductive sphere and he felt that generational change was slowly happening: *I think my daughters will approach* *these issues with better preparation than me. It could be that my daughters find a man who does more than clear, who also cooks. On the other hand, I sometimes cook. I make a quick spaghetti with garlic and oil—spaghetti aglio e olio.* I make it and I make it willingly. But look, either the men have to adapt to doing jobs they never did before or otherwise they have to keep their wives at home. There's no other way.*

Although Rinaldo by his own admission was neither willing nor able to do household chores, he did feel a responsibility to earn enough to enable his wife to stay home so that she could do them with more ease than if she had also to work outside the home. He envisioned the division of labor perhaps changing in the future in his children's generation. He confirmed that cooking was often the first chore from the reproductive sphere that men took up, and he minimized its challenges. *I like to eat well, but eating well for me can mean eating salame and cantaloupe slices. For me, that is an exceptional meal—understand? Or else two hard-boiled eggs, or artichokes in **pinzimonio,** raw, tender baby artichokes, dipped in olive oil, salt, and pepper. These are all foods that don't demand much work. It is Sergia who creates problems around cooking. When she doesn't feel like cooking, as often happens on Saturday or Sunday, she says, "Rinaldo, what shall we eat?" I give her an idea, but not so I'll have to cook. She gets angry and says, "I always have to cook."*

*"But who says you always have to cook?" So last Saturday I whipped up **spaghetti aglio e olio**—with garlic and olive oil. You know perfectly well that it only takes about five minutes to make. Then there was a cantaloupe in the refrigerator—I sliced that and sliced some prosciutto. Perfect—in fifteen minutes it was all ready. Or else, when the artichokes are in season, I'll have two artichokes in **pinzimonio.** Or else a **pinzimonio** with artichokes, carrots, celery, green onions, and radishes—that for me is a meal from God.*

Rinaldo made cooking sound easy, but failed to acknowledge Sergia's work in stocking the larder with food and in washing the pots, pans, and dishes. Furthermore, he was able to define cooking as easy and simple—something that women, due to cultural expectations, were not able to do, for they felt compelled to produce elaborate meals. Even though Sergia recognized the limits of Rinaldo's contributions, she valued the help he gave her: *Sometimes Rinaldo cooks. For example, tonight he will make the roast rabbit; he does a really good job. I prepared it, I flavored it with spices, but on the spit, he's in charge. Sometimes he'll make some kind of last-minute spaghetti sauce; a friend taught him how. Yes, yes, he cooks occasionally, but oh God, if he had to do it often, he too would get bored of it. But he knows how to make some things. The other day he made spaghetti with tomato and basil—I don't even know what it was and I don't want to learn, because if I do, he won't make it for me anymore. It was good, really good.*

Fifty-five-year-old Baldo also recognized that cooking was the one household chore men sometimes did: *Yes, it is usually the women who cook, although there are some men who like to do it. They really have a penchant (**sono portati** *proprio) for cooking and for making this dish or that one. But I just have no aptitude at all for cooking. I'd rather work overtime because I can't do anything at all in the kitchen.* Baldo's sister-in-law Laura speculated: *Why do men choose cooking? I don't know. I think they have more of a penchant to cook, to stand at the stove, than to iron or wash. I don't know what this comes from, why they cook and don't do other things for you. They don't do other chores, but I don't know if it is because cooking gives them satisfaction or whether they just have an instinct for working at the stove. Look, I don't know what a man is.*

Contributing to Raffaele's becoming his family's cook was his father's experience: *When he was unemployed, my father started to help my mother do the cooking. That was when my father began to devote himself to the culinary arts, let's say. Because my father wasn't doing anything and my mother was working, my father started doing the shopping and bringing the food home, and then my mother told him how to cook while she was sewing. She said, "Chop up this and that." So my father would set to work and chop. "Put the olive oil in the pan. Put the tomatoes in. Then put the meat in." Little by little, my father learned. They switched positions.*

I asked Raffaele if this switch in gender roles—his mother to productive labor, his father to cooking—caused any tension. He replied: *No, there wasn't any tension over this because I repeat that they had always lived in poverty. So whether she worked or he worked, it was all fine, because the poverty was the same. And although my father didn't have his factory job, he still found small jobs here and there. He helped with the cooking at home. He brought the sewing to my mother in the morning and then took it back completed in the evening. In the afternoon, he found other little jobs to do, understand?*

Having his father as a model surely made it easier for Raffaele to take on cooking himself, but he did nothing in the home except the cooking: *My wife rarely cooks, but here's what happens: my wife has to wash all the dishes. I don't do that because I just don't have a penchant for dishes (**non ci sono portato**); a woman has more of an inclination to be more precise in washing. With detergents, I just don't know where to begin. Yes, she finds dinner ready when she comes home for lunch, but she also finds a mountain of dishes to wash, understand? So when she has finished eating, before she returns to work, she washes the dishes and puts everything back in its place. I cook and she cleans up.*

Raffaele professed incompetence in washing dishes—literally, he said he "was not carried toward" doing them. Women, he implied, were "naturally" better at housework. He went on to say: *My daughter does the other domestic chores. When she returns at lunch, while I cook the spaghetti, she makes the beds and straightens up the bedrooms. She does all the bedrooms and cleans the bathroom. That's her job, because she gets home a half-hour before my wife, at twelve-thirty, while my wife returns at one. As soon as Laura walks in, we eat, because everything is all ready. However, at a quarter of two when we have finished eating, my wife goes to do the dishes and my daughter leaves right away to go back to work. The only one who does absolutely nothing is my son Piero.*

Men and Production

While men did little around the house, work outside the home, *il lavoro,* was the most important component of masculine identity. Seventy-five-year-old Massimo was succinct about manhood: *A man must work at a trade, and find himself a job, an occupation. Family is always an important part of being a man.* Males and females agreed that the primary job of a man was to work outside the home and earn a living to provide for his wife and children. Forty-eight-year-old garment worker Laura said, *The only obligation men have is to go to work; there's nothing else. There are many men who go to work, come home, change their clothes, and go out and have fun—that's it; they have no other concerns about the family or the children.*[8] All my male subjects described at length their work histories. They articulated a self-definition centered around productive labor and, as we saw above, ignorance and irresponsibility for reproductive work.

Rinaldo described manhood: *If you ask me what a man should be and do, I'll answer on the basis of myself. First of all, a man has to maintain his family economically. This is obvious. What else? He has to respect his wife. This too is obvious. He has to respect his children, also obvious. For a man to be a man, if he does what he believes in, he can do anything. It depends on the individual. You can't change a man's education and upbringing and force him to do certain things he doesn't want to do, because he would feel crippled; he would be wretched. Oh, a man has to work, without a doubt. Here in Italy, a man's upbringing and education would never allow him to stay home and do the housework and send his wife out to work. He would feel like a total failure if he switched roles with a woman.*

Rinaldo expressed perhaps an extreme devaluation of women's work in saying that doing it would make a man feel like a *total failure,* but all my subjects agreed that a man's main job was outside the home. Men shared ideals about masculinity articulated by seventy-three-year-old Renzo: *A man must have a will to work, to produce, and to emancipate himself. Never to go backwards. I have always had the goal of realizing myself, in one way or another. Yes, with sacrifices, and with work. . . . You need so much determination to be a man. That's it more or less. And honesty. And you must work. If you don't produce, there is nothing. If nobody produces, what would we do? First you work, you produce, then you make demands.*

For Renzo, in addition to working, caring for family was a key to masculinity: *Another responsibility of a man is the family; that's a whole huge responsibility. A great responsibility. For the children first of all, because when you have a child, your life changes. It's completely different. The husband and wife become accessories. They're unknown to each other; they're improvised. Instead with a child, you know that it is born from you, in your house. . . . When our baby was born, Grazia no longer went off to work. Today it's different. Today there is the day care center and all these things, but in the old days there was nothing and we had to make do by ourselves. The women stayed home; they kept themselves busy at home as she did, doing crocheting and all these other things. Grazia was always busy taking care of Leonardo: his behavior, his clothes, his schoolwork. That's nature.*

A rather infrangible division of labor, with men in charge of production outside the home and women of reproduction in the home, was defined as *"nature"* in Florence in the 1980s. Yet this division led to insupportable burdens for some women and inevitable conflicts and imbalances for Florentine couples. Because women's work was valued and paid less than men's, couples had to cope with the inherent economic and social inequality that underpinned their relationship. The next chapter explores several ways in which Florentines worked out the differences in gender ideology, social status, and economic power in marital relationships.

6

Balancing Gender Differences

Introduction

Thirty-nine-year-old Giovanna grew up in Florence, and at age twenty-one married an Italian-American and moved to the United States, where she raised two daughters. She returned to Florence for long visits every year, and her insider-outsider position enabled her to articulate succinctly the dilemma posed by Florentine gender relations: *Here's the situation: He works all day, and she works all day, but his work counts more than hers because he earns more money, understand? It bothers her to ask him to help, because look, women's work is never valued.*

Because women's work was undervalued, they had to do it without compensation or regard. Giovanna continued: *Sure, fine, he brings home his salary, but is that enough? If you had to pay someone to prepare your breakfast, wash your clothes, prepare your lunch and dinner, and then go to bed with you, well, look, it is impossible to put a monetary value on it. Right? Think about how much prostitutes earn. You have to realize that a woman has to satisfy the needs of so many people and it would be impossible to pay someone to do it all; it would take so much money. Women's work is taken for granted from generation to generation. But there are problems if the women are increasingly working outside the home to gain some independence. We have to get the husbands used to contributing more of themselves to the family. . . . But this is what makes the woman feel guilty—because she is asking her husband to do something in the home that traditionally the husband did not do.* The past weighed heavily upon present gender relations, making it difficult for women to ask for changes from men or for men to voluntarily assume them.

The production-reproduction dichotomy not only institutionalized unequal gender power, but also meant that women's sexuality was more closely regulated than men's because women stood for family, hearth, and home. This chapter uses Florentines' food-centered narratives to show how they expressed and managed imbalances in power through their beliefs about marriage, their family budget, and their attitudes about their bodies.

Marriage, Courtship, and Gender Ideology

Marriage was an expected state and goal for all the Florentine men and women I knew in the 1980s.[1] Because of the legacy of male economic dominance in

Italy, encoded by *mezzadria* compacts, Fascist law, postwar family law, and tradition, it was difficult for Florentine women to earn a good living by themselves, and thus marriage tended to enhance their social and economic status. Similarly men needed wives to perform reproductive services for them: to cook, clean, do their laundry, and have and raise their children. Florentine men and women eagerly sought marriage and, perhaps unwittingly, perpetuated the gender hierarchy it upheld.

Marriage was a venerated civil and religious institution in Italy. Because of Italy's Catholic roots, divorce was illegal until 1970, when the divorce law passed and was later approved by 59 percent of the population in a national referendum in 1974 (Passerini 1996b, 145). Separations and extramarital affairs have always existed, but ideally marriage was forever. It was an essential part of the *sistemazione* or "setting up" that every Italian strove to reach and that included a house or apartment, a job with benefits (originally for the man, increasingly for the woman as well), children, a high standard of living, and an old-age pension. Seventy-three-year-old Massimo spoke for many when he told me what he wanted for his daughters: *My concern was that they get themselves well established (**sistemate**), with a husband, a family, everything. . . . I wanted them to have a job, to be good people, well established. . . . And the home, yes, the home; they need to know how to maintain a home and to cook.*

Marriage was important for both men and women not only because it was essential to economic security and domestic well-being, but also because it marked an important step toward maturity and freedom from parental control, particularly for women. Forty-one-year-old Sergia said, *When I was growing up, our main goal was to find a husband. If I had to do it all over again today, if I were young today, I don't know if I would get married. But in those days, there was nothing else we could do. In the past, if you weren't married, you were looked at with different eyes. People thought: Look, she couldn't even find a husband; she couldn't even find some desperate guy to take her. Understand, that kind of thinking really bothered you. Hence you had to find a husband. . . . In those days we thought, I'll get married and finally I'll do what I want.* Sergia's aunt, sixty-six-year-old Elena, concurred that marriage represented fulfillment for women: *Getting married was beautiful because I acquired a whole lot of freedom. My father was really stern and inflexible, but my husband wasn't.*

Being unmarried carried a negative stigma in part due to the economic difficulties likely to be incurred by women. Giovanna said: *I think that Italian women are looking for support in marriage. I'm sorry to say it, because maybe it is not true, but this is what my antennae have picked up: Italian women are seeking more than anything financial support. Clearly Italian women cannot maintain themselves as well as a husband can, especially one with a profession. I think Italian women are looking most of all for economic support. I don't know if violent passions, impetuous love, and all these things exist anymore—either in Italy or anywhere else. I don't know. But I think that what a woman wants most of all is to get settled—una donna si vuole sistemare. "Sistemare" is the verb most often used.*

Almost all of my older female subjects saw marriage and staying at home as important, but these hindered women from the fulfillment of work and made them economically vulnerable. Divorced women were suspect. As sixty-six-year-old Elena said, *Here in Italy divorced women are seen as—how can I say it?—a little bit like loose women. But that's wrong. Furthermore, here in Italy at least, the fault is always attributed to the woman, at least insofar as the little old women who gossip are concerned. Always. They say, "Oh, what ideas did that one have in her head? It must be that she didn't like him anymore; it must be that he wasn't any good anymore. She must have someone else. It must be this, it must be that." That's the way it is. The fault is always the woman's. But you can't generalize; you've got to look at each case individually, because there are some men who have their little affairs. They are allowed this; up to now, they've always been allowed this; it's always been this way, that men can have their affairs. But for women, no way. They would be whores. My friend Mara didn't accept her husband's affairs—they went on against her will, but she was forced to accept them. She swallowed the toad and that was how it was. Many women close their eyes and think that it will pass, and then it passes. The wife remains the wife. But other women don't accept the affairs. You see, Mara didn't accept them; however, she stayed in the marriage. She stayed there.*

Elena articulated clearly the difficulties for women who lacked economic independence and were unhappy in their marriages. She also defined one of the central tenets of gender ideology in Florence (and Italy in general)—that women who were sexually loose or who had affairs were villified, but men who did so were accepted. Although this double standard was changing in the last quarter of the twentieth century, and pre- and extramarital sex was more widely practiced and tolerated for women as well as men, the old value on women's sexual monogamy still lingered.

Men chose their wives carefully, because they believed that a good woman was the linchpin of the family and guardian of the domestic sphere. Seventy-three-year-old Renzo made this clear: *A woman's role in society is very important. As we say in Florence, "A good woman makes a good husband. A good husband makes a good woman."—"Una buona donna fa un buon marito. Un buon marito fa una buona donna." They need to understand each other as much as possible, to help each other as much as possible. Then, for the rest, to confront it in the best way possible. Because it is not easy to put together two different personalities. Between Grazia and me things were rough—even if she was a person of infinite goodness. Men and women are different by nature. Women have certain problems that men don't have, and men have certain problems that women don't have. It's unlikely that you would find identical personalities between a man and a woman. Other kinds of men are not exactly the same as me.*

Some men are different. Even women have their defects, sure. It's hard to be a husband, but it's also hard to be a wife, right? Renzo knew how hard it was to forge a good marriage, but in spite of his turbulent relationship, he greatly admired his first wife because he felt she was a *good woman*, and a person *of infinite goodness.*

In describing his mother, fifty-four-year-old Raffaele made clear his admiration for women: *The women in the old days, like my mother, did so much; they had to have so much determination. The strength my mother had, I don't know if I would have it, understand? And there were so many like my mother. They had the children, they raised them, they took care of them, and the men just went off to work.* Raffaele admired women and admitted that most men would not acknowledge women's contributions: *I'm sorry to say this, but I think that women are much more intelligent than men, not only more intelligent, but also stronger—without a doubt. We men give the appearance of being strong, yes, but we really are weak. Women are stronger, in all ways. They are stronger in enduring troubles and worries; they bear them better than men and they take them with more philosophy. Oh, yes, there are exceptions, but normally women are stronger. This is good for men. Even if men delude themselves that they are the stronger sex, it's not true at all. Men deceive themselves in thinking they are—I don't know— powerful, but instead we are weak. Even in the field of—how can I say it?—in the field of love, women are stronger. I mean that women are stronger in all ways, understand? Yes, men are necessary, and women are also necessary, but I believe that women are much more potent than men, even though men think they are. But listen, don't believe them.*

Look, when a woman really loves, she does not waiver. Men too, but I think that men, being more fragile, are more subject to highs and lows. Oh, God, there are women who unfortunately are what they are, and men too. But I view women more positively. In fact, the woman is key to making a good family. Because the woman can make of her husband whatever she wants—remember that. It's the woman who decides everything, even if she gives the opposite impression. It is all the woman. The woman can make or break the family.

Women have a different touch, a different emotionality. They have something—nature gives them something extra, in my opinion. A lot of men would tell me that I'm a fool to talk like this; however, they would say it to defend themselves. I too feel superior to my wife and to women, eh. However, if I must reason seriously, I have to admit that women are superior, judging from their value. I give my wife credit for all her merit. I recognize her defects too, eh. But I have more defects than she does, it's true. My wife is more positive about things. She is inexhaustible—not just in bed but around the house, with the children, with everything. I give up before her; that's how it is. That's what shows that women have superior strength, in my opinion.

Women concurred with men about the stronger and weaker sexes. Sixty-one-year-old Marianna said, *Men don't get along very well on their own; they do worse than women alone. I think that even if a woman has so much to do at her job, she'll still find time to do a little bit in the house, but not a man. I've always heard that a man alone can't make it. Because they're used to having everything done for them, the bowl of soup prepared and placed in front of them. Oh, if they don't have anyone to prepare it for them, they get by, they prepare it for themselves, but it's more of a sacrifice for them than for women. I say that men alone find themselves much worse off than women alone.*

The fact that women believed that men could not make it alone and could not do certain household chores of course reinforced the cultural necessity of women taking care of men. Giovanna affirmed that Italian women developed their identities based on doing things for others: *Maybe the value of marriage is to say, "When I am seventy years old, I will have this companionship, good or bad, for better or worse. It will give me something to do in the house. I'll cook a bowl of soup for my husband." Understand? It means that there is always a house to clean and there is always something to do—for another person. The woman who doesn't have something to do for another person finds herself dead and lost. For herself she does nothing. For her whole life she has been doing things for her husband.*

Women were inculcated with expectations that they find fulfillment through caring for others, and it was hard for them to resist these expectations. Giovanna expressed the dilemma of trying to place her own needs ahead of her family duties: *In this sense of personal aspirations conflicting with domestic roles, it's hard for me. It's hard, and it's hard to explain how and why. Maybe it's because I myself place these obstacles before me. Yes, I think it is precisely me and no one else. My family, my husband, are fine. . . . It is I who have to overcome this tradition that lies behind me. I'm the one who has to reconcile the roles of mother, wife, and woman who wants to live a life.*

Other Florentines managed to reconcile their diverse roles by establishing complementarity with their husbands. Elena's husband had died of cancer about five years before I interviewed her and she was still extremely bereaved. She described her marriage as one where they shared tasks and supported each other so as to overcome their individual shortcomings and weaknesses: *I really miss my husband because it seems that I leaned on him for so many things even if in other ways he was weaker than I am. For example, I don't know, if he saw a little blood, he fainted right away. However, I felt supported and protected by him— something that you unfortunately can't get from a woman. Yet he always told me that he felt very weak and that I gave him strength for so many things—that's how it was. Maybe we counterbalanced each other.*

I remember that my husband helped me so much, especially after he retired. Before that, there was little time, because he left in the morning, he returned at noon and ate in a hurry, and then he had to leave again to go back to work. I always tried to have everything ready so that he could eat and go straight back to work. But after he retired, he certainly did help me. He helped me wash the floor, he helped me cook, and he came with me to do the shopping so that he could carry the heavy bags. He thought of everything, in short, everything, everything. . . . Why was he so willing to help me? Perhaps it was because of his great love.

In Elena's vision of marriage, love was the fundamental basis of their partnership that induced her husband to help and support her: *Giorgio showed me so much solicitude and so much tenderness—I was struck by that right away. He was like that right up to the end. Affection, if it is reciprocal, is beautiful. But if it only flows in one direction, then it is useless. It's better to break off and let it go.* Fifty-four-year-old Baldo had a similar vision of marriage: *I think love in a marriage is the most important thing. If there isn't reciprocal love, a marriage is really lacking. The primary thing is to love each other a lot.*

Sixty-one-year-old Marianna had been married three years when I interviewed her, and she too emphasized reciprocity and compromise as the bases of a good marriage: *I think men and women have to help each other. Renzo gets up in the morning and does all the shopping. He knows I have this bad back and he helps me. I wash all the dishes and that doesn't bother me, but he has suggested that we hire a woman once a week to come in and do the heavy cleaning. But I said, "No, as long as I can do it for you, I will do it." He doesn't do all that much in the house, but he helps me wash the windows and take down the curtains so I can wash them. And it's already a big help that he does the shopping. He comes back in the morning and brings the newspaper, the bread, other things. Sometimes he goes to the market there in Piazza delle Cure, and other times he goes to his butcher friend and gets the meat, so really that's a big help. Plus he gets what he wants. How can I know what he will like? You've got to live together to know it.*

Marianna described their negotiations about food to illustrate how they got along: *We talk in the morning, "Shall we make broth today?" So then I cook what we decide and make him happy cooking things that he likes. Then we're both happy. You know, I have a little anxiety when I cook: "Let's hope it comes out well," because I'm not used to cooking for others, understand?*

Sometimes he goes out and comes back: "Look, I brought you some beans (fagioli). I went to the Caldini's to get beans and they also had peaches, and I bought some." Fine. Tomorrow beans and peaches. Sometimes . . . he says, "Look, I'm going to the market and I'm going to get asparagus. Tomorrow we'll have asparagus for dinner, all right?" Yes, that's fine. Look, I don't have any desire to ruin my days by arguing about these things. First of all, I don't have days to ruin, and then if he brings something home, he knows I like it too. He says, "I'm going to the Caldini's. I'll see what they have."

I reply, "Get whatever you want." Because I like everything, it's fine with me. Because listen, we're here, if I'm going to cook, what does it take? It doesn't take very much. I'm the one who worries that it won't come out well, but I try my best. Marianna's willingness to eat whatever her husband wanted was typical of the women in the United States whom DeVault (1991) studied. They deferred to their husbands' food preferences and in so doing subtly reinforced men's privilege.

Marianna defined compromise around food as key to marital harmony: *I think that men and women have to help each other. The other day I was talking with a friend named Fulvia. She was telling me about her husband's character and I had no idea how he was. Oh, others had told me a little bit, but she said to me—listen to this—"Oh you think Ercole is such a good man, but he isn't good at all. Listen to what happened today. It was one o'clock and I was in the bathroom and the pasta got a little bit overcooked. Look, as a result of that, we aren't even speaking to each other."*

No way, listen, I wouldn't even think about it, you know, because we're just not like that. Sometimes Renzo and I will talk. "Look," I say. "This dish really didn't come out very well."

"No," he replies. "It will come out better the next time."

That's how we talk. You can't live the way she and her husband live; it's just not worth it. I said to Fulvia, "Your husband—couldn't he just let it go?"

"Oh, no," she replied. "He will hardly say a single word to me."

He's crazy, for heaven sake. That's no way to have a relationship. Men and women have to help each other. For a man to make such a big deal about over-cooked pasta seemed preposterous to Marianna, but men in diverse cultures have used dissatisfaction with food as an excuse to berate their wives (Charles and Kerr 1988, Counihan 2002, DeVault 1991, Ellis 1983).

Other women were explicit that the basis of a good marriage was talking about problems and making decisions together. Forty-eight-year-old Laura said, *There are couples where the husband wants to rule and the wife doesn't want to be ruled—then you've got problems. But in most families, husband and wife decide things together. I'm content because I just want to get along well with everyone. I like to be with my husband and so I don't care what he does as long as he takes me with him or else we stay at home together. I don't care at all what we do as long as we're together. In my home we try to reach agreement with ourselves and the children. We don't try to create problems for each other but rather seek a path that works for everyone if possible. What I care about is that there's harmony and tranquility in the house, and that we're all getting along—for me, that's so much.* Laura followed her husband's lead to preserve family harmony.

Forty-one-year-old Sergia described ideal husband–wife relations: *What kind of a man do I want for my daughters? First of all, not a man who commands but one who talks with his wife, consults her, and makes decisions with her. . . . Affectionate, he has to be affectionate, that's the most important thing. Affectionate and always so, not just at the beginning when they start going out, but he has to continue to be so. . . . Here's something else that is important for me—a man most of all must be willing to discuss things with his wife. In every marriage there are misunderstandings and times when husband and wife don't get along for whatever reason. When these things happen, they have to try—and the man especially has to try—to talk about things, to understand each other, and to arrive at a good resolution for both of them. . . .*

Women have to speak on equal terms with men and be considered equal as well. I do not believe that women are inferior to men—more impulsive yes, but inferior no. On the contrary, there are women who are directors of companies and they are sharper than the devil. I don't consider myself inferior. Oh, yes, things are changing greatly between men and women, eh. The big changes happened in my generation. If you look at my parents, my father has always commanded and that was that. But I have changed a great deal with Rinaldo, and most of our friends are like us. The essential change is that women can speak their mind now. They decide things together with their husbands, and if there is something they don't like, they don't do it. Both men and women must have their say. For Sergia and others, the crucial characteristics a married couple needed were mutual affection, a willingness to discuss problems, and an ability to make compromises. Each partner also needed to have an equal voice in discussions, even if his or her role was in a separate domain. This give-and-take of affection and negotiation also had to extend to economic power.

Economic Power and Gender

Florentine men and women had unequal economic power because of the relatively inflexible division of labor and because women's work of both reproduction and production had lower value than men's. Men also had greater access to and expectations for employment. Forty-eight-year-old Rinaldo from Prato, a well-known textile and commercial center, commented on gender and how it affected access to resources in his generation: *Women did not have the same business opportunities as men. Oh, I know some women who are incredibly capable. Some women are entrepreneurs who have crushed their male competitors and emerged as tops in their field. But there are also women who don't succeed, not because of their lack of abilities, but because of their formation. First and foremost, they didn't have the freedom that men had. By the time we were teenagers, we men were already discussing various work possibilities at the bar. But young women didn't and still don't hang out at bars or clubs. Women didn't pile into a car with three or four girlfriends and head for the beach on Sunday and talk about work the way we young men used to do. Oh, maybe a few women did, but only a very small percentage. Most women have not had the same formation that young men have had.*

Men and women had different *formation.* Because men were socialized to productive work at an early age, they tended to be less conflicted about it and better prepared for it, and they had greater access to resources. Marriage improved most women's access to resources but did not necessarily give them economic autonomy. Giovanna said, *My impression is that in Florence the man is the one who runs the family, especially in regard to the financial and administrative issues, and the women are kept outside of all that except for the few businesswomen that exist. In general, women who are mothers of families seem excluded from the financial matters. In short, I think I see that the women walk a half a step behind the men.*

Women's lack of economic autonomy contributed to their subordination. Because many women who worked did so outside the formal economy, they earned little and lacked benefits and retirement pensions. In Renzo and Grazia's marriage, Grazia lacked financial control, even though by Renzo's own admission she worked just as hard as he did to build the family handbag business; however, he controlled the money. She never received wages and had to ask Renzo for every penny she spent. This economic imbalance was an important reason why they fought and yet also why Grazia stayed in the marriage. Elena told how Grazia maneuvered around Renzo's control by describing a time she saw Grazia making up a package of tomato sauce, cheese, bread, and other things. Grazia told her that she was making the package for Renzo's brother Massimo. He and his family were going through hard times, and she had compassion for them because she had plenty and they had little. But Grazia told Elena not to tell Renzo because he was *tirchio—stingy* and would begrudge her giving the food to his brother. Similarly, Sergia went around Rinaldo's control by budgeting her food money to have enough to purchase things for herself, to avoid the humiliation of having to ask Rinaldo for money. Yet Grazia's and Sergia's experiences were only some of a number of different ways spouses worked out the household finances.

Renzo's second wife, Marianna, was financially independent because she had her own job and then later her own pension. She underscored how important this was to her: *I'm new at everything to do with marriage, but I'm doing fine with it. First of all, I have enough money to survive, and I don't have to ask anyone for anything. This is a great thing, and it's the most important thing. I'm not saying it because I like to brag, no; I'm saying it because at least I know I'm secure. If you don't have anything, maybe, who knows? Instead, the way I am is fine. I'm well off, he's well off, we are both well off.* Marianna recognized the benefits of having her own job and income. Yet such a pattern was anomalous in the postwar period, when women's labor-force participation in Italy was among the lowest in Western Europe (Balbo and May 1975–76).[2]

Except for Marianna, my older female subjects depended on men for their financial well-being. While all of the men worked for money outside the home, most of the women gave up their salaried jobs at marriage. Many did piecework in the home while their children were young, and some returned to salaried jobs after their children were grown. The family budget was sometimes controlled by the husband who gave his wife an allowance for household expenses; this pattern was followed by Renzo and Grazia, Tommasa and Marco, and their daughter Sergia and her husband Rinaldo. Sometimes the husband gave his pay envelope to his wife, who controlled the budget and gave her husband a monthly allowance for his pocket money, like Valeria and Baldo, and Elena and Giorgio. Sometimes husband and wife managed the budget jointly, like Berta and Massimo, and their daughter Laura and her husband Raffaele. One couple, Caterina and Sandro, kept their paychecks separate and used them to pay for their own luxuries as well as different portions of the household expenses. Sandro paid for the rent and their vacations; Caterina paid for food and household products. Administration of money in the family was one important measure of marital relationships and respect. Like other gender behaviors, it seemed to reflect family traditions. Furthermore, in families where the women worked not at all or for less pay than their husbands, their access to their husband's earnings was a major factor in their status.

Sixty-six-year-old Elena was an interesting case. She defined herself more through her family than through her work, although she labored for almost thirty years in the family bakery. She was a key player in the business because of her long hours and good rapport with clients, yet she received no wages or pension contributions. Men—first her father and then her brother-in-law Marco—ran the bakery and controlled its profits even though Elena and her mother provided labor essential to the bakery's success. But although Elena did not earn money, she had a strong position in her marriage because her husband Giorgio gave her control of the family budget: *Everything Giorgio earned, he brought to me, everything, down to the last cent. And then he said, "Give me some money so I can buy cigarettes." Or he said, "Listen, I'm out of money. Would you give me a little please?"*

I answered, "But for heaven's sake, you can take what you need. You know where the money is—in the bureau drawer."

He said, "No, no, no, no. I gave it to you. You are the one who administers the money and you have to give it to me." He never went and took money by himself. At the end of the month, he brought me his pay, and then I administered it all by myself, all of it. He trusted my budgeting. He didn't even have this example at home because he told me that his father gave his mother a sum for the shopping and that had to be enough. The rest of the money he kept himself. He didn't squander it because he didn't have any vices; however, he did not give it to Giorgio's mother. Instead, Giorgio right from the start gave me his entire paycheck.

The situation of fifty-four-year-old Baldo's parents was similar to and different from that of Elena and Giorgio. His parents were of peasant backgrounds, and his father became a cabinet-maker. Like Elena, Baldo's mother was first and foremost a housewife, although she always did piecework for wages. Baldo explained: *My mother continued to work after getting married. Like so many women in Empoli, she wove straw onto wine flasks. Oh, she worked so much. . . . What my mother earned covering wine flasks paid the interest and principal on the loan for my father's carpentry shop, and what my father earned served to keep us alive and to keep the carpentry shop going.*

But in spite of her earnings, Baldo's mother had no economic autonomy. Baldo continued: *Something that always bothered me about my father was the way he treated my mother about money. He did it wrong. Even though my mother worked, my father controlled all the money. He didn't give her a monthly amount, or even a weekly amount. No, every day before my mother did the food shopping,* she had to go into my father's shop and ask him for a few dollars. That was something that I never liked, and I told my father so again and again. But my father said, "That is the way I've always done it." I didn't like it, because for God's sake, every day she had to go into his shop and ask for money. Didn't he know she needed it? At least he could have given her an amount each week to cover the food shopping and the things we children needed. It's not like the poor woman bought anything for herself—have no fear. She had few clothes and I don't know if she ever went to the hairdresser—maybe once a year for Christmas or Easter. Yet she always worked and earned money.

It seemed like she was begging when she went to my father. It seemed like he didn't trust her, or that she was spending money unwisely, but that wasn't true and he knew it. So why did he treat her that way? It was the way things were in those days. That's the way men were. They had to be in charge of everything. It was like he was saying to her, "But don't tell me you already spent all the money I gave you yesterday?" But it was the men who didn't bother themselves with budgeting. My father didn't even know how much bread cost, how much butter cost. He knew how much a glass of wine cost because he went to the bar to drink it. In the morning when he had breakfast, he didn't want to think about the fact that if he ate an anchovy with his bread it was going to cost something. That's the way they all did it in those days; the husbands gave out money in hiccups. And if they gambled it all away, the wife and children just had to put up with it.

Because of Baldo's distaste for his father's ways, he followed a different strategy: As soon as my brother and I started working, we gave our mother our pay. After seeing her asking my father for money every morning, as soon as we were big enough to go off to work, we immediately changed the system. Furthermore, when Baldo married, he gave his wife Valeria control of the family budget. He said, At the end of the month, I give my paycheck to my wife and she takes charge of all our expenses. Sometimes I used to do extra jobs to make a little supplementary income so as to be able to leave my entire paycheck for the house. With two children and with her not working, well, I had to do my best to earn what I could. After I gave her my paycheck, she was completely in charge. I said, "Here's the paycheck. Look, you do as you want with it." In general, she is the one who does the food shopping every day and makes all the purchases, even for everyone's clothes. Valeria thus had an important source of power in her family related to her culinary responsibilities that compensated for the fact that she did not earn very much money herself. She said, My husband always left the family budget in my hands. Let's be clear, it wasn't because I demanded control. He worked and brought me his paycheck to cover the household expenses. Then he tried to work extra to pay for other things, like his car, and going out. Note that Valeria made it clear that she didn't demand control, which she implied would have been unseemly, but was given control, which was fine.

Valeria's sister Laura and her husband Raffaele preferred to administer the budget together. As Laura said, Raffaele and I pool our pay and then we take out *what we need when we have to do some errands. We shop for food every day.* Being able to take the money she needed to buy food rather than having to ask reinforced Laura's economic parity with her husband. In his family of origin, Raffaele's mother controlled the money: *Before I got married, when I was work-ing I gave my pay to my mother and then she gave me spending money—"vizi."* *She knew that I spent, let's say, three dollars a week. Every Saturday I was paid and I brought my salary to my mother. I gave her my pay envelope and my father gave her his, and every penny was needed. The pay was so miserable that my mother used it all just to keep us alive. She needed all our earnings to pay the rent, to buy us clothes, to eat, to live, understand?*

Raffaele's parents' experience accorded with the fact that among my sub-jects, the less-well-off couples were more egalitarian about money than the more wealthy. Forty-five-year-old Rinaldo, the financially successful owner of a dyeing factory, did not share control of the family budget with his wife Ser-gia, but rather gave her a monthly allowance. Sergia, like her mother before her, was one of the few of my female subjects who did not work after marriage. Rather she devoted herself to the life of a well-off bourgeois housewife, run-ning the household and dedicating herself to her children's welfare.

Sergia's husband Rinaldo did not value women's labor in the household and expressed ambivalence about the importance of paid work for women: *Is eco-nomic independence important for women's status? Well, that depends on the husband they find. My wife is not economically independent, but I don't think that she has fewer rights than I do at home. If she has fewer, it is perhaps because of her upbringing—but I don't think she does, no, no, I don't think so. It's not that she doesn't have rights because she doesn't bring home any money. There are cases of women who work and they are still treated badly by their husbands and not taken into consideration. I don't think women's status depends on their earning—but maybe it does a little bit. However, I don't think that is the determining factor in the family balance of power. However, when I think about what I want for my daughters, the most important thing is economic independence.* Although Ri-naldo hedged about the importance of economic autonomy to his wife's sta-tus, he was clear that he wanted his daughters to have it.

He continued: *I want my daughters to have their own work, a profession that they like. . . . I hope they find their own work either as a dependent or in some pri-vate or public business. Oh, I think it is absolutely right that they work; it is indis-pensable. Today they just can't hope to marry someone who will support them. That would be absurd. No, no, such a hope is out of place today. It would shrink their choice of husbands, eh, by a lot. Furthermore, I want my daughters to have a choice whether to work or not. I don't want them to be forced to stay home because they have no profession. If they marry someone who after a year of marriage or after twenty years no longer needs them to work, they'll have a choice to stop. Un-derstand? But today—given how much things have changed lately—I don't think it is easy to marry someone who can support a family on one salary alone. Fur-*

thermore, if they have their own job, they won't be a burden on the family budget, understand?

Rinaldo's wife Sergia evinced ambivalence about her lack of economic control and about men's power in the family: *When I say a man can have all the responsibilities, I mean those having to do with work, the family budget, and the big expenses. Rinaldo takes care of the electric bill, the telephone, the heat—all these bills. I'm not the kind of woman who wants her husband to come home with his paycheck and entrust me with the entire family budget like so many women. No, no. I prefer that he give me a monthly amount of my own (**un mensile**). Oh, God, I want it to be a generous amount, because I try to use it not just for the household costs, but also for my own expenses, without having to ask him for more. I use my money to pay for the household food and for clothing for the girls and me. . . . But I say to him, "It's not right, it's not fair, because when I have to buy myself a new dress, I can't do it with my money." I don't manage to save much. "I can't do it," I tell him. "I have to come and ask you for more and I don't like to ask. I too work at home. Why should I have to ask you for money?" So then at one point I decided to go get a job, but then I quickly realized that I would earn more by staying home. So that's how it is. The Italian male is like this. He likes to be in charge of the money and know exactly how much there is.* Sergia wanted a good share of her husband's money but was willing to let him have control, but perhaps she said that because it was her only choice.

Sergia's blunt recognition that she could "*earn more*" by staying home than she could by getting a job reflected the unequal opportunities for men and women in the workplace, especially higher up the earning scale. Sergia, however, also learned from experience how total her husband's control of money was: *One time I had my own checking account. I had fun with it, but Rinaldo immediately took it away from me. When he said I could write my own checks, one day I took them and I went into Center and I bought some clothes. Right away he said, "No, listen, it will be better if I take away these checks, because when you need something, you just ask me for the money." So now I have to humiliate myself and I don't like this. Many times I do without something rather than ask him for money. Or if I can't do without something, I try to put aside some money from my monthly allowance until I have enough. I usually manage.*

Control of the food budget gave Sergia some monetary control, but not very much. She rationalized: *Listen, I entrust a lot of responsibility to men. I'm not an ardent feminist (**una femminista sfegatata**). I'm fine with a man having all the responsibility as long as there is collaboration and discussion with his wife. But in short, the man can have the essential responsibility. I think women are more impulsive sometimes. So it's good to have the man make the serious decisions because I think men are less impulsive and more reasonable—they weigh things more carefully. Oh, maybe just my husband is like this. I don't know. I don't know. I only know him.*

Interestingly, Sergia repeated the very gender stereotypes that had angered her cousin Giovanna. Sergia did not challenge her husband's economic dominance, perhaps because she benefited from his considerable earnings. Furthermore, Sergia herself was raised in a relatively well-off household, and her father Marco was the man who said in Chapter 5, *When it comes to paying, I pay.* Sergia said she wanted Rinaldo to be in charge, but she also resented his financial control and the humiliation of having to ask for money. She also wished she had her own work and felt that her life lacked satisfaction because she did not have it.

Giovanna commented on how middle-class Florentine housewives sought compensation for the services they performed for husband and children: *I've noted that the values of the women here—not all of the women but so many of them—focus on material things more than anything else. For example, I see these women caring a lot about having a Persian rug, a mink coat, a beautiful house, understand? The new furniture, the house redone, the floor just so, the sheets perfectly embroidered, the bedspread exactly the right color. Yes, beautiful things are nice; however, I think many Italian women's aspirations stop at this level. . . . I have one friend who has a beautiful house. She's well off and she goes on vacation with her family every year. However, I see all her ability used up day after day with all her obligations to take the children here, to go there, to buy new clothes for the boy, to shop for new shoes for the girl, to sign them up for school, and to talk with their teachers. In short, is this a life? Is this all there is? . . . Italian women give a lot. They feel that they are recompensed when their husbands buy them a fur coat or a gold ring or a diamond.*

Some women did have access to money and goods through their high-earning husbands, but it was an access granted or withdrawn at men's will. Being financially dependent on their husbands made women vulnerable in their marriages, which they had to put up with even if things went bad or if the husband had affairs. As Elena said, *There are many reasons why a husband and wife stay together in spite of not getting along. Sometimes there are reasons of economic interest. My God, if a woman is independent and can survive by herself as well as she can with her husband, well then at a certain point she can say, "I'm self-sufficient and I'm washing my hands of this, and that's that." But if the woman is economically dependent on her husband, how can she make it without him? So then she bows her head and stays there. Oh, there are so many cases like this. If a woman quits her job to have children, then she will have the challenge of getting back into the workforce and all that.* The production-reproduction dichotomy in the 1980s undermined women's economic power, for the lack of value in their own work made them all too often dependent on men, who often were equal and benevolent partners, but sometimes were controlling despots.

Body and Gender: Commodification and Resistance

Women's economic disadvantage meant they had to attract men to maximize their standard of living—a fact that affected gendered body image.[3] Florentine women struggled with increasingly prevalent images in the media and fashion that promoted female objectification and thinness (see Figure 6.1). Whereas older people cared more about good food and convivial meals than staying in shape, younger women experienced growing cultural pressure for body beauty and thinness. Twenty-year-old Piera said, *I have so many friends who get massages, exercise, and eat little—they take aerobics and exercise classes. They pay attention to what they eat, every single thing. Men do it too. They go to the gym, they pay attention to their physique, however, less than the women; it's logical. When the men go out to dinner, it's not like they watch everything; no, it's more likely you find one who eats one thing and then another; they eat. It's logical; they're less concerned than women. There are also fewer who are fat. There are more fat women than men. I don't know why, but that's the way it is. There are women who are fixated, who weigh themselves, who go and exercise and watch what they eat.* Piera resisted such pressures as she described below, but increasing numbers of Italian women fell prey to a cult of thinness.[4]

According to forty-one-year-old Sergia, media pressure on women's bodies was growing: *There's a lot of talk about being thin in this culture. If you open the newspapers, the magazines, they are all about shape and diet. They are full of the little image of the little lean woman. When you look in the mirror, you see her and you say to yourself, "Mamma mia, how fat I am." You feel like a traveling ball of lard. You see images of beautiful clothes worn by beautiful little women. You see advertisements for hairdos and shampoos, all with these very thin little women. This tells you that you are out of this world if you are fat.*

Sergia described her upper-middle-class female friends who were mostly stay-at-home mothers: *I have many friends who diet occasionally, almost all of them. They eat these powders instead of food. Many, many friends are careful about their weight. Now at this time of the year, as summer approaches, almost all of them diet. They slowly lose a little weight because they feel ugly; they don't like themselves. If they have to put on a bikini, they don't like themselves at all. It's not that they really need to diet, but they think they will be more attractive thinner. They all want to have a lean silhouette. They play tennis to sweat and lose weight. They do aerobics to keep their thighs and bellies from sagging; they do massages. The goal is always this—to have a beautiful body, to be presentable, to wear pants with tranquility, and to put on a bikini without fear.*

This focus on thinness was not typical of the first two-thirds of the twentieth century, when the majority of Italians struggled to get enough to eat. During the Fascist years, as Chapter 3 described, propaganda exalted a plump, maternal body. In the 1980s, many Florentines expressed disapproval of a woman who was too thin, as Elena did by saying of her daughter after a long illness, *Sembra ciucciata dalle streghe—She seems sucked by witches.* Furthermore, Florentines felt that eating together established literal physical similarities between family members and defined the body not as a product of personal moral concern and control but as a "natural" product and reflection

Fig. 6.1 Billboard at bus stop in Viale dei Mille, Florence, summer 1984: *"Miss Vantaggio, più magro, più sexy, più tutto"*—"Miss Advantage—more thin, more sexy, more everything"

of the family. Valeria's relatives were almost all on the plump side. She said, *Nature made us this way. There are those who can eat as much as they want and they keep their shape just fine. Instead there are those who watch what they eat, who suffer, and still get fat. My children are like me. Many times my daughter Caterina has said, "I don't know, both Arturo and I take after you. All we have to do is eat a little and we gain weight."*

Valeria's son Arturo echoed his mother: *All of us in this family have a large body build and so I think it is just something that we carry with us.* His sister Caterina concurred: *We are all fat in this family.* Their cousin, Piera, echoed them: *All of us in the family are nice and plump—bell'e pasciucuti. Our cousins in Florence too. We're all nice and abundant—bell'e abbondanti. I don't know; it's our constitution; it's logical.* They concurred that people's bodies were given by their families, along with their eating habits. As Piera said, *In this family we eat; we don't hold back.*

Similarly Teti (1995, 4) found that up until the 1970s, for Calabrian peasants, "plumpness came to be considered as a symbol of well-being and alimentary happiness, of beauty, wealth, power and dominance" that they associated with the elite. Thinness represented the peasants' lot of unending physical labor, misery, and a meager diet. But in the last third of the twentieth century, attitudes toward fat and thin changed in Calabria as the Italian economic miracle brought dietary abundance to all. When all could be fat, it lost its prestige, and today, "a fat body is no longer fashionable, indeed it is negatively perceived" (Teti 1995, 23).

At the end of the twentieth century, in Calabria, in Florence, and in the United States, thinness in women was associated with the upper classes, as it was with Sergia's friends. She described them: *Yes, these women are all wealthy, very well off. This has a lot to do with it. Those with less money don't have the time or the resources to go and waste on massages and tennis. Furthermore, the wealthy people frequent certain ritzy environments where there is a certain competition in clothes, fashion, and body beauty.* This competition for beauty sometimes alienated women from each other (Whitaker 2000, 278).

Not only did the Florentine upper-middle-class women work on their bodies to fit into the standards of their elite culture, but according to Sergia, they also linked thinness with their allure to men, which was key to their self-worth: *My friends pursue dieting to be admired because they are always dependent on men. They can't live without men courting them and making them feel like women. They need this because they are unsatisfied in life. To feel like women, they need to feel loved, pleasing, still attractive. They need to feel that even at forty years old they can still make a conquest of some young man. Perhaps the women who are most unsatisfied and thus most restless always want to realize themselves through their body. They have no other way to fulfill themselves. The life of a housewife is oppressive, so they go out with a beautiful body and they feel compensated.*

Sergia's words implied the subjugating dimensions of her friends' upper-class lives; they were dependent on men's attention for self-worth as well as survival. She recognized that the media reinforced this patriarchal value system by using women's bodies as commodities, and she felt that women were complicit in their own objectification: *Seeing women's bare breasts has become normal in Italy—on television, in magazines. Ever since it has become accepted for women to sunbathe topless, you've seen a lot more breasts in advertising. Yes, it is a form of exploitation to expose women's breasts in advertising. It makes the woman into an object, of course. Just like the issue of going on all these diets turns us into objects too. There's no way out. But it is women themselves who go along with this. We women turn ourselves into objects. It comes from advertising and these models who are paid millions to objectify themselves. It is men who put it all into action, no? In these newspapers it is the men who initiate it all—the photographer and the writer who use the women. The women go along with it to get paid or show themselves off, or who knows why? It begins with men, but the women go along with it. That's the way it always is. The women do it because they need the money.*

Florentines knew that the objectification of women's bodies made them, as Elena said, *vulnerable.* They said that young women were worrying about being thin and dieting, whereas in the past most women thought more about being wives, workers, and mothers, than about cultivating their bodies with exercise routines and diets. The pressure on women to mold their bodies to please men seemed to be linked to women's economic dependence and lack of self-fulfillment, a situation assured by the Italian economic imbalance and ideology favoring men.[5]

Men's cultural power was manifest in their caring little about their weight and being defined as the pleased rather than the pleasers. Sergia described male body ideology: *Men don't worry about their weight the way women do, but, you know, large men are not unattractive. Plus men do not have all the competition in newspapers that women have. Women continually confront an image of how they are supposed to be, but men do not see images of other men in the press. Men are allowed to be normal like so many you see around. It's more the woman who has to be perfect. I don't think men with a little extra weight get a complex about it the way women do.*

Sergia recognized the different standards held for women and men: *Women have to attract physically and sexually as well as in other ways. But men can attract even if they aren't great-looking. I don't think women focus on men's looks alone. Men can attract with their character, their behavior, their way of looking at you, and in so many ways. It isn't necessary for a man to be beautiful.* Sergia's opinion was confirmed by male subjects who expressed a general sense of well-being in their bodies regardless of their shape. Fifty-four-year-old Baldo explained: *Men are less obsessed about being thin than women. A woman who is fat is afraid that she won't find a husband. But a man even though fat doesn't have this fear. He says to himself, "I can always find a woman who is fat like me. On the contrary, the other men will leave her for me; they will shun her." That's the way it is. The first worry a girl has when she reaches age twenty is, "I won't find a husband." Even the thin ones have this fear.*

The double standard for men and women in regard to bodily beauty defined women as suppliants for men's approbation. This belief was most explicitly voiced by twenty-eight-year-old Sandro: *Our mentality about men and women may be wrong, but it persists. Women worry more about how they look. It comes from the fact of wanting to look a certain way as a person and of wanting to be pleasing in a general sense, not necessarily pleasing to a specific person. This comes from an old idea, a mentality persisting from the beginning that it is the woman who has to please the man and not the man who has to please the woman.*[6] *Maybe nowadays we are both doing everything to please each other, and maybe this old mentality is changing, but it still endures. I know many women who are obsessed with being fat, but instead they are not fat. Men worry less; in fact, men are more likely not to give a fig about how they look. This is just due to the old mentality that is beginning to change, but it has always accompanied the woman. The woman has to please the man; it is not the man who has to please the woman.*

Sandro articulated a Florentine gender ideology that privileged men, and this privilege was reflected in a widespread proverb: *"Moglie e buoi dai paesi tuoi"*—*"women and cattle from your own villages."* This proverb implied men's right to choose, and linked women with animals as the ones to be chosen. Not all of my female or even male subjects embraced this ideology; however, they all saw women as responsible for nurturing and feeding others, cultural practices that sanctioned men's claims to be served, and hence pleased.[7] But while some of my female subjects accepted men's right to judge their body, others did not. Twenty-year-old Piera commented about her generation, born in the 1960s: *I know men who harass their wives or girlfriends about their weight. I wouldn't stand for it. It wouldn't be the thing for me. They badger their girlfriends to lose weight. The girls pay attention to them, but if they said it to me, after two days, they would be out the door. But their girlfriends pay attention. And the girls aren't even fat; they are just sick in the head in my opinion. And even if they were fat, so what? It's not something to harass them about. I don't know why they do it, because it has never happened to me and it never will. It would be impossible for me. Yes, it's a form of male power. They make their girlfriends uncomfortable. My attitude is, if you want me, I'm like this. If you don't want me, you don't want me no matter how I am. You just can't marginalize what you are.*

Piera projected a strong sense of self and refused to let a man control her eating or her looks. She also prioritized the pleasure and sociability of eating over fasting to lose weight: *For me, if we're all in a group on a Saturday or Sunday evening and we decide to go out to eat, am I going to go out to eat and then I can't eat? I have to eat a little salad with no dressing? No. I like to eat the way everybody else is eating. I can't suffer my whole life just to be thin.* Yet Piera was dissatisfied with her weight, as increasing numbers of Italian women were.

Sergia reported that her slim fourteen-year-old daughter had started to worry about being too fat: *The other day, Eugenia said to me, "Mamma, look, I too have cellulite."*

"Oh, come on," I said. "Where do you have it, Eugenia?"

"Look," she said, and effectively on her bottom she has those little depressions. It begins even at the age of fourteen, eh. She said, "Look, even here on my thighs I have it."

"Oh, forget it," I said. "You'll see, later it will go away."

"I'm not going to eat anymore," she announced.

Women's ambivalence about their bodies mirrored broader cultural upheaval. In the 1980s, Florentines were losing touch with old theories advocating a harmonious balance in food, body, and health, and they were focusing more on the body as aesthetic object. At the turn of the millennium, increasing numbers of young Italian women watched and worried about their weight. Liuccio (1998, 269) stated, "We are all in fact exposed to homogenizing and normalizing ideologies relative to 'femininity' and feminine beauty; the equation thinness = success, in our culture, places constantly in danger the preservation of alternative ideals of beauty." A study of almost 10,000 young people between the ages of 13 and 19 found that 45 percent of the females called themselves fat and were not satisfied with their physical condition, whereas 64 percent of the males were satisfied and only 24 percent defined themselves as overweight. Almost half of the teenage girls dieted and a little less than half exercised, whereas 80 percent of boys did some sports and 60 percent practiced sport or exercise at least three times a week (*La metà delle ragazze si vede grassa,* 2002). In the focus groups I conducted in 2003 with university students, several young women defined thinness as an important social imperative, and almost all of the students knew at least one person, usually female, who suffered from anorexia nervosa or bulimia.

Florentine men and women dealt with the economic and ideological imbalances imposed by the production/reproduction gender dichotomy in many ways. While they lived in a society where men's work and contributions were formally valued, they espoused an informal value system that validated women's strengths and accomplishments. In some couples this went beyond lip service and resulted in women having some economic autonomy through control of the family budget. In other couples, men putatively valued their wives but denied them economic independence. In few families did the men contribute much labor to the reproductive sphere, and when they "helped," their contributions were far less than women's. In families where the women did not work outside the home, or where they had mothers or daughters to help them with the domestic chores, the women managed, but they all recognized that working outside the home made their situations difficult. Chapter 7 focuses on the ways that eating together constructed family and community, while Chapter 8 looks at how Florentines perpetuated the imbalance in gender relations through child rearing, especially through habits of feeding the family.

Commensality, Family, and Community

Mangiare insieme è la base della famiglia.	*Eating together is the foundation of the family.*

Baldo

Commensality and Relationships: *"The table unites us"*

Forty-five-year-old Rinaldo, the father of two daughters, described what the family meant to him: *Listen, here in Italy still, and I hope in other countries as well, the family is the starting point. It is the foundation. It is in the family where everyone finds support. It is the place where you can find help any time you are in need—whether it is a need for money or affection and security. I say the family has to be the foundation.... For us Italians, the family is important, very important.* The family consisted of those one regularly ate with, and included the broader extended family at larger ritual meals for major holidays like New Year's Day, Easter, and Christmas.[1] Seventy-five-year-old Massimo expressed his continuing closeness to his brother Renzo by saying, *Today we still celebrate holidays together, Christmas and Easter always.*

Meals set boundaries between the family and outsiders. Marriage was cemented by the two families eating meals together again and again throughout the years. Commensality—literally sharing the table—was an important means of social connection, for it brought people together around the pleasurable act of eating.[2] Even though family size shrank greatly over the course of the twentieth century, Florentines in the 1980s still valued their families and insisted on eating together every day, even as they recognized that several forces including television, restaurants, and the rapid pace of work undermined commensal meals. While most families still ate both *pranzo* and *cena* together in the early 1980s, by 2003 the numbers who ate a big noon meal together had dwindled considerably, but many Florentines still reconstituted the family for *cena* as often as possible.

The family was the place where Florentines expected to find emotional and financial support. It was closed to outsiders and meals established its boundaries. Sixty-one-year-old Marianna spoke of her family in the 1920s and 1930s: *Whenever it was time to eat dinner, my father didn't want anyone but the family. He said, "When we eat, the family united and that's all." Always, always, always.*

Sixty-six-year-old Elena expressed a common attitude: *I feel a stronger attachment to my relatives than to my friends, naturally. The difference is the fact of consanguinity—how can I say it?* She continued: *We Italians believe that we must try to keep the family united as much as possible at any cost, and we are rather closed in the way we live our families. We're not used to having lots of friends come to the house. We never did when I was a child. . . . Our parents taught us this. When we were at friends' houses and we saw them putting the tablecloth on the table, we went home. That's what I was taught and that's what I did. My friends did the same. When they were at my house and they saw us setting the table, they said, "Ciao, ciao," and left.* Meals were central in constituting the family and outsiders were not usually included.

Parents' dedication to children was expressed not only through feeding them, but also through spending large sums of money to raise them and help them get *sistemati*—"set up"—at marriage, often at considerable sacrifice.[3] Parents strived for enduring family unity. Fifty-four-year-old Raffaele, father of two children, described child-rearing: *You know, we had continual sacrifices because, understand me, little children cost a lot—to dress them, send them to school, feed them. It was all toil, a continual life of struggle. However, you see, you can endure it well when you have tranquility and health. . . . I worked really hard, and it would have been bad if in all this toil there had been discord. But fortunately there were no ruptures and we went forward with love and harmony—*d'amore e d'accordo.*

Going ahead with love and harmony meant that in their old age, parents were likely to have their children around to help them. Florentines believed that the family provided security for the children as they were growing up, and for the parents as they grew old. Seventy-five-year-old Massimo spoke about his feelings for his family and his contentment to be sharing a household with his daughter: *I like living with Valeria's family—I do it willingly. I've always been amenable to living with them; it's better than living alone. I don't like being alone because I've always loved conversation. Both inside the family and outside it, I've always loved discussion. I think it is a great satisfaction to have my children nearby and I feel unhappy when I'm alone. I feel more tranquil with them. . . . When you are young, you can do so many things—go out for a walk, go here and there. But when you're old, you stay at home and what do you do? Living with my family brings more conversation, more harmony, and more courage to confront life. At least that's how it seems to me.*

Meal Division of Labor

Family meals were very important; in the 1980s and still in 2003, women were almost always in charge. Even when a man cooked, one or more women helped shop, prepare the food, set the table, serve the dinner, clear the table, and wash the dishes. Rarely did men help with more than cooking and food shopping, even in 2003. Yet although women performed the bulk of the food labor, they also had full places at the table. Whenever something was needed, to be sure, a woman leapt up to get it, but all the women I knew also sat at the table and enjoyed the food with their husbands, children, and other family members. Usually, a woman made sure the entire meal was cooked ahead of time so that when the family sat down to eat one course followed another, and she did not have to get up and cook in the middle. The *secondo* in Florentine cuisine did not have to be piping hot when it was brought to the table, so the cook could make it while the pasta was boiling, and then serve it after she cleared the pasta dishes away. One of several women got up from the table frequently during the meal, but in extended family homes they shared the tasks and were able to sit a good part of the time. As women got older, they sat more, and younger ones took their place.

Family Meals: Pleasure, Tension, and Socialization

Because, as Leonardo said, *there was this incredible routine around meals,* they were an important means by which Florentines reproduced the family.[4] They were often pleasant but sometimes tense. Fifty-four-year-old Baldo spoke succinctly: *For our family, eating together has always been important. We developed a relationship around being at the table together, passing that hour, hour and a half chatting, talking about the problems of this one or that one. Food calls us together—it is the basis of our relationship—especially in this house, because we eat so much. My wife loves to cook, so we always begin with many dishes; maybe even when we're only having a little meal among just us, it never ends. Meals are a real pleasure. And the pleasure is not so much in the eating as in finding ourselves all together. . . . The meal is the foundation of our family.*

Baldo's emphasis on the centrality of gustatory pleasure to family meal interactions was confirmed by a study comparing Italian and American family meals, which found that "Italian families gave priority to food as pleasure over all other qualities" (Ochs, Pontecorvo, and Fasulo 1996, 7). The food logs (see Table 7.1) kept by my Florentine subjects in 1984 confirmed the generally convivial and positive meal environment, as well as the "*incredible routine*" they involved. Of the eight people who recorded their meals for a total of fifty-three days, all had three to four meals a day, usually *colazione, pranzo, cena,* and sometimes a midmorning or midafternoon snack (*merenda*). Except for Elena, who lived by herself and ate many meals alone, and except sometimes for breakfast, people ate all their meals in company: "with the family," "all together," "all reunited," "with colleagues," or with spouse, parents, or children. The other activities they reported while eating consisted mainly of conversation: "talking," "conversing," "chatting," "in dialogue," "joking and laughing," "talking about this and that," and rarely "watching television." Before eating, they reported a variety of feelings, many of discomfort, such as "tired," "hungry," "rather down," and "I was really hungry!!" ("*Ci avevo una fame!!*") After eating, they almost always reported feeling good: "better," "much better," "relaxed," "quite good," "good," "very good," "so good," "great," "really good and

Table 7.1 Facsimile of the food logs compiled by Florentines, summer 1984

DIARIO GIORNALIERO DEL MANGIARE

Nome: _Massimo_

Giorno e data: _2 agosto 1984_

condizioni speciali _____

Ora	luogo	che cosa hai mangiato e quanto?	da solo o con chi?	altre attività mentre mangiavi?	come ti sentivi prima di mangiare	come ti sentivi dopo mangiare
7,30	cucina	un quarto di latte con caffè e pane arrostito	Da solo	Ascolto la radio	Avevo appetito	Soddisfatto
13	cucina	minestra in brodo con lesso e pomodori conditi e frutta, caffè	con la moglie	Conversando con la moglie	Molta languidezza	Bene
21	salotto	pasta alla pomarola, braciola ai ferri, frutta e caffè	con la moglie, un amico, e la Valeria, le figlie	parlando	Voglio di mangiare	tranquillo

euphoric," "much better than before," "satisfied," "tranquil," "satiated," and "full." Only four reported feeling poorly after eating—"bad," "sad," or "depressed"—but they had felt that way before the meal. Overall, meals almost always resulted in people feeling better.

Laura confirmed the generally positive atmosphere of meals and their integration into family life: *In our family, we like to be at the table precisely for the pleasure. Eating together with the whole family has always been important for us, maybe because it is a habit. Meals are the only time when we are all together.* Laura's eighteen-year-old daughter Piera told an anecdote that linked her favorite food—pasta—to her comfort in her family, and the lack of pasta to her distress when she was away from home: *I like to eat pastasciutta best of all. I eat tons of it. . . . I eat pastasciutta at any hour; just let someone give me some and I eat it, no matter what time it is. I like pastasciutta in all ways, even with fish. . . . We eat spaghetti every day, at both lunch and supper—at least I do. One time I went to the beach to stay with a friend of mine. I was there two days without eating pasta and I was badly off. I telephoned my father to come and get me because I could not stand it anymore. I could have stayed another couple of months with that girl, because her family was very well off, but I could not stand it anymore. They never cooked pasta. They ate only cold-cuts and sandwiches, sandwiches and cold-cuts. Oh, I suffered from a longing for pastasciutta. When my father arrived, he took me right away to a restaurant to eat it. I was really badly off. I was suffering. I think I was miserable also because they led a life completely different from my family. They slept so much and they didn't get up until four in the afternoon. They ate a sandwich at four and then they went to the beach. Then they went to bed. In short, it was a really different lifestyle and I wasn't used to it.* Piera linked **pastasciutta** to her personal equilibrium, her family, and her customary lifestyle. Her discomfort at her friend's house crystallized into a distress with their food habits, and her reintegration into her own comfortable family occurred through eating her beloved pasta. Her missing was visceral, felt literally in her stomach, hungry for the pasta that was the heart of her family meals.

Meals were important because they affirmed the family, produced sociability, and conveyed sensual and convivial pleasure on daily and special occasions, and also because, as Leonardo said, *The table is the vein of the family.* Meals provided a forum for working out family problems, and several of my subjects reported tense meal interactions. Elena did not eat as a girl because of her parents' dissension (see Chapter 8). Leonardo said, *My parents had a wretched relationship (**un rapporto disgraziato**). There were tensions at meals. Certainly, everything came to the table . . . and I remember it well; it was very tense, especially in my home. Because my father came home, we sat down, all of us there. All the knots in the comb came out (**venivano fuori tutti nodi del pettine**). . . . Often there were scenes; they often came out at meals. I suffered from these things; I certainly didn't enjoy them.*

Leonardo's cousin Sergia had similar memories: *When I was little, I had to be quiet at meals, and that was all. Me, quiet, mute, listening. I was an only child. I didn't like meals at all as a child. I couldn't leave the table, because my parents' upbringing was that the child had to stay seated until the parents had finished. And in those days they loved to sit at the table, as they do today. They loved to spend hours at the table. Therefore I had to stay there to wait until they finished and I had to shut up.* **Mamma mia,** *what torture! I got this knot in my stomach; I didn't eat; my stomach closed up. When I started to get older, when I was at that critical age of thirteen or fourteen years old, I went days without eating. So I asked, "Mamma, can I take my plate and go out into the garden to eat?" So I went into the garden and then I would eat. When I stayed with them, no, I couldn't. I was so thin, so thin, look, you could count my ribs. Depleted.*

Sergia's inability to eat reflected her discomfort, anxiety, and silencing. The closing of her mouth meant the closing of her stomach as well. Only after she found her husband—*someone to talk to*—and had her children did she really begin to feel comfortable at meals. Yet she reported, as many did, that difficult decisions were made at meals, decisions concerning the family budget, the children's school and work, the parents' retirement, and other crucial matters. Her husband, forty-five-year-old Rinaldo, said, *We often work out our problems at meals. Eating together in the family is important. . . . We always eat together in the evening; we never eat separately. The evening meal is the only time during the workday when we are all together. If you were to take that away and have us all eat at different times, I would be upset.* Because meals were a meeting place, they were an important locus for working out the family balance of power. Rinaldo went on: *Sometimes my wife and I have arguments at dinner. We bring our problems to the dinner table. If we have an argument in the morning, we avoid each other during the day. . . . It happens at dinner that we go back to the arguments.*

Similarly, forty-eight-year-old Laura described how she and her husband and two children confronted their concerns at meals: *When we're at the table, we discuss, we argue, we have all kinds of discussions. If we didn't do it at meals, there would be no other time. We all have our own lives. Already the television has eliminated some of our conversation, because there's the news and then maybe there's a film. Someone says, "Everybody quiet—we've got to watch it." But if in addition to the television, we stopped eating together, well, then, good-bye to everything, understand?* In spite of television's incursion, Laura clung to meals for their importance in maintaining the family equilibrium: *I think our meal-time discussions have kept us from having huge fights and discord in the home. We've always tried to discuss things together, and the table is when we do it. Except for that, we never see each other. It's important because we can talk about so many things. The children need to know what is going on in the house, because they're already grown up enough to understand the family situation and everything about it. The table unites us. We're all together and we can talk about any-*

thing, any problem, the children's or our own. . . . If we didn't have our meals, together, everything would fall apart.

Laura's husband Raffaele confirmed her statements about the importance of family commensality and television's threat to it: *Meals are very important in my family. They are the sole, the only time in which we all get together—the children, me, my wife—and we can talk, notwithstanding that now the television has disrupted things. In spite of television, lunch and supper are still today the family meeting place. We are all used to eating together at the same time every day. That's when we are all together. The children talk about their issues, we talk about ours; we can argue, we can fight. However, it's great in my opinion, great to get together, and to do it while we're eating makes it even better. It is the only time when there is a dialogue in the family. If I had to go and seek out my son to talk to him, I would never do it. But instead, it works well at the table; we sit down, we eat together, and we talk. I have things to say to him, and he has things on his mind to say to me. . . . Then my wife gets involved and says, "He's right." So then my wife and I argue about it. In short, there is a dialogue that I think is really positive even if we argue. Things are bad when there is no dialogue; that's the way I see it. Lunch and supper are the forum for this dialogue.*

Raffaele and Laura's children demonstrated that their parents had been successful in socializing them in the importance of meals. Piero said, *Meals are important in my family. . . . We talk. We sit at the table together and we talk about problems, about work, about everything. We talk, we argue.* His sister Piera concurred: *I think the only thing that my father demands is that we all be at the table together. Really. Always . . . if you are not home at eight o'clock for dinner, mamma mia! When we're at the table, he wants us all to be together. Of course, he doesn't prohibit us from going out to dinner with friends, but if we're home for dinner, we all have to be at the table at eight o'clock. He has always held to this really strongly. Maybe because it is one of the few moments when we find ourselves all together. Meals are very important.*

Eating Alone

Meals were the main forum for expressing and reproducing family life, and family was the linchpin of sociability. The compelling regularity of meals could provide structure for people who lived alone like Marianna: *I always kept the habit of preparing a meal. I would return from work, set the table, sit down, and slowly, slowly I would eat. Eating meals is a habit that you can't give up, because if you start neglecting that, you are lost. On Saturdays, for example, I used to work overtime. So at home on Friday evening, I prepared my dinner for the next day. When I got home, I set the table like this, with wine, water, bread, the other foods, everything nicely like that, and then I ate.* She continued to have proper meals, because they were the mark of a social existence, which itself was a mark of being fully human.

Whereas Marianna clung to having meals because she felt that without them *"you are lost,"* Elena seemed to recognize that she was indeed lost after her husband died, and her neglect for meals expressed her solitude: *When I was left without Giorgio, everything having to do with eating changed, because it became something mechanical. I have to eat to stay alive and that's it. I have just lost all desire to cook, to eat the delicious things, the good things that I used to make. Why should I cook, when it's only for me alone?*

Oh, every now and then I get in a frenzy to cook something, I don't know, a minestrone or some pasta with cheese. But rarely. Usually when it's time to eat, I just grab whatever I find—ham, a lot of ham. I keep it in the refrigerator and eat it with bread. Sometimes **mortadella.** *Cheese, have you ever eaten* **stracchino** *cheese? You spread it on bread. A fish fillet. Often a sandwich for lunch and dinner, precisely because I just don't feel like cooking. Sometimes I buy those cans of processed food or frozen food and I heat them up. But I don't like them very much. I just eat them for a change.*

While Elena bought processed foods to keep herself alive, she recognized that they were not fully social the way homemade foods were: *I never serve them to guests, absolutely not. First of all, that would seem rude to me. In Italy, you know, if we invite someone, we like to give them food cooked by ourselves, even if maybe it's not excessively good. But it's made with love. It is not good to offer food already prepared. I'd rather cook something myself. But when I'm alone, why would I bother? Why in the world should I devote myself to cooking? Understand? I just don't have the desire to do it. But the desire is probably latent within me and it explodes when I have guests, because then I say, "Oh, yes, now that I have this person coming, well, then, I'll make this thing." Understand? For example, tonight I made you spaghetti with* **pomarola*** *sauce. It's been so long that I've been longing to make* **pomarola,** *and so I said, "Now that Carole's coming, tomorrow I'll sit her down and we'll eat together, and I'll make* **pomarola.***" Do you know it's been years since I've eaten* **pomarola***? Oh, yes, what do you expect, that I make* **pomarola** *for myself alone?*

Making a meal meant creating a social life, and while Elena cooked enthusiastically for guests, she barely cooked for herself alone: *Yesterday evening I didn't feel like eating, so I just had a dish of* **semolino**[5] *with butter, and that's all. Today I ate a little ham with bread, and that's all. Every now and then I cook—for example, I cooked yesterday because Sergia and her children came for lunch. I made a roast with fried potatoes and cooked greens. In short, I cooked. But if I am alone, why in the world would I go to the trouble of making all those things just for myself? . . . Eating alone is disgusting and shameful and disastrous.* Elena's comments revealed the interconnected importance of meals and sociability, and how solitude paralleled the decline in commensality. After her husband Giorgio died, Elena's failure to eat normal meals was a symbol of her solitude. Marianna's insistence on having normal meals when she was living alone was a way to cling to healthy civility; however, she was not always able to vanquish solitude: *The only time I felt alone was at the holidays. . . . I suffered from the lack of a family. There, that was the time that I felt its absence.*

Eating with Friends

Just as commensality—eating together—reproduced the family, it was also a primary means of forging and soldering extrafamilial relationships. As social distance increased, eating together decreased, became more formal, and/or took place outside the home. For example, often a group of young people or several families would make an excursion to the countryside for a *scampagnata*—a picnic or a festive meal at someone's farmhouse. I went to many of these *scampagnate* at an old stone farmhouse (*casa colonica*) rented by a group of friends outside of Florence. Sometimes we cooked masses of pasta, or roasted meat, or sliced some *salame toscano* and ate it with thick slices of Tuscan bread. Other times we roasted chestnuts (*bruciate*) over hot coals in the massive stone fireplace, or toasted bread on the coals, rubbed it with raw garlic, and soaked it in olive oil to make *fettunta*. Another time we made pizza out of dough bought at the bakery and baked in the wood oven still remaining at the farmhouse. There was always plenty of good red wine that we bought from the peasant family down the road who still worked the land.

Florentines loved going out to eat with friends for the simultaneous pleasures of food and conviviality. Raffaele said, *We have a group of friends and not a week passes that we don't go out to dinner together. We get together for meals, sometimes in the countryside, sometimes there's a dinner at one's house, sometimes there's a dinner at my house, sometimes we go out to eat. Between one thing and another, we're always eating when we get together.*

Raffaele and Laura took me on a *scampagnata* in the countryside with some of their friends from Empoli. The following are my field notes on this occasion:

We went to Cerreto Guidi in the countryside near Vinci, where live Berto, his wife Giulietta, and their twenty-eight-year-old son Giacomo. This was where Raffaele had been evacuated (*sfollato*) during the war. He and Berto are the same age and they have remained friends ever since. So they get together regularly for these *scampagnate*. Berto and Giulietta are real *contadini* (farmers) and have always lived and worked on the land. Berto has only been to Florence twice in his life, even though it is only 35 kilometers away, and he has never seen the sea, 50 kilometers away.

Dinner was brought and cooked by Raffaele and Laura and their friends from Empoli, Ricardo and Dorotea. Raffaele made *spaghetti come ci pare**— "spaghetti as we like it"—with olive oil, garlic, parsley, tomato, and hot pepper— *peperoncino.* Berto and Giulietta would not eat it after trying it because they said it was too *piccante*—too spicy hot. To me it seemed barely hot, but Berto said, "*Mi frizza la lingua*"—"My tongue is burning." Raffaele and Ricardo grilled the meat in the big fireplace in the kitchen—one of Berto's rabbits killed the day before and some pork chops and steaks roasted over coals. Dorotea prepared the salads, one of tomatoes dressed with olive oil, vinegar, and salt; the other of lettuce, tomatoes, and raw onions, also dressed. There was bread. There was wine of Berto's production and another kind of wine Raffaele had bought from a friend in Vinci. At the end of the meal, a *prosciutto* went around the table, not of Berto and Giulietta's production because they don't keep pigs, but one bought from a neighboring farmer. After all this food, there were *biscotti di Prato,* the hard cookies made with almonds, and a thick, sweet Aleatico wine in which to dip them. Dinner was consumed with great speed, confusion, noise, and competing conversations.

In addition to *scampagnate,* young people like Piero and Piera occasionally had formal meals in a country *trattoria* or *ristorante* or gathered with their friends at a local *birreria, pizzeria,* or *spaghetteria*—all relatively new phenomena in 1984 discussed further in Chapter 9. Piero spoke of the role of these new locales in his social life: *Maybe sometimes before going to bed I'll eat out. I'll have something like a plate of spaghetti at around 11:30 or midnight. Here there are several places—a birreria, a spaghetteria, several pizzerie—where they make things quickly. Sometimes I might have a plate of prosciutto or mozzarella, or a plate of french fries with ketchup, and a beer, with my friends. Because some of our friends own the birreria, practically every evening we meet up there. Sometimes we just stay there, we drink, we eat, we hang out. We all gather there, and we know just about everyone there because it is not a very big place.*

In the 1980s and still in 2003, eating out with friends involved different foods and a different context from eating meals at home. University students in 2003 reported getting together to eat with friends often, usually at restaurants or at each other's apartments, but less often at their family homes. One student wrote, "Living in a 'little' city like Florence, the little, inexpensive, restaurant of the neighborhood becomes a site of congregation, where everyone, either in person or by sight, knows everyone else. Food creates a place where people socialize." Occasionally my subjects had friends to their home for meals, but not often, and they had to be good friends. Having guests made the meal a more formal occasion, which served to acknowledge and mark the greater distance between friends than between family members.

Sergia and Rinaldo regularly socialized with a group of several couples around meals. They sometimes went out to eat and at other times ate at one another's houses. Sergia and Rinaldo had an upper-middle-class income and lifestyle, and they had purchased and tastefully renovated a spacious old Tuscan country farmhouse where they lived, about twenty minutes by car from downtown Florence (*Centro*). They paid an older former peasant couple to run things: the husband to work in the fields and cultivate a wide array of crops, especially olives; the wife to help with the housework, cooking, chickens, rabbits, and food preservation. This reconstitution of peasant farming enabled Sergia to resolve the culinary insecurity she described in Chapter 5 by cooking simple, genuine Tuscan cuisine from the produce of their farm using the traditional wood oven and cooking fireplace of their farmhouse. She cooked rustic but easy dishes that were special because they were no longer accessible to her middle-class urban friends: *We get together often with our friends, a group of about ten or fifteen couples. We used to go out to eat, but now we prefer having all our friends here in the house, even though I don't like to cook. . . . I make things that my friends can't make because they live in the city—things like charcoal grilled meat, pork when we kill the pig, things they can't eat because they don't have any way to make a fire. During the winter, we build a fire in the fireplaces and we roast meat. And when we slaughter the pig, we give them a couple of sausages, they stick them onto forks, and they roast them on the fire. . . . After the olive harvest when we have just pressed the new olive oil, we invite all our friends here for fettunta**—toasted bread rubbed with a garlic clove and soaked in olive oil.*

Sergia and Rinaldo successfully cultivated an active social life through their ability to offer Tuscan *cucina casalinga* to their urbanized friends. Marianna described how in the 1950s and 1960s she constituted a social life at work with the other unmarried women through eating together at lunch. Without a family of her own, these friendships forged through meals were very important to her: *Yes, yes, I had friends at work. We were really good friends. We always went out to eat or ate together in a room there at work. What do you want? We were all young. Sometimes we cooked eggs in that room. Other times we put beans on the fire in the morning and we left them there to cook while we worked. Someone would come in and ask, "What do we have to eat today?"*

"Join us. We've got this to eat, and we'll get this other thing, okay?"

"Let's eat here, eh. We don't need to go out; we can stay here in the office and set the table and we'll eat." And maybe someone went to get a little sliced ham sometimes, or we got some frankfurters with artichoke hearts. We all got along really well.

*The others used to tease us because we were a little group (**un branchettino**). "Are you even going to bring your beds in here?" they joked. We were always together and we ate there at midday. When there was still the cafeteria,[6] we ate there, and if not, we walked down to Via Tavolini and we bought some food and we added what we had brought and we all ate together. . . . They used to tease us because we were a little group, all girls. Two were separated from their husbands; two or three of us were unmarried, including me. None of us had to worry about taking care of a house.* Because she did not have a family, Marianna constructed social relationships with her coworkers by eating together and trying new foods that were different from the *cucina casalinga* eaten at home.

Shopping and Social Life

For city dwellers, daily neighborhood grocery shopping was another way of constructing social relationships. Italians had a long tradition of localized neighborhood shopping that was reflected by the large numbers of small shops relative to supermarkets in 1960, in 1984, and even in 2003 when, however, small stores were suffering a significant decline. In 1960, 95 percent of

Italian food purchases took place in small neighborhood stores, not supermarkets (Helstosky 2004, chapter 5). However, in Italy as a whole, between 1991 and 2001, small shops declined 24 percent from approximately 254,000 to 193,000; between 1996 and 2000, the number of supermarkets nearly doubled from 3,696 to 6,413 ("Italy Losing Mom-and-Pop Shops" 2003). In the 1980s, there were few supermarkets in Florence, and many people shopped several days a week in local stores, but in 2003, there were many new supermarkets, and more of my informants reported using them more consistently.

In the early 1980s, older folk, especially women who did not have jobs outside the home or retired men, practiced daily shopping on foot near home for fresh goods to be immediately consumed. People often relied on serendipity for meal planning, cooking something that struck their fancy on their daily shopping trip to the local greengrocery (*frutti-vendolo, ortolano*), butcher shop (*macelleria*), delicatessen (*pizzicheria*), general food store (*alimentari*), and bakery (*panificio, forno*). Shopping every day sustained people's ongoing relationships with other shoppers and favorite grocers with whom they passed the time, exchanged gossip, and discussed meals. The younger people, however, increasingly relied on bigger and fewer shopping trips with the automobile, and used the supermarket more heavily than local specialty shops.

In summer 1984, two of my subjects recorded all their food expenditures for a week: seventy-three-year-old Renzo, who lived with his wife Marianna; and fifty-year-old Valeria, who lived with several family members. Both went shopping in their local neighborhoods—Renzo in Piazza delle Cure, and Valeria in L'Isolotto—at least once every day (except Sunday, when most stores were closed), and made purchases at between one and three stores per trip. Valeria went every day to the *pizzicheria* (delicatessen) for at least her daily bread, but also for items like mozzarella, pasta, pepper, olive oil, anchovies, capers, gorgonzola, butter, and *baccalà*. She also went every day to the *macelleria* (butcher shop), where she purchased minute steaks, liver, *ossibuchi* (veal shanks), chicken, and tongue, and to the *ortolano* (greengrocer), where she bought eggs, fruit, tomatoes, plums, apricots, and string beans (see Table 7.2).

Renzo went to even more stores than Valeria in a week. He visited the *macelleria* for roast, steak, minute steaks, and *lesso* (meat to boil); the *forno* (bakery) for bread and cookies; the *vinaio* for 20 liters of wine; the *pizzicheria* for ham, eggs, cold cuts, and tuna; the *ortolano* for Swiss chard, fruit, fresh beans, tomatoes, potatoes, cherries, peaches, cabbage, and watermelon; and the *lattaio* (milk store) for milk. The traditional shopping pattern followed by Renzo and Valeria and others was embedded in an urban life centered in neighborhoods, each with its essential services and stores.

Women forged social ties while shopping by exchanging recipes. For example, fifty-year-old Valeria, a passionate cook, said, *I learn new dishes sometimes when I'm out doing the shopping. I hear a woman say, "I made this; it was great; this is how I did it." So then I have to go home and try it out myself.* Marianna

Table 7.2 Facsimile of Valeria's family's weekly food expenses, summer 1984

LA SPESA FAMILIARE PER UNA SETTIMANA

C. M. Counihan 6/84

Nome: *Valeria*

Giorno	ora	tipo di negozio	spesa in lire	acquisto	fatto da chi
6-7-84	9	Ortolano frutta e pomodori	13000	Ortolano	Valeria
		Pane e mozzarella	5370	Pizzicheria	
		Braciole	9000	Macellaro	
7-7-84	8:30	Macellaro	20900	Ossibuchi fegato	Valeria
		Ortolano uova frutta	14200		
		Pane pepe pasta	4900	Pizzicheria	
8-7-84	10	Macelleria	4500	Braciole	Renza [a neighbor]
		Pane	2650	Pizzicheria	
		Pizzicheria	4500	Olio	
9-7-84	8:30	Pizzicheria	8100	Pane acciughe gorgonzola	Valeria
		Macelleria	4500	1 braciola e 3 petti di pollo	
		Ortolano	9400	pomodori susine albicocche	
10-7-84	9:30	Pizzicheria	5600	pane pasta burro	Renza [a neighbor]
		Macellaro	4200	petti di pollo	
		Pizzicheria	6500	baccalà	
11-7-84	9	Pizzicheria	4600	pane capperi	Valeria
		Macelleria	20500	pollo lingua braciole	
		Ortolano	11200	frutta fagiolini uova pomodori	

also described exchanging recipes as a form of social interaction: *Often I hear women talking in the shops when I go to do my shopping. That one says, "You know, I make it like this."*

"Oh, really, signora, how do you do it? Oh, really, like that? Would you tell me how you make it?" And so she tells me how to make it. We used to exchange recipes at work too. Remember that little cookbook that you gave Renzo, **L'Orto in Casa** (The Garden in the Home)? *I found a recipe in there for rice with artichokes—* **riso coi carciofi.** *So I told one of my colleagues about it, "Oh, you should taste this. I made rice with artichokes, and oh, it came out good."*

She replied, "How do you make it?"

I said, "I'll bring you a little cookbook tomorrow, and you can read it there. You will see how you can make it well." Daily shopping and trading ideas about cooking were important ways that Florentines connected with people beyond the family. They came together on the familiar terrain of cuisine—a terrain they shared, felt strongly about, and discussed endlessly.

But in 2003, supermarkets were making significant inroads on neighborhood stores all across Italy, and Florence was no exception. People who had access to supermarkets used them because they were convenient, pleasant, up-to-date, less expensive, and some believed they had fresher foods than smaller stores due to their greater volume, as Giovanna said in 2003: *Well, my mother's neighborhood doesn't have too many food stores—two or three. There is a small fruit and vegetable store where you hardly see anybody; there is a deli store at the corner, a beautiful deli. They have wonderful specialties. It's very expensive and I don't see too many people in there—I don't know how they survive. There is one butcher store, which is working okay. They're good. The bakery's working; it gets very busy because people like to have their fresh bread every day. But for the most part there aren't too many little food stores that are making it. For the most part people go to the supermarket or to the little neighborhood market (***mercatino***, see Figure 7.2) which has two or three food stands with vegetables, or delicatessen-type things. They sell olives and marinated mushrooms and cold cuts and stuff like that, breads,* **porchetta** *(roast pork). The person that has a little store and sells a pound of oranges for twice the amount of money as the supermarket or the stand outside—how much longer are they going to stay open? There are a lot of shops that are closed, right?*

In 2003, one university student remarked that she had rediscovered the local neighborhood stores as a student, because she had no car and thus could not frequent the supermarket. Another remarked that he liked to shop at the outdoor markets because they were "places still within reach of our pockets, where foods can still see the light of the sun and breathe the open air." He liked the neighborhood stores where "there is still human contact with the vendor," but the supermarket was "a world where the winner is what costs the least." The supermarket responded to the consumer society, he said, creating the ability "to consume as many times as we want."

While the overall national trend has been the decline of small stores, my observations in Florence in early 2003 indicated that their success or failure depended on location, neighborhood, and competition. The historic center of Florence had few food stores of any kind, and those that existed were very expensive. Locals who had money or no alternatives frequented them, as did tourists, but locals who had cars shopped at the nearest supermarket. Just across the Arno River from the Centro Storico in the San Frediano district, small neighborhood stores were flourishing. In about a ten-block area, I counted twenty-four retail food outlets, including three ambulatory stands at the entrance to the Boboli Gardens in the Piazzale di Porta Romana.[7] There were several delis, greengroceries, and bakeries, as well as three wine stores, a milk shop, a fish store, a tripe vendor, one large self-service grocery store, and several butcher shops (see Figure 7.1). In addition to the twenty-four I counted, this neighborhood had other food stores on some of the side streets as well as a daily *mercatino* with four or five food stands in Piazza Santo Spirito (see Figure 7.2). In this densely populated area relatively inaccessible by automobile, the small stores were thriving. However, friends living farther from the center of Florence in areas more easily accessible by car frequented the Esselunga, COOP, or Standa supermarkets on a regular basis to benefit from ease and economies of scale. Supermarkets undermined but did not extinguish the daily social interactions of neighborhood shopping, and Elena in 1984 and in 2003 found her local COOP a welcoming and pleasant place to pass the time.

Crossing Social Boundaries: Meals and *Fidanzamento*

In the 1980s, most Florentines ate the majority of their meals at home with the family, and outsiders were rarely present. Hence, meals were extremely important in creating the new family ties that formed between in-laws at engagement and marriage. The official engagement was called *fidanzamento in casa*—"engagement in the home." It was marked by the betrothed (*fidanzati*) "entering into the house" (*entrare in casa*) and "eating in the house" (*mangiare in casa*) of each other's families. Betrothal was celebrated by a special meal, even when times were hard. Massimo described his engagement to Berta in 1929: *I liked Berta's company, her conversation, and her family. I said, "This is the shoe for my foot (**Quest'è la scarpa per il mio piede**)." Now instead, she's the slipper for my foot (**la sciabatta per il mio piede**)! For our engagement we had a special light meal (**merenda**). We ate fennel-flavored Tuscan salami (**finocchiona**) at the **merenda**. I'll always remember it. We had it with bread. And wine. There wasn't even a cake.*

Their marriage was also celebrated with food:

Massimo: *In 1933, we got married.*

Berta: *We invited friends and relatives.*

Massimo: *We had a breakfast at my house in Trespiano. Not lunch—breakfast, with caffelatte and homemade cookies for everybody baked by my aunt Lisa. There was a kind of cake—a **panettone**.*[8]

Fig. 7.1 A meat and poultry store in Via Romana in March 2003 with two of the many *motorini* that make Florence the *motorino* capital of Italy

Fig. 7.2 Fruit and vegetable stand at the *mercatino* (little market) in Piazza S. Spirito, March 2003

Berta: *Yes, we had these big **panettoni,** and inside there was either a little chocolate or a little marmalade. They sliced them up in pieces for everyone.*

Massimo: *Afterward we went to the church for the wedding and then right after the ceremony we left for Rome.* Massimo and Berta marked their wedding with commensality, although it was a modest repast in comparison to the weddings held in the 1980s and to some of those held before World War II. An old Tuscan woman in 1977 remembered that at weddings in her village of Valiano, "*mangiaveno e beveveno a crepa pelle*" (sic)—"they ate and drank to split their skins" (Coppi and Fineschi 1980, 193).[9]

The first meal of the *fidanzamento* was a major step for my Florentine subjects because it marked the beginning of a lifelong commitment not just between husband and wife but also between their two families. It was a step that all of my subjects cautioned against taking lightly. Massimo said, *We don't believe in bringing home a boyfriend or girlfriend to eat unless it is serious. So as not to break a trust, so as not to have remorse about knowing someone and then dropping them. Getting engaged in the home is always a serious thing. We feel apprehensive about having people come into our house and get all worked up about it.*

It's a bother. Well, if that person is coming into the house because it is a serious affair, we say, okay. If he wants to be a fiancé, if he wants to be a husband, fine, but if not, if he is coming to waste time, he can go to the Cascine Park; there are plenty of pastimes there.[10] For us, it's a formal event when a person presents himself in our home. He presents himself for a reason—the reason of marrying our daughter. But if he is coming to say good day and good evening and then he goes away, why is he bothering to come here?

Massimo's son-in-law, fifty-four-year-old Baldo, was vehement on prudence in establishing relationships: *In my youth, before we got engaged, we looked carefully at the girl's family, just as the girl assessed the boy's family. Getting officially engaged was a big step; you felt a new responsibility. You made a tie with the parents. The only time I did that was with Valeria. I didn't go into any other girl's home. Why not? What for? I could go out with plenty of girls. Why bring their parents into it if it wasn't serious? In fact, before having my family meet Valeria's, I went to meet her parents by myself. Because my father said not to bring the families together if I was planning to back out. And he was right. Why bring the parents in, either hers or mine, and do the whole engagement ceremony, if you know that you are really not convinced that you're going to go all the way to marriage with that girl? Why bring the parents in if you're going to go out for two or three months and then break up?*

My son-in-law Sandro feels the way I do. He and my daughter Caterina spent four years going together "outside the house." In those four years they had two months of crisis, when they broke up, but then they got back together. From that time Sandro said, "If I come into the house of your parents, I want to be sure that we are going all the way. I don't want to know your family, or have you meet mine, and then find ourselves breaking up. Because if that's the case, then we could just avoid involving the family groups, mine as much as yours." When he did finally come to the house, he became another son to me.

Baldo passed along to his children the same careful beliefs about getting engaged in the home: *I always said to my son Arturo, "Listen, it's useless for you to have us get to know someone unless it's going all the way. I prefer you to find the right girl first. Listen, I was young once too, I know how it is. . . . Look for the shoe that fits, and when you have found it, think carefully." In fact, with Maria he didn't have us meet her parents right away. We waited a long time. I told him, "Before you enter the home, brush the dust off your pants outside. She too will brush the dust off her skirts." That's the way we think. Our reasoning is this: Why do you want to bring this girl home and have us meet the families if you're not sure about this girl? What for? There's no need to bring the families into it. Introducing the families creates a tie, a bond between the families. Before Arturo and Maria got engaged, who were her parents to me? Just people. But after we have come to know them, they are no longer just people, understand?*

Essentially, after eating together, Maria and her parents became part of Baldo's family. Commensality established ties of intimacy among Florentines—an intimacy that implied reciprocity, care, and serious commitment. Baldo continued: *In the beginning, I wasn't at all convinced about Arturo going here and there with his **fidanzata** (fiancée) to eat. I didn't like it. Because I kept thinking—and maybe here my ideas are a little backward—I kept thinking that if they had taken the wrong step and they broke up, her people would think about Arturo, "Look at that shameless fellow. He came here to eat." I would have tortured my son for creating these difficult conditions. So I said to Arturo, "Before you introduce me to her parents, I want to know that you are sure. But are you sure?" Engagement is a commitment you make with a family—a commitment that I believe you keep until the end.*

The principle is, don't compromise the families. And, in fact, Arturo thought about it and took his time. The young people today have plenty of freedom, so I don't see the need to bring the families together if after two or three years of dating they're going to make fools of everyone by breaking up. Interestingly, in the 1980s, Baldo was more worried about his son eating with his girlfriend than sleeping with her. Arturo did eventually become officially engaged to his girlfriend Maria. He "entered her house" and started eating meals regularly there. Arturo had unusually picky eating habits that his mother indulged, even though picky eating was contrary to Florentine ideas about proper socialization of children. His in-laws indulged him as well. Arturo said, *From the moment I entered their house, they have always treated me like a son, and they learned my tastes right away. They have adapted and they even make me a minute steak (**braciolina**) every evening. To tell the truth, my mother-in-law has always thought of the **braciolina**. She always makes a special little pan for me no matter what else she makes.* Interestingly, he equated his mother-in-law making the special foods he liked with being "treated like a son," showing again how commensality incorporated new people into the family. And from the time of their first meal together, in-laws started using their affinal kin terms to refer to each other.[11]

Caterina's husband Sandro became *another son* to her parents Baldo and Valeria, and Valeria continually renewed the tie by feeding Sandro. When he became terribly busy working as a dental technician and trying to set up an independent business, he worked through the lunch hour and stopped going to Valeria's house for the delectable three-course lunches she prepared for her family every day. Valeria took pity on him and started making him *panini*—sandwiches—which gradually became more elaborate and more like the workers' meals of the past. Valeria said, *Sandro started working harder and stopped coming here for lunch. So at the beginning I telephoned him, "What are you eating today?"*

"Oh, nothing," he answered. "It doesn't matter."

*Some days he didn't even eat. This happened once, twice, and then I said, "Oh, Caterina, listen, we can send him sandwiches; at least he'll have something to eat." It's not possible that one does not eat. (**Non è possibile che non si mangia**).*

*At first I sent him many sandwiches with cold cuts. It was winter and I sent him sandwiches made of head cheese (**soprassata**), or **prosciutto**, but then I was sorry to send just that, so now I send him sandwiches with what we're having at home. I send sandwiches of **frittate** with vegetables, or of refried meat and onions (**lesso rifatto con le cipolle**), whatever I happen to have. Today I sent him liver and potatoes in a sandwich.*

Sandro loved Valeria's cooking, and he and Caterina regularly ate with her family and his. He said, *We eat at least twice a week, even three times a week, at either my mother and sister's house or at Caterina's mother's house. Saturday and Sunday we never eat at home for **pranzo** or **cena**. Add one day during the week, and we're already out three evenings a week with our families. But it's not that we go there for the eating, eh; that has nothing to do with it. We go because by now it's a habit of ours, a tradition let's say, that we go there to eat. Ever since I got married, I have never eaten Saturday or Sunday dinner in my own house.*

Eating together with the families constantly renewed their ties, but they could be binding and sometimes oppressive ties, necessitating constant attendance and interfering with other possible plans. But Sandro enjoyed the company and the food at his in-laws': *I will say that I really like my mother-in-law's cooking. She makes a cuisine that is characteristically Tuscan—things like **trippa alla fiorentina**, **lampredotto**, the kind of things that I really love. With a modest expense you can cook delicious things. For me, you can put steak and **lampredotto** next to each other on two plates and I will take the **lampredotto** and leave the steak. My mother-in-law makes—what can I tell you—tripe, eggplant with pesto, eggplant in sauce, **baccalà alla livornese**, and **frittate** of all kinds—I don't think anybody knows how to make **frittate** the way my mother-in-law does. She makes so many things, and I tell you sincerely that she is an excellent cook. . . . I had never eaten pork rind (**la contenna del maiale**) and I ate it for the first time at Caterina's house. There I've eaten many things that I had never eaten before and that I love.*

All my subjects agreed that when a couple broke up after being engaged in the home (*fidanzati in casa*), it was very difficult. After they had forged a relationship of interdependence and affection between families as well as between the betrothed, the loss of that relationship was emotionally painful and embarrassing. At the *scampagnata* described above, I took field notes on such a breakup in the peasant family where we spent the day:

> I talked at length with Giulietta, the mother of the family, while she washed and I dried many dishes. She gave the impression of being deeply sad, and talked mostly about her son Giacomo's ex-*fidanzata,* Amalia from Milano, with whom he broke up after they vacationed in Algeria together last summer. Giulietta said that her husband Berto resisted the girl for a long time. He didn't like her because she and Giacomo slept together. But finally the girl "entered into the house" and she was a big help to Giulietta. Berto's mother was sick, and Amalia cooked so Giulietta could take care of her mother-in-law. Giulietta said Amalia

cooked exotic things like *risotto alla milanese** (Milanese-style rice with saffron) and *petti di pollo con panna* (chicken breasts with cream) and used a lot of *peperoncino* (hot pepper), which Berto didn't like. During the dinner, Berto complained about the spaghetti cooked by Raffaele being too hot, and he went to the cupboard and pulled out a packet of hot pepper. He said, "Look, this has been here since Amalia and Giacomo broke up." She had brought it into the house, but Berto didn't like it. The hot pepper was a gravestone marking the death of that relationship.

A disliked food symbolized the end of a disliked *fidanzamento,* which had been inaugurated by food, and was renewed on a regular basis by the daughter-in-law cooking for and eating with her affinal family. The fact that Berto never accepted Amalia's cooking was a sharp symbol of their incompatibility.

Forty-five-year-old Rinaldo affirmed as vehemently as Baldo that he didn't want his daughters bringing boyfriends to eat at the house unless they planned to marry, and he criticized his sister's family: *My sister has become a seaport—a porto di mare—in the sense that her daughter's boyfriend is always coming and going. I think that parents have the right to their own privacy.*[12] *My sister and her husband never know if the boyfriend is going to be there for dinner—the boyfriend, eh, because they are not even engaged yet. Engagements are going out of fashion. They even sleep together at my sister's house, eh, and that just doesn't sit well with me.*

Listen, I don't plan to accept boyfriends of my daughters into my house at an age when it is highly unlikely that their relationship will finish in the traditional manner. . . . I am fine with the idea of having a group of my daughters' friends to the house, even for dinner. But what I won't accept is to have one boyfriend come to the house by himself and I have to accept him in my home, and then six months later, I have to accept another. I won't stand for this. So I've already told my daughters, they can present to me a boyfriend when they are ready to say, "This is the man I'm going to marry." But I don't want them to include us, their parents, in all their romantic attachments until they are ready for marriage. They can go out with their boyfriends, but I cannot accept them bringing a boyfriend home and thinking, "Who is this boy?" And then a year later, they bring another one home, "Who is this one?"

I'm happy to have a group of my daughters' friends come to the house—to a party, a volleyball game, a dinner, whatever. I accept that. But what I won't accept is to have a single boyfriend come here, plop his bottom on the chair, and not get up again. Why do they have to bring me into it? It goes back to sexual issues. If my daughter wants to go to bed with some fellow, that is her business, because, after all, there's nothing I can do about it. But I want my rights, just as she wants hers. Let her go to bed with him if she wants to—that's her business—but not in my house.

Rinaldo articulated a link between the sexual relationship and the commensal one, a link made in many cultures.[13] Florentines often used foods to stand for sexual acts or parts, for example, *il bacello*—the pod of peas or fava beans—stood for the male sex organ and was used in jokes about copulation. *La fica*—from *il fico,* the fig—represented the female sex organ in vulgar slang. At festive restaurant dinners and *scampagnate,* there was often ribald joking around food and sex. Rinaldo did not want to have his daughters' boyfriends at his house to eat because he did not want to acknowledge their sexual relationships except in the socially sanctioned context of marriage. While times had changed and premarital sex was more common and accepted in the 1980s, parents still did not want to acknowledge it.

Belief in the significance of eating in the future in-laws' home persisted among the younger generations in the 1980s, even though they had acquired far more freedom to go out alone together before marriage. But subjects who came of age later demonstrated radically altered social mores. Eugenia and Ondina, who were 14 and 12 in 1984, in 2003 at ages 33 and 31 were both living with boyfriends who ate regularly at the home of their parents, Rinaldo and Sergia, even though neither daughter was engaged or had imminent plans to marry. Their mother Sergia said, *The ring doesn't exist anymore—L'anello non esiste più.* Interestingly, in 2003, Rinaldo had completely changed his conviction of nineteen years earlier. He said it was a *bischerata*—a Florentine expression meaning an idiocy—and he no longer held to it. He had realized that he had *an unconscious jealousy—una gelosia inconscia*—which dissipated as time went on. One of Sergia and Rinaldo's daughters' boyfriends had lived in their house for over a year, but later she broke up with him. They were sorry, they liked him, but so it went. And furthermore, they said, *the term fidanzato no longer exists; it is too much of a commitment (è troppo impegnativo), and now they say "my boyfriend" ("il mio ragazzo") even if he's forty years old.* Although times were changing, some Florentine university students in 2003 were still cautious about becoming "engaged in the home." Crossing the family threshold to share meals was traditionally a big step for Florentines because commensality marked family, and family depended on trust and reciprocal respect—feelings that Florentines did not readily hold toward outsiders.

The pleasure of eating good food and the conviviality of pleasant meals incorporated outsiders into the family and consistently reinforced ties between family members. My subjects all felt that meals were the foundation of the family, and that if meals fell away, the family would be in trouble. As the most important locus of family interaction, meals also played a crucial role in the socialization of children, which the next chapter examines further.

8
Parents and Children:
Feeding and Gender

Introduction

Fifty-year-old Valeria defined Florentine attitudes toward child rearing: *Parents have so many responsibilities toward their children—everything. They have to help them get set up as best they can and help them economically if necessary. For my children I have made so many sacrifices. I do without a dress for myself, I do without eating a steak for myself, so I can give something to my children— that's the way I am.*

This chapter examines how parents, especially mothers, talked about the socialization of gender roles and ideology in their children through foodways in the early 1980s. This was a time when small family size coincided with relatively large numbers of women not working outside the home, so children had an "unprecedented amount of nurturing from their mothers, compared to the past" (Whitaker 2002) when families were large, children did productive labor at a young age, and mothers were extremely busy. But in the 1960s, '70s, and '80s, many households had women whose main occupation was caring for children and husbands, which had an undeniable effect on women's status and on gender definitions.

Many feminist researchers have discussed how the production-reproduction dichotomy and women's almost exclusive care for infants have contributed to, as Harding (1981, 139) put it, "patterns of [male-]dominating social relations."[1] Florentine women, like many the world over, were almost totally in charge of child rearing and they defined this as one of their most important responsibilities. It was inaugurated in pregnancy, continued with breast-feeding in infancy, and symbolized throughout the child's life by the mother's feeding. Because women did all of the infant care and most of the child rearing in a context where these activities were taken for granted, there was an asymmetrical socialization of gender that continued from generation to generation. Girls learned to cook, feed, and "spoon out the soup," while boys learned to expect the brimming bowl before them. Feeding involved care of others rooted in self-sacrifice. It involved deference to the needs of others and suppression of the woman's own needs or desires (cf. DeVault 1991). Thus feeding reproduced unequal gender relations.[2]

Yet, paradoxically, feeding spouse and children gave Florentine women some influence and power because it created dependence and appreciation in others. But it was an ambiguous form of power because it depended on giving something that had emotional but not economic value.[3] Because women were the primary feeders of infants, children, and the family, they had an enduring visceral relationship with and influence over offspring that men did not have, but also bore most of the hard work of taking care of them. Teaching them to eat Florentine cuisine was a process of instilling in them a whole way of life, with its rhythms, flavors, and beliefs. As children grew, they learned appropriate food-related behaviors. Children's important transition from dependence to autonomy could be expressed through the feeding relationship.[4] In this chapter, I present my subjects' narratives about how feeding—in pregnancy, breast-feeding, and lifelong meals—structured parent-child relations.

Women's Responsibilities in the Family

As we saw in earlier chapters, Florentines—men and women both—defined women as primarily responsible for reproductive tasks, including raising children.[5] As thirty-nine-year-old Giovanna said, *Once the man has turned over his earnings to the family, he feels totally free of all other obligations. Oh, yes, I've seen some fathers interested in their children's progress, but their interest involves information rather than participation. In fact, all the women that I know do the cooking, the shopping, and the cleaning. In general, the running of the home is always a "big business" here.*

A major part of the "big business" was bearing, feeding, clothing, and socializing children. Women attached importance to their role by taking pride in their sacrifices, and they upheld the naturalness of female altruism by criticizing women who shirked responsibility. Valeria explained: *I know one woman. She began to leave her son home alone when he was nine or ten years old and she went dancing until two or three in the morning with her husband. Imagine leaving a child home alone in the house at nine or eight or ten years old to go dancing! What if something happens, the child turns on the gas or something, anything? He's a young man now, but she goes away and leaves him alone for Easter, for Christmas; he's always home alone and she goes off and does her own thing. She doesn't give a damn about him. . . . Those are not even mothers, right? She just doesn't seem like a proper mother.*

Valeria condemned her neighbor for putting her own pleasure before her child's welfare, and by implication Valeria thus validated her own sacrifices: *But for me, whatever I can do for my children, anything imaginable, is my satisfaction. I am so happy to do it that I feel badly if I can't do something. When I can do something for them, it's better than doing it for myself.* Valeria was the quintessential altruistic woman who subordinated her own needs and supported the patriarchal values and practices of her culture. She worked to sustain her family and raise her children with little reward other than her own sense of fulfilling a cultural ideal based on self-abnegation, which she defined as appropriate maternal behavior.

Forty-one-year-old Sergia established clear priorities: *For me the woman's chief responsibilities are taking care of the children. The man can't look after them because of his job. Now if the woman works, things get difficult. In fact, the children of parents who both work are raised differently from those who have a mother who looks after them every day, day in and day out. The responsibility of a woman for the family and the children is so much, if she looks after them as she should.* Sergia reinforced the given social order where child rearing belonged to women, and where doing it right meant doing it full-time.

Sergia's husband Rinaldo supported this same social order and commended his wife for taking care of their children: *Look, here's something that I would not know how to do and for which I give credit to the women, especially to my wife. She has a patience with the children that I myself absolutely do not have. She has to sit there for hours and hours explaining things to them. . . . The few times that they have asked me, "Daddy, look, how do you do this math problem?" I have had to make a great effort, not to solve the problem but to have the necessary patience. It's hard for me. So I would rather go off to work and let my wife handle the child rearing.* Although in the 1980s and 1990s Italian birth rates were falling toward the lowest rates in the world, motherhood continued to be a central part of female identity (Whitaker 2000, 277).

Feeding in Pregnancy

Women's responsibility for and attachment to children began at conception and was expressed in attitudes about eating in pregnancy. Florentines believed that what the mother consumed affected the fetus directly, and urged her to eat certain foods and avoid others to nurture the baby and ward off harm. They believed that women had to eat for two and that the unfulfilled desires of the mother—*le voglie*—adversely affected the fetus. In these beliefs Florentines affirmed the essential connection between mothers and children that held throughout their lives.

Sixty-six-year-old Elena described her memories of pregnancy that highlighted her link through food to her baby: *All those women that I had around me—my aunts, my mother, my grandmothers, my great-grandmother—they all said, "You've got to eat for two. You can't eat for one; you've got to eat for two." And because I had a great desire to eat, because I was always hungry, I really threw myself into eating.*

Elena recounted beliefs about *le voglie* or "the desires" of pregnancy that were widespread in the 1940s when she was pregnant.[6] These beliefs linked the mother's food cravings in pregnancy to her child's physical appearance and food preferences after birth; *la voglia* referred both to the mother's unfulfilled desire and to the birthmark on the child that resulted from it. Elena remembered: *Yes, people were supposed to give a pregnant woman everything she desired, yes, yes. I remember that my grandmother—my old grandmother Lisa—as* soon as she found out that I was pregnant, she brought me snails to eat. Yes, because the desire for snails—**la voglia delle chiocciole**—is very dangerous. If the baby is a girl, this **voglia** is no threat, but if it is a boy, something terrible could happen. The penises don't develop on boy babies who are born with the desire for snails. In the old days, that's what they used to say.

So, anyway, my grandmother hurried to bring me all these snails to eat. She went out to gather them and she brought them to me already cooked. But years later, I found out that they were not real snails. She had not been able to find real snails, full with the little veil over them. So she made up a delicious filling and she stuffed it into all these snail shells and then she cooked them in the way that we cook snails. I tasted that same flavor, I ate them, they were really good, and I didn't even think about it. I learned this years and years and years later. She did this for me precisely so that I wouldn't have the desire for snails, to convince me that I had already eaten them so that I no longer had to worry about the **voglia delle chiocciole**. She told me years later, "You know, those snails I brought you when you were pregnant? They were absolutely not real; they were false." She told me this later when there was no longer any danger, because the baby had been born a girl.

Interestingly, Elena's story revealed her grandmother's awareness of the psychosomatic nature of *le voglie*; it was the belief that she had eaten snails rather than their actual consumption that protected Elena. Harelip was another condition believed to stem from unfulfilled pregnancy desires that people tried to combat. Elena said, *As soon as I was pregnant, my grandmother cooked me . . . a little piece of hare. The hare was so the baby wouldn't be born with a harelip (**labbro leporino**). Once the pregnant woman has fulfilled her desire for hare, there's no more danger of the baby being born with a harelip.*

Apergi and Bianco (1991, chapter 5) found similar and different prohibitions for parturient women among rural Tuscans in the Mugello region near Florence. Their informants reported restrictions on pregnant women eating herring because it was excessively *calorosa* (heat-producing), cabbage because it was *ventoso* (wind-producing), and pork because it would make the baby cry. They affirmed that the desires or *voglie* of the pregnant woman had to be satisfied to prevent damage to the baby. Some of the common desires they named were for strawberries, raspberries, wine, apples, chestnut flour, and polenta. Failure to satisfy a desire for mushrooms would cause the child to be born with a mushroom-shaped growth on the head, for bread would cause boys to be born with a blockage in the penis, for snails would impede penile erections, for eels would cause incessant movement or love of swimming, and for hare would cause a harelip.

Traditional food beliefs emphasized the important symbiotic relationship between mother and child during pregnancy. Elena was pregnant from February through November 1945, a time of extreme food scarcity in Florence. She was hungry all the time and craved specific foods: *I remember that when I was pregnant there was little to eat. I had to eat whatever we could find. One time my father managed to buy a whole large salame. I remember that he hung it on the kitchen wall. I was just pregnant, only two or three months, and I looked at that salame and I said—oh, I remember it well—"Oh, my God, that salame will be good; oh, that salame will be good." And then, as soon as they found out I was pregnant, they sliced it right away and gave me a piece. But nevertheless my baby was born with the birthmark of that salame. She was born bald, completely bald, you know, without a single hair on her head. And right here on her little head, where I always touched myself to push back my hair, she has a birthmark exactly in the shape of a slice of salame. Thank goodness I touched myself up here.*

Yes, because I always remember that a neighbor woman had repeatedly said to me, "When you become pregnant, listen well, if you see something that you want to eat, don't ever touch yourself on your face; always touch yourself where it won't show. Remember, always do this." Because then the "desires" will come where you cannot see them.

Do you know that Giovanna really loves salame? It is one of the things she always wants to eat when she comes to Florence. I always buy two or three whole ones when Giovanna visits. She goes to the refrigerator and cuts herself a couple of slices of salame, not at meals, but during the day, between one meal and another. As soon as she gets here, she begins to feel a craving for salame. Elena linked her hunger and cravings in pregnancy to Giovanna's lifelong food preferences. Elena believed that a parturient woman's food habits intimately affected her baby's personality, appearance, and hungers. She had to manage her cravings and eat properly to nurture and protect her fetus.[7] She revealed the Florentine belief that a mother was intimately connected to her children, a belief that persisted even after the baby was born and that was expressed and sustained through lifelong habits of maternal feeding.

Breast-feeding

Breast-feeding predominated in Italy in the first half of the twentieth century, when it was viewed as essential to babies' survival. Wet nurses were eagerly sought if mothers died in childbirth, had no milk due to malnutrition, or belonged to the upper classes and chose not to breast-feed. But Whitaker (2000, 249) tells us that "by the late 1950s and early 1960s, there was a growing tendency to renounce breast-feeding," and by the mid-1980s, there had been a significant decrease in the duration and prevalence of breast-feeding relative to the first half of the century.

Breast-feeding involved an intimate corporal connection between mother and infant. As Anna Freud (1968, 443) wrote, "All human love begins as 'stomach love.'" She pointed out that infants' earliest and deepest emotional connection was through food to the person who provided it, traditionally to the mother through breast milk. For some Florentine women like Elena, this corporeal intimacy with the child was wonderful: *I loved breast-feeding. For me it was such a beautiful thing that I never would have stopped, never. I had a lot of milk, even though I was slender and not very robust. I had so much milk that I could nurse as many children as I wanted. And I found other children to nurse whose mothers didn't have any milk. They asked me if I would nurse their infants and I was so happy to do it. I would have nursed all the babies in the neighborhood, I liked it so much.*

Elena adhered to traditional beliefs that underscored the intimate connections between mother and child through breast-feeding: *You know, Giovanna had six grandparents who all told me what to eat. I had to eat farinata—flour cooked in water and flavored with a little olive oil—next to the sink. My grandmother told me, "Go and eat it next to the sink. That will make your milk come." Well, I don't know where they got those ideas. And every morning I ate farinata. They thought that this made good milk—sweet-smelling and nutritious milk. You had to eat it next to the sink. You had to eat fennel because it also made the milk smell good. You couldn't eat beans, or pork, because they said that those foods would give the baby a stomachache. And you couldn't eat onion either, because they said that the baby wouldn't like the milk because it would stink of onion. Everything that the mother eats, they said, shows up in the milk. The milk takes on the taste of our foods, like when we eat asparagus, the milk comes out sour and distasteful.*

Two proverbs collected by Apergi and Bianco (1991, 129) in Vicchio di Mugello near Florence affirmed the connection between the mother's diet and her breast milk: *"il latte viene dalle minestre, non dalle finestre"*—"milk comes from soups, not from windows," and *"il latte viene dalla bocca"*—"milk comes from the mouth." Elena shared these beliefs and was proud of her fruitfulness: *So I followed my grandmothers' instructions and ate everything that the baby loved. And it worked well because she really sucked. Oh, yes, she was a really good nurser. My milk spilled out from my breasts. I remember that the baby slept in her bedroom back behind the bakery, between one breast-feed and another, while I stayed in the shop and waited on customers. I used to make mad dashes back there every little while to check on her because her room was a little bit removed from the bakery. But I continued to work in the bakery, and at one point I remember a customer saying, "Signora Elena, your baby is hungry."*

"Oh, God," I said. "Do you hear her crying?"

She replied, "No, no, no. It's you who are losing your milk." They could see the milk spilling out onto my apron, the white apron that I always wore in the shop. They could see the milk coming out.

And so, "Yes," I said. "Yes, it's time; it's time for her to eat." It was beautiful. The customer's remark underscored the Florentine belief of the interconnectedness of mother and baby. The mother's milk spilling out of her breasts was a clear sign to Florentines that the baby was hungry.

Elena exemplified the idealized contentment that breast-feeding was supposed to give mothers and she also spoke about it as a form of power. *I loved breast-feeding most of all, because at that moment the baby belonged completely to me, that's why. In that moment, she was really all mine. And I thought about it. I said to myself, "Look, the baby is growing because I am giving her my milk, because I am giving her life. I am giving her nourishment." And it seemed to me to be such a beautiful thing that I never would have stopped. And, you know, when I should have stopped, I didn't because I liked breast-feeding so much.* Elena continued to breast-feed her child for pleasure and violated Florentines' sense of measure that we saw in their concept of **gola** in Chapter 2. She said, *So then my grandmother said to me, "Stop giving that baby your milk. It's not doing anything for her anymore; it's water." But instead, every night before putting her in bed, I loved to give her a drop of milk. I realized that it couldn't be of much nutritive value, especially because the baby ate everything already; she ate everything. I breast-fed her just for love.* Elena's narrative underlined many meanings of breast-feeding. It was literal creation of life through nurture. It involved an extremely close emotional and physical connection to the child that had to be broken some day, even against the mother's desire, to allow the child to mature. It was deeply fulfilling to Elena and to most of my female subjects.

My older subjects—Elena, Valeria, and Laura—breast-fed their children for eight months to a year in the 1940s, '50s, and early '60s. Elena, Grazia, and Marianna's mother nursed other infants as well in the 1940s. Leonardo defined the woman whom his mother Grazia nursed along with him as his *milk-sister—sorella di latte*.[8] Of all my subjects, only Sergia did not breast-feed; I describe her experience below. My younger female subjects—Piera, Caterina, and Maria—planned to nurse the children they desired, and in 2003 Caterina and Maria told me that they had indeed breast-fed their infants for about three months. My subjects approved of breast-feeding for several reasons. Laura, who nursed her two children born in the early 1960s, said, *Fa sempre meglio— It is always better, at least that's what I've always heard everyone say. It's a natural thing, so why go and look for something else? If a woman doesn't have any milk, she doesn't have any. But if she has it like I did—I had so much—why should I take it away? Why? It gives you a stronger sense of affection, you feel—oh, God, maybe another woman doesn't feel that way. But for me, it is a beautiful thing. I find it a beautiful thing.*

Several women said, *è una cosa naturale—it's a natural thing,* or *è una cosa bella—it's a beautiful thing.* Valeria elaborated: *I nursed my children for eight or nine months. They ate solid foods too, eh, how they ate. Then I gave them a drop of milk for the pleasure of it. I reprove a mother who doesn't nurse her children. For me it was a great satisfaction to breast-feed mine. I don't know, it seemed to me—I made them, I put them into the world—and it seemed like I was giving them life when I nursed them. It's a beautiful thing for a mother.*

My older subjects disapproved of women who did not breast-feed, particularly those who did not breast-feed out of concern for their figures. Such selfishness contradicted their notions of maternal altruism. Forty-eight-year-old

Laura said, *There are young women who are afraid of ruining themselves and so they don't want to breast-feed. Understand, nursing a child means you have to eat, absolutely. You can't be dieting because then the milk won't come. So when you're nursing, you tend to get fat, to ruin your figure, to lose your shape, and so many things.*[9] *So a woman doesn't nurse and she goes on a diet so she returns to her former shape. I never even thought about these problems. Breast-feeding is something natural—why should you take it away from your baby?*

For women to rank maintenance of their own attractiveness higher than nurturing their baby contradicted the Florentine ideal that women put their children first. Sixty-six-year-old Elena elaborated: *I've heard of some women who don't like breast-feeding. I think it's because they are afraid of ruining their figure. I don't know, that might be the reason. I can't see any others. It doesn't seem like a good reason to me. If a woman ruins her shape, what's wrong with that? What kind of a reason is that? I'll tell you the truth. I nursed Giovanna and I would have nursed her a lot more, but I never ruined my figure. I stayed the same as before and I never even thought about the possibility that breast-feeding would have ruined it. I stayed the same as before. Even in regard to the husband, have a little patience. If a woman's figure is ruined, it's because she had a baby, because she nursed it. That should be a reason for tenderness from the husband towards the wife in my opinion. It's not her fault—it's nature.*

Sergia was the only one of my subjects who did not breast-feed her children, and she was emphatic that vanity was not the reason: *Let's be perfectly clear, it's not that I didn't nurse them because breast-feeding ruins the breasts, eh.* After the birth of her first child Eugenia in 1970, Sergia did not have enough milk to feed her adequately (a common problem for new mothers who have to develop their milk supply in response to their baby's needs). Unfortunately her doctors told her to supplement with formula (something that breast-feeding advocates oppose, because only the infant's sucking builds up the mother's supply). In Italy at this time, most breast-feeding mothers including Sergia had a scale to weigh the baby before and after each feeding to make sure she or he got enough.[10] This practice of the *doppia pesata* (double weighing) created anxiety and stress for Sergia. Getting up in the middle of the night to weigh, nurse, weigh again, mix adequate formula, and feed again exhausted her, so she gave up the breast-feeding and put Eugenia totally on formula, after which both mother and daughter did much better. When her second daughter Ondina was born two years later, Sergia nursed her only once, in the hospital, and gave her formula from then on.

Sergia insisted that formula had been fine for her children, and because she disliked breast-feeding, it was much better for her: *Breast-feeding really bothered me. First of all, I didn't like it at all; I didn't like it; it bothered me. I felt badly. I don't know; it bothered me. This sensation of this baby who was sucking at my breast was just something that I didn't succeed in—maybe because I didn't have milk. In fact, my mother always said to me, "Do you feel the let-down reflex? You have to feel it; you have to feel the need to give your milk." I said that I didn't feel it. Hence it could be that it all depended on this. Furthermore, I was very, very anxious. In short, I didn't like it at all. No, no, breast-feeding was a negative experience. . . . Perhaps I disliked breast-feeding because I was so anxious; perhaps it was because I was exhausted by everything that went before. . . . It bothered me. I felt weaker. I couldn't hold myself upright. I didn't have energy to do anything. You know, breast milk is a food; you've got to regenerate it yourself, with your organism. If you physically don't have sufficient strength—in fact, I didn't have any milk, which showed that I just couldn't do it.*

Interestingly, whereas for some Florentine women the intense bond with children through breast-feeding was wonderful and fulfilling, for Sergia it was *disgusting*. She was caught in the vice of changing cultural mores that simultaneously extolled breast-feeding but made it difficult to do successfully. Because it was so highly valued as a sign of good mothering, she felt she had to affirm her maternal devotion to her children and her pleasure in feeding them even though she did not nurse them.

Refusing Food, Refusing Connection

For children to refuse food was to protest against their expected role of being compliant consumers of parental values and ties. Connection with parents was suffocating at times and rejection of food expressed a need for distance or a sense of distress. When Giovanna was growing up an only child, her mother Elena was continually anxious about something happening to her. It was a challenge for Elena to allow Giovanna independence and not be overprotective, and she gave in only reluctantly and at her husband's urging to Giovanna's rejection of the breast at one year of age. While identification and connection with her mother were important for Giovanna, in adolescence they may have felt suffocating. Her father presented an alternative figure of attachment that helped her gain distance from her mother.

Elena told a story about *baccalà* (dried codfish) that metaphorically demonstrated how food became a way for Giovanna to identify with her father Giorgio. Elena said, *My husband Giorgio loved all foods. There was only one thing that he didn't like—**baccalà**. He never learned to like it. This was perhaps because when he was a boy he took so many blows in being forced to eat **baccalà**. A bit a **baccalà** and a slap, a bit of **baccalà** and a slap—from his father—because he had to learn to eat everything. The child learned, but he just really couldn't ever stomach **baccalà**. I tried the same thing with Giovanna. Then it just made me upset. I said to myself, "Why in the world am I doing this? If she doesn't want to eat it, she won't eat it." Understand? Giovanna was just like him. She didn't like **baccalà**, only that; she was just like her father. . . . You know, I think she still doesn't like **baccalà**. She is really her father's daughter, the same, the same. But, look, for me, **baccalà** is the best thing to eat in the whole world. That's why I couldn't understand why she didn't like it. Me, for **baccalà**,*

I would do crazy things for baccalà. I love it to death. Although Elena loved *baccalà* and believed that children should eat what was put in front of them, she overcame her urge to force Giovanna to eat the food she hated. She allowed Giovanna to express her independence and identification with her father by refusing *baccalà*.[11]

Because eating was a form of acceptance and connection, refusing to eat communicated powerful messages of rejection or distress. In Chapter 2, Rinaldo described how he hated the odious duck in peach sauce offered by his clients in Paris, but he had to eat it to avoid insulting them. Similarly, Baldo described how much he detested fish, especially crustaceans. Once when visiting friends in the coastal city of Viareggio, they served him fish soup. He tried to eat it, but after two bites he felt literally sick and had to stop, telling them that he had already eaten. *It was an offense,* he said, *but there was nothing I could do about it.* Not to eat food offered by others signified hostility or anguish. Anorexia nervosa—the refusal to eat—was a powerful and disruptive disorder. While my subjects in the early 1980s knew only a few people who had anorexia nervosa, Sergia recollected long periods in her childhood when she had difficulty eating due to her stressful family situation (see Chapter 7), as did Elena.

Elena could not eat as a child due to angst over her parents' troubled marriage. When she spoke of vomiting up worms in Chapter 2, it was almost as if she were trying to vomit up the poison of her parents' dissension. She said, *As a young girl, I never ate. I would go even a week without eating. I realized as an adult why I didn't eat—because in my house there was discord between my father and my mother. . . . I felt so much anguish, so much fear, and I have this defect that when something bothers me, my stomach closes, and I can't eat. That's what happened to me then, without my knowing it. I heard my parents arguing and my stomach closed and I couldn't eat. . . . They fought because my father was jealous of my mother.* For Elena, eating meant and depended on family harmony.

Because her family was discordant, she could not eat and her food refusal was a loud cry that her parents heard because of how important children's eating was: *So then my parents were extremely worried about me—not eating today, not eating tomorrow—it was bad. I remember that my father always returned home with something in his pocket, and he said to me, "Look, if you eat tonight, look, this is something for you."*

"Daddy, let me see. What is it, what is it?"

"I'll give it to you after you have eaten." So then maybe I tried a little harder to eat. He brought me—I don't know—a little toy, a silly little thing, a candy, or something like that—to make me eat.

Elena's story was revealing because it contrasted dramatically with the normal Florentine expectation that children eat with gusto whatever is put in front of them. Her food refusal was a call for attention, to which her father responded with gifts but not with the tranquility she craved. Children's eating validated mothers' skill and altruism, and mothers were always exhorting their children—*"Mangia che l'ha fatto mamma"*—*"Eat because mother made it."* Giovanna said, *My mother pushes me to eat . . . because she likes it, and because she also fulfills herself doing this for me. Do you understand? It gives her pleasure.* Mothers were supposed to express love through food and children were supposed to accept that love through eating. Going without food was a meaningful protest against distress.

Eating and Parent–Child Ties: Nurturing Male Dependence

Food refusal made an especially powerful statement in Florence because eating together was central in constituting the family, as was shown in Chapter 7. Feeding was an important way that parents socialized children, as seventy-three-year-old Renzo made clear: *A father has so many responsibilities toward a child. Everything, everything. . . . You've got to teach a child respect. You've got to tell him, "When it's time for dinner, we're all at dinner. If there's this to eat, there's this for everyone and nothing else."* Interestingly, although he did not prepare the meals, he felt responsible for upholding the family moral order by enforcing rules about consumption.

Fifty-four-year-old Raffaele defined a similar imperative that children eat the food put before them, and thus incorporate family tastes and values along with Florentine cooking and culture: *Here's another thing about meals—they serve to get children used to our cuisine. Our possibilities are what they are, and when we cook, we make one meal only, understand? It has to satisfy everyone, because we only cook one meal. Sure, there are foods they like better and those they like less, but little by little they get used to different things. They just can't pretend that I eat a minute steak (**braciola**), but they don't like it, so I have to cook them a sirloin (**bistecca**). No, if today there is minute steak, there is minute steak for everybody. Maybe tomorrow we will eat the sirloin, and then there will be sirloin for everybody, understand? . . . I was raised like this—in my home there was one dinner. You either ate that or you did without. I always followed this habit and I've always done fine. My children eat everything. I've never said, "I don't like this." If my children don't like something, I say, "Well, if you don't like it, leave it on your plate. If you get hungry, you'll eat it." Then they eat it.*

But in spite of these values articulated by fathers, some children did not eat everything and were indulged by their mothers. Eighteen-year-old Arturo was a fussy though hearty eater. He lived at home with his parents and grandparents, and divided his meals between his house and his fiancée's house. He had narrow tastes that focused on pasta, meat, and potatoes. He was famous in the family for liking expensive foods like **petti di pollo** and **braciole**—chicken breasts and minute steaks. In Florence, people often cooked **braciole** as a second course—broiled, cooked in tomato sauce, fried in olive oil, or breaded (**alla milanese**). They were definitely a symbol of modern cuisine and had been rarely eaten by my older subjects in childhood. That Arturo ate little except **braciole** was a source of irritated comment by many family members, who felt it showed him to be improperly socialized and spoiled (*viziato*). As Arturo's great uncle Renzo said, *At dinner Arturo's house seems like a restaurant. "I want a steak, I want this, I want that." You can't have this in a family—four different things to eat for supper. They're spoiled. If there's this to eat, there's this for everybody.* But Arturo's mother Valeria pampered him and cooked what he wanted. She made the *braciola* especially for him along with the other delectable and varying meals she made for the others.

Arturo reflected on his restrictive food preferences: *I'm more open about foods than I used to be. Before, I didn't eat anything except **bracioline** and chicken breasts. I didn't eat anything else. Now I try a little harder to taste new things. Then I ate **bracioline**, chicken breasts, roast beef. No vegetables. Potatoes or tomatoes, and that's all. Many, many evenings I dined on caffelatte and cookies. And **pastasciutta,** oh, yes, that was never missing. I ate little in terms of variety but a lot in terms of quantity. I don't know why I was fussy, but from my early childhood I didn't accept other foods. I just never did. I grew up being fussy, and I never managed to break the habit of eating like a baby and I never tried new things.*

Maybe this was the fault of my family, but I don't think so, because, on the contrary, they eat everything. So it was totally me who refused to try new things. I don't know how much my eating reflected my lack of maturation. I don't know; maybe it did. Maybe my eating habits did reflect a certain wish in me not to grow up. But only in eating, because in no other way did I try to stay a child. I started to enlarge my diet two or three years ago when I started going out with Maria. Being with her, maybe this caused me to change. However, I think more than anything it was my own maturation. In these years that we've been together, I made a big change from being rather closed to being quite open. Arturo made an explicit connection between being spoiled through feeding and being immature. He linked his limited eating habits to his family even if only to refute the connection. However, his mother always fed him whatever he wanted and made herself indispensable to him by catering to his narrow eating wishes.[12] This is an example of how some mothers nurtured dependence in their children, especially their male children. By indulging Arturo in his picky eating, Valeria exemplified the self-sacrifice typical of the maternal role and created expectations in Arturo that his wishes would be met by women, even if they caused extra work.

While many boys were socialized to expect service and special treatment, and were not encouraged to perform household chores, most girls were taught to pull their own weight, which was of course essential if they were to grow up to run households and nurture their own expectant spouses and children. Sixty-six-year-old Elena raised her daughter to help in the home: *Giovanna had to learn to be self-sufficient very early because I couldn't be there. I had to be in the bakery. Hence from when she was very small, she had to go out and get the milk, prepare her breakfast, wash herself, dress herself, and go to school. Because I just couldn't do all these things. She had to manage by herself.*

Like most girls and in contrast to most boys, Giovanna was raised to be competent in the household. Thirty years after her own childhood, Giovanna reflected in 1984 that the gender division of labor in the household had not changed: *The daughters help a little. They dry dishes, make their beds, maybe help with the dusting, do a little shopping, and run a few errands, nothing special. But the sons do nothing. Nothing. There is already a predetermined attitude towards the boy from an early age that he is the king of the house. Being used to this treatment from a very young age and all through his teen years, a young man naturally seeks a wife who treats him the same and doesn't ask him to wash the floors and do the dishes. . . . The male child—**il figlio maschio**—has always been more important than the female. This fact affects both the man and the woman—it's like a chain, understand? To satisfy her husband, the woman takes on not only the role of wife, but also that of mother to him.* Men benefited from the privilege of service first from their mothers and later from their wives, while women were expected to pull not only their own weight in the home but that of the men as well.

Mothers reproduced the imbalance in the domestic division of labor by requiring help from their daughters but little from their sons. Fifty-year-old Valeria explained: *I've tried to teach Caterina and Arturo how to tend to a family—how to manage money and budget expenses. . . . Caterina has become accustomed to doing everything in the home—cleaning, cooking, washing, in short, everything, whatever has to be done. Oh, heavens, it's not that as a girl Caterina did much housework. However, later on we reached a point where we needed her to help out, when Baldo got sick and I stayed with him in the clinic for almost a year. She and Arturo were alone at home with only my parents, and they had to manage. However, I think these are things that you learn when you have to; all it takes is determination. These are things you can do wrong once, twice, three times, fine, then you learn them. All it takes is the will to do them—cooking, housework, washing, all these things—where there's a will, there's a way.*

But Valeria admitted that her son did nothing in the house: *Arturo doesn't do housework now, but maybe he will learn when he is with his wife. Perhaps our Italian system is all wrong because I never managed to teach him. Maybe I didn't try hard enough to get him in the habit of doing housework. I don't know. I don't even know how to explain how this came about. Oh, goodness, if he sees that I need some aid, he helps me. In short, Arturo has assisted me many times. However, it is not like he has a penchant for housework like Caterina or any other girl; they throw themselves into it. Not Arturo—I think it's partly his character. Nevertheless, I hope that when he is with his wife, he helps her. If they are both working outside the home, it is right that he help out. I think it's right; they are equal. But wait and see. Men don't do it. My son-in-law Sandro doesn't do any housework at all. No, no, that's the way Italian men are.*

Valeria felt that men should help at home, but she lacked conviction to change them, saying *that's the way Italian men are,* and she admitted her complicity in her son's failure to help: *I think it's the fault of the older mothers. I think the mothers accustomed their sons to having everything done for them. I don't know. I didn't succeed in getting Arturo to do anything, because I would grumble at him and grumble at him about leaving his clothes all over the place, but then I always went and straightened everything up. It was partly my fault because I gave up nagging and cleaned up after him. But with Caterina, it was enough just to tell her, and she always straightened her things up. Even if she did it badly, at least she did it. You only had to tell her once or twice. She liked doing it. But Arturo, you had to tell him three or four times to get him to clean up. And then it's our fault too because we always blame the women if the house is messy, not the men. So why should the men clean? It's not their problem.* This last comment was telling because Valeria showed one powerful mechanism in socializing gender hegemony by blaming women for any failings and letting men off the hook.

Valeria pointed out how mothers socialized their children with beliefs essential to male gender privilege: that household chores were women's duty and men had a right to expect domestic service. Sixty-six-year-old Elena also acknowledged women's complicity in men's domestic incompetence: *Most men in Italy only do the men's chores; they don't do women's chores. . . . But it's something for which we women also bear the guilt. I remember one time when my husband Giorgio was still alive. I was doing some taxing household chore—I don't remember what—when it started to rain. I had the clothes outside drying on the line. So Giorgio said to me, "Don't worry. Continue what you're doing. I'll bring the clothes in off the line; otherwise they'll get soaked." Look, I didn't want him to go out on the terrace to get the clothes and bring them in. I didn't want him to do it, because I thought people might see him from the other apartments and think badly of me for making him do this chore. So you can understand the prejudices about what men should do start from us women. It's our fault as much as theirs.*

Not only did mothers free their sons from domestic labor but so did fathers, who usually did little in the home themselves and supported this male privilege. Raffaele commented on his son's domestic incompetence: *The only one who does absolutely nothing in our family is Piero. He eats and he's off. And yet he lives here too. So why does he do nothing? Well, it is evident that he just doesn't have the inclination. He does nothing, utterly nothing. Oh, if you ask a favor of him, he does it. It's not that he's indolent—but would you have him cook? He would poison us all! Would you have him wash dishes? For the love of God! Nothing, he eats and he's off. He's got the good life, yes.* Raffaele suggested that boys' exoneration from domestic work was traditional and excused it on the grounds of disinclination and lack of skill—self-reinforcing attributions.

Furthermore, women and men alike condemned women who did not fully embrace domestic chores and child rearing, further supporting male privilege. For example, forty-five-year-old Rinaldo, who in Chapter 5 expressed his aversion for domestic chores, told a story about his own upbringing: *Because my parents were both working, they hired a woman to look after me, but she really didn't supervise me very much, so I was always playing soccer in the streets, never studying. . . . I think that today my mother might regret having worked so much when I was little. Perhaps as she has seen how carefully my wife Sergia is watching over our children, my mother has felt, "But in short, maybe I erred. I worked so much—so, so, so much—however, I didn't give my children what they really needed."* In suggesting his mother erred, Rinaldo upheld the traditional gender division of labor, even though in the next breath he recognized his mother's economic contributions to the family's standard of living: *I don't know why she worked so much, maybe because we needed the money. I think she worked for need, not in the sense that we were risking hunger, no, absolutely not. But they felt it was necessary, understand?*

Similarly, sixty-one-year-old Marianna upheld the norm that women carried primary responsibility for rearing and feeding children, even though she herself—by not marrying or having children—did not conform to it: *I always worked, so I don't know what to say. But maybe the mother should stay at home to take care of the children. Because if a child stays home alone, comes home, and eats nothing but a sandwich, and then goes out until seven or eight in the evening, it's not a good thing; at least it doesn't seem good to me. Yet maybe I'm wrong; it could be that I'm wrong. But I think that more than anybody else the mother should care for the child. And if she really needs to work, there are day care centers, schools. But the children grow up without loving their parents; they love their teachers or their babysitters more than their parents.* Marianna, like most people in her culture, felt that the mother should raise the children or risk losing their love, even though she recognized the benefits to women of working: *But a woman wants to work to have her freedom. Women like to work, I think, because I know I always went to work willingly.*

Burdens and Conflicts for Younger Couples

Most of my subjects, younger and older alike, recognized the value and increasing tendency of women to work outside the home, and several of the older people, especially the women, realized that this put the younger women under a heavy burden. Fifty-year-old Valeria said, *All the young women want to work today, but how can they manage everything? Unless one of the couple has a really good job, they both have to work. If they don't, they can't make it. There is no way—with one salary you can't survive anymore. . . . Women who work outside the home are really squeezed tightly, because they have to do all the work in the home too. They have to cook, wash, iron, clean, even if they only do the minimum, but they have to do something.*

Yet even as women were increasingly trying to enter the workforce, men were neither helping with the housework nor relaxing their demands. Sixty-six-year-old Elena said, *Most Italian men don't do anything around the house. If a woman is a housewife and works only at home, everything is fine, but if she has a job outside the home, I don't know how she can do it. Here the men are not content to eat a sandwich at lunch. They want a first course, they want a second course, vegetables, and then maybe even a dessert. They want all this, twice a day. For working women, the situation is tragic. . . . They have to work in the house when they get home and do what they can. They have to get lunch ready for the next day after dinner. They never have any peace, understand? They're always running.*

Even though the men recognized the dilemma, they were not eager to assume more housework. Forty-five-year-old Rinaldo commented: *Oh, sure, my daughters will need to learn how to cook, that's important—for them, for their husbands, for the whole family. But it becomes problematical for women who work. In those cases, the women have to ask their husbands to make a sacrifice, because I don't think it is right that when they both work outside the home that the husband does nothing in the home. . . . Yes, in the past when the women didn't work, the house was their job. But now the women work. How can they take care of the house when they are working full-time? Who does the cooking? Who makes the beds? So look, you tell me, you're a woman, don't you see the women overburdened (***sacrificate***)?*

Forty-eight-year-old Laura underscored the fact that younger women and men were ***sacrificati*** and attributed this to their heavy workload and also to the fact that neither were used to housework: *The younger men and women are always overburdened, always **sacrificati**. They are used to doing very little around the house. They go to work, and then when they come home, what do they do? They need to do something, but they don't have much time to do anything. So when they get married and have their own families, they surely find themselves overburdened trying to cook and clean the house and do all the other chores.*

But Laura felt that men had made some progress: *These young men are already more open to helping their wives at home, or doing some housework, or cooking, or taking care of the children. This is happening in many couples, much more often than before. In our generation it's rare to find the men even cooking, the way my husband Raffaele does. Instead, in the younger couples, they both work, the men know that they have to do more. I think their minds are more open, and they understand more, including the sacrifices of their wives. I don't know. I think so, because you can see already among many young couples that the husband gives his wife a hand if they are both working. But still, the woman always bears a heavier burden. Try to find a man who will wash clothes—a man won't wash. Iron? A man won't iron for you. In short, the housework, maybe they'll sweep, give a quick pass with the mop, but never as well as a woman does it— that's logical. A man can watch the children and take them out. But, in short, it remains to be seen whether they can do as much as the women do. We will never get there. But at least we will be a little better off.* Although she and others noted that men were doing more, Laura was not optimistic about men being equal partners in doing housework. She expressed the hegemonic ideology that men might *give a hand* but simply were not as capable as women in the home—*it's logical.*

Maternalism and Sacrifice

Women upheld patriarchal ideology not only by condemning women who shirked their domestic duties, but also by shouldering a heavy load and defining themselves through sacrifice.[13] We saw in Chapter 6 how Florentines defined women as *sacrificate*—sacrificed or overburdened—for carrying out the lion's share of reproductive chores along with productive work as well. This concept of sacrifice carried over into child rearing, as fifty-year-old Valeria said, *A child demands sacrifices—but not sacrifices for their own sake, sacrifices if you want to maintain a child respectably. There are many sacrifices. . . . I think parents have an obligation to take care of a child if they put it into the world. After all, the child didn't ask to be born. In my opinion, parents shouldn't ask a lot from their children because it is we parents who give them life. They didn't request it.*

Parents—especially mothers—owed it to children to sacrifice for them, but if all went well, Valeria said, the children would reciprocate: *Then if we raise them well, they help us. I see mine; I have no problems with them. However, we should not be demanding of them. I sincerely believe that if in old age I find myself in bad shape, I would be really sorry, more sorry for ruining their lives than for myself, understand? I tell you that I think they should put me in some place, in one of these nursing homes where everybody should go. Otherwise I will ruin my children's lives. That's what I have seen in my experience. For example, there is this neighbor. She cannot go out of the house because her mother refuses to stay alone for an hour. And this woman isn't even in bad shape; she's fine. However, she won't even stay a half hour or an hour alone. So my friend is never in charge of herself to go out to dinner, or to the movies, nothing. Is it right for that woman to ruin her daughter's life? She didn't ask her mother to make her.*

Oh, you will see, if I am in need, naturally I will want my children to help me, of course; that's the way we are. But in short, if they do it for me, if they try to help me, they have to want to do it. It has to come from them. It is not right for me to say to them that they must help me. They have to feel it themselves, and they will feel it if they have affection for the family. They will feel it by themselves. I look at mine; they have kind feelings. I never ask them anything. It's really rare that I ask something, because they see by themselves when I am in need. It just doesn't seem right to me that I impose on them that they have to help me and then I ruin their lives by burdening them with too much. Valeria believed that she should give much to her children, but ask little, and hope that she managed to instill enough affection in them so that they would help her if she needed them. Most likely it was going to be her daughter who helped her, rather than her son, because the socialization of children allocated nurturance and care to women.

A cultural ideology of sacrifice defined Valeria and other women through self-abnegation and contributed to affirming children's and men's rights to service. It also set up an impossible impasse for the women and men of the younger generation. They believed in equality in principle, but found it difficult to achieve in practice, because of the persistent ideology of female responsibility and sacrifice. Florentine babies began to imbibe gender inequality in utero. Changing years of socialization was extremely difficult. The Florentine family was a critical institution of what Antonio Gramsci called "civil society," whose institutions functioned to reproduce the practices and beliefs upholding gender hierarchy through socializing children. In Florence, as parents, especially mothers, talked about feeding and eating, they demonstrated the socialization of gender behaviors upholding male privilege.

Food and Gender: Toward the Future

La parità dei sessi non c'è.　　　*There is no sexual equality.*
　　　　　　　　　　　　　　　　　　Caterina

Introduction

Caterina was twenty-six in 1984, newly married to Sandro, and working as a cashier in the COOP supermarket. She was blunt in her claim of unequal gender relations, yet she was mildly optimistic: *Only in the latest generation have things begun to change. . . . Today's girls are not the girls of before who liked to show their boyfriends how competent they were in washing, ironing, cooking. The girls have changed, eh, and the boys are changing too, but slowly.* This chapter focuses on how and why younger Florentines were experiencing and altering gender relations centered on foodways.

My six younger subjects' food-centered narratives described their cultural experiences of gender, work, and family in Florence in the 1980s. Born between 1956 and 1964, they were in their early to mid-twenties when I interviewed them in 1984. Four were the siblings Caterina and Arturo, Caterina's husband Sandro, and Arturo's fiancée Maria, all of whom lived in Florence. The other two were Caterina and Arturo's cousins, Piero and Piera, who lived 35 kilometers from Florence in Empoli. Their stories address the following questions: Who would prepare, serve, and clean up after meals? How would women handle the competing demands of working outside and inside the home? Would men "help" with reproductive labor, and would they move beyond "helping" to become equal partners in running the home? How would cuisine and its associated practices and beliefs change?

The younger subjects' experiences were both similar to and different from their elders', and were radically different in one important respect: the younger grew up with abundance rather than scarcity. In the 1980s, as the economy became more market oriented, women increasingly turned to wage labor to earn the money needed to participate in the consumer economy and the social value that went with paid productive labor. But women consequently felt new pressures in the family. Men and women both recognized women's need for economic independence and the importance of their contribution to the family economy, but they struggled unsuccessfully to attain balance in child rearing and household chores. They struggled with the conflict between the increasing trend toward "parity or formal equality between women and men" in the public sphere and the continuing lack of equality in the home (Passerini 1996b, 145). And with less time to cook and declining interest in the traditional cuisine, they gradually changed their consumption habits toward processed and restaurant foods. They had higher standards of living than their parents and valued quantity as well as quality.

Men, Women, and Work Outside the Home

Among my young subjects, both the men and the women wanted to work at paid jobs. Men still defined their identity in terms of work outside the home, and everyone assumed they would work. The younger women wanted the independence and the money that a paying job provided, and younger men supported this desire, but they still defined it as conflicting with women's traditional reproductive duties. Neither men nor women were clear about how they would manage the basic household chores of shopping, cooking, cleaning, and taking care of children while both husband and wife worked outside the home.

My subjects also confronted a difficult job market with high unemployment and too many unfulfilling jobs. Twenty-two-year-old Maria, for example, had two years of secretarial school after middle school and went through a "*calvary*" at the unemployment office and at various temporary factory jobs without finding a permanent job, which she needed to get the financial security to marry and have children. She complained: *If you want a job where you can earn enough to start a family, it's difficult. It's difficult to find a decent job with a regular salary, and without that, it's useless to start a family. There are enough problems without adding the burden of not having any money. Then there's the second problem of getting a house. That's very important. It's hard to find a house to rent that isn't incredibly expensive. The only thing to do is to buy a house, but that too is expensive, and again we see the need for two salaries.* Younger people were caught in a difficult situation: they needed jobs to live the middle-class lifestyle they had come to take for granted, but jobs were exceedingly hard to get because older people had a lock on the good ones. In 1997, unemployment still remained particularly high for young people under age twenty-nine, who composed "70 percent of the unemployed in Italy" (Blim 2000, 171). Even if they found jobs, they still had to balance work with household responsibilities, and this fell mostly on the females.

Maria's fiancé, twenty-one-year-old Arturo, also had problems getting a steady job that he liked. He completed the eighth grade, then worked as a warehouse supervisor, construction worker, and plumber's helper, and he was still searching for a permanent position. He articulated the same identification of manhood with working that the older men expressed: *For the future, first of all, I would like to have a job, but nowadays getting a job is a big problem. A person who has a job is already fortunate. Then I would like it to be a job I like—I hope* *also for this. I would like to have a tranquil family and enough money to live (**i soldi per campare**). I'm not saying I want to roll in gold, but I would like enough money to support my children and my wife well. That's the essential thing. But today it is a big problem to attain material well-being. There are problems finding a job, finding a house, starting a family, and, in consequence, problems of living. How can you live if all the roads are closed to you?*

Arturo articulated a conflict between the lack of jobs and the need for both husband and wife to work. He felt another conflict because ideally he would prefer his wife to stay home: *Today it's no longer the man alone who is responsible for supporting the family. Today we are in two, and it is right that we both decide things together. But if I could have a job and my wife could stay at home, I would be more content. I don't know if I feel this way because my family was like this, with my father at work and my mother at home, but I think it's better for the children. However, it's logical, if my wife wants to go to work, well, I can't impose anything on her; she's free too. Taking care of the children is both our responsibility.*

Even as Arturo recognized that he should help with child rearing, he left himself an out: *I don't know if I'm wrong; however, I think the woman is more successful at raising children. That is, even the children themselves have a greater attachment to a maternal figure. I've never tried with children; maybe I could raise them, maybe I could adapt. I would like to stay with the children—it's not that I'm reluctant. Maybe we could do a switch and have her working and me at home with the children; however, I would feel like—I won't say a kept man (**un mantenuto**)—but I think I would rather work than stay home. I think a person keeps the imprint of the family he grows up in, that's the thing.*

Arturo's sister Caterina reflected that same family "*imprint*" when she spoke about work versus children, and revealed an attitude of maternal sacrifice similar to that of her mother Valeria, but with the added frustrations of a working woman: *Would I give up my job to stay at home? I would do it for my child, because it seems right to take care of him myself and not have to take him to my mother's in the morning and go and get him in the evening. That is a tragic situation in my opinion. It's the fate of all the children nowadays. But listen, for God's sake, nobody told you to put a child into the world. If you have a child, you do it for your own satisfaction. Then what do you do? You wake the child up in the morning with the alarm clock. There are children who are like office workers already, used to getting up with the alarm at seven every morning. Then you rush to take him to your mother's house; then your mother takes him to nursery school. One day the father picks the child up at school; another day the grandmother does.*

I see it with my sister-in-law. When does she see her son? She starts work in the bank at eight in the morning and leaves at five-thirty in the evening. She sees her child between five-thirty and seven. . . . When children are little, they really need their parents, and that's the time a parent should stay home. In fact, why didn't my sister-in-law have a second child? Not because it would inconvenience her, but because she says, "For whom would I have another? I haven't been able to care for this one. For whom would I have another? To whom would I give it?" Sure, she *would give it to her mother to watch, but for whom would she be having it? In my opinion, she's right. I want to have a child; actually I would like to have two. But I think it will really plunge me into deep shit. When you have a child, you sign the death sentence. So maybe one would be enough.* Caterina reflected an enduring maternalist ideology linked to why Italy today has the lowest birthrate in the world—9.3 children per thousand, which is lower than the death rate of 9.9 per thousand (ISTAT 2000). She revealed the continuing cultural belief that mothers should care for children, which persisted even into the late 1990s when Italy had fewer dual-wage-earning couples than all the other EU11 countries (Blim 2000, 172).

Both Arturo and Caterina lamented the difficult job market. Caterina had a permanent job, but she hated it. Unable to land a nursery school teaching position, the job for which she trained, she instead worked as a clerk in a COOP supermarket, like increasing numbers of Italians in the last quarter of the twentieth century, when supermarkets grew considerably (see Chapter 10). Caterina was torn between wanting a job for independence and hating the monotonous labor of the cashier: *Working is important to me. It's important for economic satisfaction and because I don't like staying home. But I would like to do my real work—teaching nursery school. I realized when I was substitute teaching that maybe I arrived home tired to death—because you know with children there is so much chaos, you need a lot of patience, and they tire you out—but I never looked at my watch. Time flew. That's what happens with a job you do willingly, the time flies past. . . . But working in the supermarket, you say to yourself, "Madonna, it's not one o'clock yet." You can't go on; you can't do anything but lament how slowly the time is passing. In my opinion, that's a bad way to work. It's tragic. But I think most people are in this situation today. I don't think there are very many people satisfied with their jobs. Most people just do the work and thank God that they have a job.*

Working in the supermarket is monotonous. It doesn't give you much satisfaction. Every day you are there at the cash register punching in prices. In short, you really don't need much of a brain to do it. All you have to do is know the prices, and sooner or later, even if you are a mule, you learn them, for God's sake.[1] You have to stock the shelves, but who is it that doesn't know how to put a box on a shelf? Come on. It's always the same work and it's really monotonous. Sometimes I get moments of crisis and I get depressed and want to quit. I want to look for another job. Maybe someone who has only finished eighth grade knows that the choices are few for career or job. But I say to myself, "How come—I studied, I went to school, and I have to work here?" I just reach a crisis point where I say, "Madonna, I can't stand this job anymore."

Caterina gave up on her desired career as a nursery school teacher because jobs were so hard to come by, but she still wanted to work: *I tried staying at home without working, and look, it's really sad. It's enough to cause a nervous* breakdown. *It's sad for a young person to be at home all the time. It's an awful sit-uation. Furthermore, you can't buy anything; you can't go out and satisfy a whim and say, "This month I'm going to splurge and spend a hundred dollars on some-thing," because you always have to go and ask your parents for money. You can do that as long as you're going to school and studying, but later it's bothersome. When you're young, you can be a burden on your parents, but later, you have to have your own independence. So I work for my own independence and I also work to supplement our economic situation. We have many expenses, you know. . . . I think that work has the compensation that at least it enables you to get some satis-faction—without it, you'd kill yourself. If you have a job that doesn't satisfy you, you want to kill yourself, but if it gives you satisfaction, that's different.*

For Caterina, satisfaction came not from the work itself, but from the abil-ity to consume that it afforded: *But if you just have a job to have it, the only good thing is—the best day is the day you get paid. Then maybe you burn your salary all at once. There are many who splurge and spend their pay all at once just to get some compensation. Maybe after two weeks you don't have another cent. You'll be at the start again, waiting for payday. But at least you indulged yourself with a new pair of $150 shoes. Right then and there, that is your satisfaction. What I mean is that you are reduced to those satisfactions. Maybe you get angry when you get paid because your pay is so little; it's always so little. On the one hand, you can't wait to get paid; however, on the other, you are there counting up your pay and saying, "Oh, it's always less, it's always less." That's the way it is.*

Because of her boring and unfulfilling job, Caterina's only satisfaction was the consumption her salary permitted. Her husband Sandro was luckier be-cause he had a job he loved as a dental technician and had recently started his own business: *At first we just had a dental laboratory, but then we also opened a dentist's office in the center of Florence so as to have a steady and dependable source of work. Furthermore, this enables us to see beyond just the birth of the tooth to its installation in the mouth, which brings a greater gratification. . . . It's a satisfaction, a real creative satisfaction in short. . . . After the dentist makes the impression in the office, he sends it to us and we make the tooth. It is really exact-ing work. It demands precision not only in the work itself, but also in keeping the laboratory neat, putting the tools away, keeping it clean. It cannot be a mess with things left here and there and all over the place. When you do this work, you have to work in a clean, neat, and precise manner—that is really important.*

Yet even though the work was satisfying, it was onerous and stressful: *My partner and I have been working very hard in this period. I've been going to work at seven in the morning for the past seven months. At noon, sometimes I eat, sometimes I don't, because I have so much to do, and I have to consign the work at two or two-thirty. Sometimes I don't even eat, or other times I take ten or fifteen minutes to grab something, no more. I work until eight or eight thirty in the evening, and so I'm putting in my thirteen hours, continuous hours, and it is really tiring. Moreover, our work is stressful—not physically but psychologically and mentally. You always have to work with precision, under a lamp, with every-thing in miniature dimensions. In short, you've got to be really exact and careful, and so it is very wearing. You reach the evening and you are destroyed, psycholog-ically exhausted.*

Sandro, like most men, felt responsible for the material well-being of his family: *Why do I work so hard? First of all, because I like it. I like it, but further-more, nowadays if you have work, you better keep it. There is the economic di-mension. Because I'm young, I have a lot of expenses, the house, everything. In short, we need the money. . . . I want to save money to be able to affront any nega-tive situations—that's my idea. However, it's not that I can put away very much, because we still have a lot of expenses for the house and the car. If one day I have a more tranquil economic position, well, maybe then I will try to dedicate myself to having more fun. But for now, I don't feel I can do it; sometimes I just don't have the energy to have fun.*

However, even though he was stressed from the long hours, he enjoyed what he was doing: *The work gives me not only economic satisfaction, but cre-ative satisfaction as well. I think doing work you love that you have studied to learn is the maximum. Having a job you choose yourself and do willingly—that's the best. So even if I have had to make sacrifices in the beginning to get started, still I find myself well off. I have made the sacrifices willingly because I like the work.* Sandro encapsulated the burdens and benefits for a man from the cul-tural division of labor that imposed hard work to support the family but en-abled him to have a job he liked and eschew household chores.

Sandro strongly supported his wife working: *I want my wife to have her own independence, and to have her independence it always goes back to the fact that she needs to have a job. It's a wheel that turns, no? And you never find a way out. This is important to me, because when my father died, my mother didn't have a job, and she found herself in dire straits—she had nothing. But if she had had a job, she wouldn't have had to go and ask for money from my uncle. That was trou-blesome even though he helped us willingly. For this reason, I would like my wife to have her own independence.* Caterina did work, but, like many women, she earned less than her husband, which had implications for economic power in the household.

Sandro described their financial arrangements: *Here's how we do the family budget. I'm in charge of what I earn and I don't ask Caterina for anything. . . . She administers her own income, but clearly she puts a certain amount into the household and food expenses. Then I take care of everything else. For example, we're about to go on vacation—I'll pay for that. I pay our condominium expenses, the telephone, gas, furniture—all the other household expenses. I don't say this to brag about myself, but clearly the salary that Caterina can earn as a cashier is very different from what I earn. So, logically, I have greater possibility to take care of the many expenses we have incurred in setting up the house—all because of the luck I have had in being able to go into business on my own. Nevertheless, I do rec-*

ognize that the $750 a month that my wife earns is very useful. I make between $1,600 and $3,000 a month, usually around $2,000 a month more or less, sometimes $3,000—it depends. As in many Italian households, the husband made a significantly higher salary than his wife. Because Sandro's work was better paid and he worked longer hours, he was able to repudiate domestic chores.

Gender and Work in the Household

The imbalance in earning power between Caterina and Sandro complicated their efforts to manage their household. They were well on their way to being *sistemati*—"set up." They rented a two-bedroom apartment from Sandro's uncle that overlooked a busy *piazza* in Scandicci, a small town west of Florence that had been subsumed into its urban sprawl. The apartment was noisy because there was a bar below it, and the ear-splitting buzz of motorbikes— many without mufflers—pierced the apartment day and night. However, it was spacious and full of light, and given the scarcity and expense of housing in Florence, Caterina and Sandro felt lucky to have it.

Caterina worked in a supermarket far from her home in Scandicci, but near her mother's place in the *Isolotto* neighborhood of Florence. Since she usually worked the *orario spezzato* (discontinuous workday) from 8 A.M. to 1 P.M. and 5 to 8 P.M., she had lunch at her mother's and stayed there to rest during the break. Sandro also worked near *L'Isolotto*, so he either ate at Valeria's, or Caterina brought him lunch. Sandro and Caterina both worked long days, leaving home early in the morning and not returning until 9 or 9:30 at night, still needing dinner. They received a great deal of help from both of their mothers, but still felt extremely stressed and without adequate time for housework or recreation. They confronted challenges and conflicts around the housework as the following exchange reveals:

Sandro: *Look, I like to have a neat house, but I don't want to become a slave to it. I mean if the bed is unmade, let it be for one day, two days; we'll get around to it.*

Caterina: *Look, all men are like him. Okay, there are a few who are more inclined to helping. My uncle Raffaele always does the cooking.*

Sandro: *Okay, I agree. He always does the cooking; however, he never washes a single dish. Tell the truth.*

Caterina: *He has always done the cooking.*

Sandro: *Caterina, you hinder people. A person does it once, twice, and you always have to follow behind cleaning up after him.*

Caterina: *Listen, there never was a third time.*

Sandro: *Okay, there never was a third time, but I washed the dishes twice—*

Caterina: *I don't remember the second time. . . .*

Caterina and Sandro expressed tensions over the housework because they had different standards of neatness and different expectations of their roles due to their gender socialization. They articulated a picture of impossible resolution. Caterina explained her point of view: *My husband is never home. He works all day long. When he gets home, honestly, to ask him to help me cook, what am I going to say?* "Help me fry this minute steak (**braciola**)." *No, if I were cooking great things, I would say,* "Give me a hand." *But to ask someone to help me cook a minute steak seems absurd; in short, it borders on the absurd. So I certainly do not ask him to help me cook a minute steak.* She was reluctant to ask for help because she felt her own efforts were so modest.

A second problem was Caterina's high standard of cleanliness. She said, *I'm the type that nobody pleases the way I please myself. In fact, one time Sandro washed the dishes, and when he was done I went in and checked the job, and he said,* "That's it. I won't wash the dishes anymore for you." *Because, he said,* "I can't please you no matter what." *In truth, I am really exacting, and he knows it. He did a good job too, you know; it's not that he did anything wrong. Knowing me, he tried to do his best; however, he is more careless by nature. . . . I like my own precision.* Interestingly, Caterina complained that Sandro could not meet her standards of neatness in the house, but he spoke of how *clean, neat, and precise* he was in his dental work.

Clearly, precision was not sex linked, yet Sandro did not bring his precision home—both for lack of training and lack of inclination, both of which most women had and most men did not. This emerged in Sandro's discussion of his efforts to wash dishes: *Let me tell you this story. In the early days of our marriage, I went in to wash the dishes. Logically, I did it the way I knew how, and, of course, as far as I have ever known, there are always splashes of water when you wash the dishes; at least I don't know how not to make them. I sincerely washed the dishes as best I could with my limited experience—I don't have a degree in it, after all. Well, I washed everything, but she didn't like how I did it. She didn't like it once; she didn't like it twice; well, now I just go and watch television while she does it. I mean it was absurd.*

Because his male socialization gave Sandro neither domestic skill nor motivation, he used Caterina's criticism as a justification for no longer trying. She articulated the stresses coming from their different socialization: *Look, when I do the cleaning, I do it right. Rest assured that if I clean the bathroom, I clean it so that there is not even one hair on the floor. But then maybe five minutes later Sandro arrives, and bam, he goes into the bathroom and leaves the whole sink dirty. All he did was wash his hands. Madonna, that makes me angry! So then I say,* "How is it possible? I washed the bathroom yesterday evening. We're only the two of us and we're hardly ever at home and yet the bathroom is already dirty. What will people think?" *Is it possible that in the morning he shaves and then I find the sink full of hairs? It makes me furious. However, understand, it is due to habit. The men have been raised in a certain way. . . .*

Oh, he's not one of those men who come and check on you and say, "Oh, Caterina, the bed needs to be made." *If the bed isn't made when he comes home, he doesn't say a thing. It bothers me more than him, because for God's sake, if people come over and the bed isn't made, it looks bad. . . . So I do the work; I make the bed. I don't want to appear disorderly. But if it were up to him, he wouldn't see anything. He wouldn't say anything. But it's my cognition that says, "Friends are coming over." Our friends are young people like us, but it still bothers me if the house is a mess. Why? Maybe because I've been conditioned. Furthermore, don't think that our friends will say, "But look at these two, they still haven't made the bed at nine in the evening." No, they say, "Look at her. She is a real slob. She left the bed unmade." That is how it is. Rest assured that if people come over to the house, it's not the man who sees the bed unmade. The woman sees it—for example, my mother, or Sandro's mother.*

My mother comes over and says, "Oh, the house! You left the bed unmade." Or else, "There's a mess of stuff all over the place." Understand? They don't say anything to him. They say it to me. I'm the one who looks bad. Nobody says anything to him. That's why it bothers me, understand? But also, sincerely, I don't like leaving the bed unmade either.

Caterina complained that cultural expectations placed on her all the burdens for keeping the house in order and all the opprobrium for its imperfections. This made it very difficult for Sandro and her to change: *I don't think it is possible in our relationship to divide up the household tasks more equitably. Because I'm the type, I repeat it, who is only satisfied by myself. I like the way I do the housework. Sure, you might satisfy me too; however, I have to tell you how to do it. If not, you won't satisfy me, and I'll redo the whole thing later because I won't like it. . . . I want it done right, understand? I am just too picky when I do my housework. He's more laid-back about the house. If I'm going to ask him to do things, I have to accept what he does. . . . I can't tell him how to do it, because then he says, "If you don't like how I do it, do it yourself." But look, men just aren't used to doing housework. Sure, there are those like my uncle Raffaele who has always done the cooking. There are some men who like to cook or do other things, but there are those who are the complete negation. And if a man is completely inept at cooking, you just can't say to him, "Go on and cook."*

Like many women, Caterina made excuses for her husband not helping on the grounds of incompetence, but nonetheless she resented doing all the housework: *Sometimes we argue and I say to him, "I'm fed up. I'm not your servant." I say to myself, "What am I? Am I a servant?" I'll tell you, we women wanted sexual equality (**la parità dei sessi**), but we have lost out. Because, listen, sexual equality does not exist. If I'm at work and I ask male coworkers, "Help me lift this weight," they say, "But didn't you want sexual equality? Well, then, my friend, you have to do it yourself." Understand? Every time you ask them something, they throw sexual equality into your face. Sexual equality—what is it? In the meantime, you see it at home, the men doing nothing as if they have better things to do.*

With these words, Caterina expressed the Italian situation so well defined by Passerini (1996b), who said that in the 1970s Italy moved toward formal public equity, but male privilege persisted in the household. Caterina went on:

Unfortunately, today the situation of the man is much more favorable than that of the woman. We wanted sexual equality, but things have gotten worse, not better. We haven't improved, because, look, we do all the same things that men do; at least I try to do them. However, it's not like the men try to do our work. It's rare that you find men who do the laundry or dust the house. They leave the dusting and they don't give a damn about it. If there's a soccer game on television, try to tell a man that the coffee is boiling over. He doesn't give a damn because he wants to watch the game. He says he works, that he's tired too, and with this he has done his part. I want to say that even if the woman is tired too, unfortunately, unless there is a cleaning woman, one of the two has to get busy on the cleaning unless you want to find yourself buried by dirt.

Caterina wanted sexual equality but excused men from fully helping because of incompetence. Her husband Sandro was ambivalent because he wanted Caterina to work and he knew he should help in the home, but lacked motivation: *I sincerely don't have much desire to cook, especially when I get home so late and so tired. At the beginning of the marriage, I enjoyed cooking, but then I'd get home and wouldn't find some necessary ingredients like the* **odori,** *and the stores would be closed, and so I couldn't make what I wanted. I got discouraged. In fact, it's easy to discourage me from cooking—it doesn't take much.*

However, I don't demand a lot from Caterina. Sure, I admit that we men are sometimes selfish in regard to women, because this is the way it has always been— it's useless to deny it. Maybe some day this will disappear, but for now there is still a difference between men and women. This is the way we grew up. Clearly, we still have a different mentality about doing things. We think that women have to do this, men that. However, for better or worse, I try to be as little burden as possible. Sincerely, though, there are things that I really don't think men have the aptitude to do. For me personally, if I had to iron, for God's sake, I wouldn't know how to do it. Maybe in case of need, yes, I would learn to manage. Oh, I know that women were not born ironing; it is our mentality. Although a generation or two younger than the older men cited in Chapter 5 who "*just could not do*" housework, Sandro echoed their words.

Sandro claimed the right to work less at home than Caterina because he felt he was working far harder outside the home and was producing more money, which they both spent: *Listen, for me this is the issue. It is true that we both work. However, for better or worse, I work a great deal. I work thirteen hours a day. Caterina works eight. If you are looking for equality, if we must have equality, okay, but then I want to say let's look at things all the way through. All right, it's true that I don't iron, but for heavens sake, I return home in the evening, and I am completely worn out. My wife is exhausted too, I agree. However, think about it carefully. She maybe had a chance to sleep for three hours during the afternoon, something I didn't have. Maybe she is less tired than me. When I get home, after dinner, I am completely depleted, truly worn out. . . .*

Listen, if I were working my eight hours, distributed any way you want over the day—however, only eight hours—I would be able to rest during the day and thus have more energy in the evening. If that were the case, then I would be a jerk if I didn't help at home. However, I sincerely don't feel inside myself that I am a jerk. I don't feel like a jerk, because sometimes I go off to work at seven in the morning and leave Caterina still asleep, understand? In short, if you want equality in a relationship, you have to look at everything. You can't say that two people have to do the same things at home when maybe one is half dead because he worked like a dog and the other maybe returned at six much less tired. No, that doesn't seem right to me. . . .

I have tried to explain this to Caterina—it's not like I'm working only for myself; I'm working for both of us. It's not like I take the extra money I earn and spend it all on myself. I put the money between the two of us and we chose together a certain lifestyle. If we want to go on vacation, if we want to buy a new car, for God's sake, it's not only for me, but for both of us. . . . I'm saying that if I work fourteen hours a day and I come home tired, I'm doing it for her also. I've had some arguments with Caterina about this. She says, "Give me a hand." What's this, "Give me a hand?" The other day I got angry. I'm fairly even-tempered, but then I just explode. What's right is right. If you want equal rights, that's fine with me. I'll work my eight hours like you and we'll earn what comes, and that will be the end of it. She talks, but then she likes to go into a store and spend a lot of money to buy herself an outfit. I don't mind; I'm glad she does it, but I would never spend three or four hundred dollars on an outfit. If she wants to spend money that way, fine, but she has to accept that if I am killing myself at work, I am doing it for her too. If she wants equality, that's fine with me, but be careful about what you ask for, in short.

Look, if I worked less, I would help my wife when I came home. Clearly I don't know how much I could help her, but I would surely give her a hand. That's completely fine with me. I would be happy to do it. . . . However, if some days we don't make the bed, then we don't make the bed—that's how I am. If I have to go out or if someone is coming over and the bed isn't made, I don't give a damn. But Caterina flips out. For me, that is absurd. Take the bathroom—yes, I agree, it has to be clean. You will say that I should clean it. I am perfectly in agreement about this too. But Christ, this is the problem. For my wife, the bathroom is filthy if there is one hair out of place. It's absurd, understand? If I clean something, she comes to see if it is clean enough and she goes over it again. At that point I say, why in the world am I doing it?

Sandro and Caterina revealed the challenges of managing housework. It was still perceived to be women's job, by women as well as by men. At best, men were beginning to think they should "help," yet the young men had not been raised to do housework, and most were awkward and incompetent. Raffaele spoke of his son Piero in Tuscan slang: ***Non fa una sega nulla in casa***—*he doesn't do a darn thing around the house.* Piero believed that *sexual equality is just,* but he just could not bring himself to do housework. His sister Piera commented: *My brother doesn't lift a finger in the house. He's worse than the majority of men. I don't know why, but I think it's a question of character. If he finds something on the ground, it's not that he lowers himself to pick it up; he leaves it there; he passes over it. Piero is disordered. He's been accustomed badly. It comes perhaps from us, my mother and me, who are always behind him picking things up for him. Because if we left it there, maybe, sooner or later, he would pick it up. But my mother is always ready, always behind him doing every little thing that he could do himself.*

Piera contrasted male and female socialization: *It's different with me. I'm not saying this out of jealousy, but for me it's different, because I'm a girl, I'm a woman. If I see something out of place, I am supposed to put it away. But instead, if Piero finds something out of place, it is not important for him to put it away, because there is always my mother and I to do it. In Italy we think that it's the women's job to do the housework, and so my parents raised me to help at an early age. I would feel badly if I didn't know how to do the housework. It's always good to know how to do it. In fact, I think that it is an instinct we women have—when we see disorder, we straighten it up. It always comes back to the fact that we do it. We don't give it a lot of weight. We don't push very hard against it—we're not there yet. We might think about protesting our burden, but then the idea passes and we do what we have to do.*

Piera knew that women were complicit in men's not helping and she used deterministic language in explaining women's assumption of housework as an "*instinct.*" She was not optimistic about changes: *If I have a son, I hope to raise him to do a little more than my brother. I hope, but then you never know. You have to be there. It is difficult to raise a child. There are so many responsibilities. We could raise our sons to do as much as our daughters, but we don't. We could surely do it; however, in one way or another, the chores always fall back on the women. I hope my generation will change, and I will certainly try, but I don't know what the results will be, because, you know, they are changes that come slowly, slowly.*

While Piera hoped for changes, she feared that her fiancé would give little help: *My fiancé Andrea doesn't know how to cook, nor does he do housework, no, no, no, no. It will fall to me (toccherà a me). Then if I need help, he will surely help me. He will help me make the beds, but for the rest, it's not that he will do many other things.* Piera was prepared to be *sacrificata* like generations of women before her: *I will manage as so many other women do. Here we're all idiots about housework. We're like donkeys on Saturday morning doing the cleaning. The men don't manage to help; they don't want to help. Women do the housework, even if they don't want to, out of pride, stupid pride. The men grumble at the women if the bathroom is dirty, but it's not like they go and clean it. It's a question of masculine pride—they can't lower themselves to do certain things. That's what needs to be overcome. It is tradition that we women have to do the work and the men just sit and watch. They talk about sexual equality, but in my opinion we haven't reached even a tiny bit of it—very, very little.*

All of my subjects' words revealed how deeply entrenched gender notions were around housework and how they impeded changes toward greater gender equality. Twenty-one-year-old Arturo and his fiancée Maria encountered the same deep gender stereotypes. Twenty-two-year-old Maria said, *When I get married, I think that I'll be doing the housework, with a little help from Arturo. I hope he'll help. My father was the type who didn't do anything in the house. But I think sometimes it depends on the couple. If you have a husband who isn't a really strong egotist, you must make him understand certain things. I hope I can do it with Arturo. Based on going camping together, so far I can say that I think he will help me. He might wash the dishes if I grumble at him a lot. He's not used to helping. Maybe he can change; however, it is always harder to change someone who is not used to helping. I know I can't pretend that he will do all kinds of housework, that no. But at least I can hope that he knows how to cook.*

Maria was prepared to get little domestic assistance from her fiancé Arturo, and he admitted to a lack of motivation: *When it comes to dividing the household chores between me and Maria, I think it's a question of desire. If I get the desire to do something, I do it; however, I don't know if the chores will be shared or if it will fall to her to do more than to me (**toccherà a fare più a lei che a me**). Sincerely it could be that more will fall to her than to me.*

*It doesn't seem right to me. I'm wrong to say it's not right but to accept it; however, that's how it is. It's stronger than me (**è più forte di me**). Oh, maybe she lacks the desire too, but she will do it because it has to be done. Just as I like to sit and relax, surely she would like to do the same. So let's hope that I change. When I'm at my mother's, I don't help, because there are so many people to help, so many women. So out of my egotism, I say there are others, so I don't get up to help. This too is wrong. It's my male chauvinism (**maschilismo**).*

Arturo named his attitude and privilege **maschilismo** and attributed it to his mother's socialization of gender in the family, which was deeply embedded in cultural traditions: *My mother used to tell me to help; however, she never said it with conviction. Growing up, my sister Caterina had to help clean, and she had to do more things in the house than I did, from when we were little. Maybe my mother told me to do things; however, she said it with less conviction—that was the important thing. . . . Maybe my mother lacked conviction with me because she grew up in different times from me. When she was my age, no one spoke of having the boys wash dishes or help with the cooking. There were different ideas than there are today. Today things are changing, but it depends on the character of the people. If people understand that it is right for the couple to divide the chores equally and not have them all done by the woman, things will change. But I think that there are more men who prefer to have their wives do the household chores than there are men who share them. I think today is a little soon for change, but at least we have begun. But the old habits of having the women do things die hard,* *because today's young people grew up seeing their mothers do everything, and their mothers grew up with the habits of the older people.*

Arturo recognized that cultural conditioning rather than nature defined gender roles, and this kind of conditioning was difficult to change: *I don't think there is any difference between men and women. I will try to educate my children to think it is normal to help out, as normal as putting on their shoes. I will try to teach them to understand this better than I have understood it, even if it is difficult. I'll have to show them different habits, and this will mean a maturation for me in the sense that I too will have to do household chores. Before educating my children, I will have to educate myself a little more. However, I think that the time will come when we have our own house, our own separate life, and I will try to adapt. It will surely be a battle. I am used to leaving my clothes all over the place and finding them put away. Instead, I will have to try to put my own things away so as not to leave everything a mess. Right now, I don't feel the need to do it, probably because of the environment. But when I become a real husband, maybe I will feel a greater responsibility and maybe I will understand these things better, but for now I'm still just a boy.*

Arturo's' words reflected the difficulty of giving up the privilege of domestic service: *I think it's a mistake of the parents to spoil the children. If they get used to finding everything already done, the clothes put away, the food cooked, the dishes washed, they get used to finding everything nice and ready, and it's a struggle to change later. I think the majority of children who live with their parents are spoiled and they will continue not to help if they can get away with it. It's not that a man doesn't know how to wash his underpants—I think he isn't used to washing his underpants. However, if you make him wash his underpants, he will wash them, just like a woman washes them. It's a fact of habit. It's how we are raised. I think a man can do as much as a woman, but if there is someone who helps him, well, then, I think he is more willing to let someone else do it. He's more likely to avoid the chores.*

Forty-year-old Leonardo suggested that women were purposefully complicit in men's incompetence: *Maybe this is a strategy by woman to make sure that men need the women—among many hypotheses. Because if not, then why do the women stand for it? This is perhaps one of the many links that might be at work. "Un uomo solo"—"a man alone," yes, my father says it so many times, "A man alone, what does he do, a man alone?"*

Leonardo suggested that there was a balance of mutual need in the old ways, but as the women forged on, the men did not: *Women's liberation has not been answered with men's liberation. It is a huge problem. There hasn't been on men's side a corresponding effort. For men it was an opposite journey; they had to enter the home, not leave it as women had to do. Men had to enter and take on certain burdens—those that have to do with the condition of the home, of the family, all these things that of course have to be done. Italian men have done very, very few of these jobs. These are problems for our generation, for the famous **com-***

*pagni, the comrades in struggle, who raised a ruckus at the university, who partic-
ipated in the student movement, and so on, but then once they were married, they
discovered that they were no longer comrades but antagonists in a certain sense.*[2]
*Why? Because the women found themselves always bearing a greater burden. And
the men resisted; the Italian men resisted. I don't know why they resist, but in my
opinion it is really a question of internal education, of thinking that these things
don't have any value, that doing them is a waste of time. Why should I wash my
socks? No one values these tasks really, when instead, in my opinion, they have a
value, but it is only that they belong to a different sphere, not to that public sphere
where men are used to maneuvering, but to an internal sphere, internal to the
couple.*

In 2003, however, there were clear signs that men were shouldering more of
the household burdens than Italian men had ever done in the past. Even Arturo, although he still did not cook, said that he did dishes and helped with
other chores. One university student who lived in an apartment with two
males and two females said, "All of us do the cleaning and the cooking." Several
other students reported that males cooked often, and some even did dishes as
well. One student said that in regard to the domestic chores, "everyone, regardless of sex or age, gives a hand." Of course, it is one thing to cooperate in a student apartment, another to buck cultural conditioning in a traditional
marriage.

There was evidence in 2003 that Italian men were becoming more involved
with fathering, after decades of being largely absent from hands-on child care.
Law 53, passed in 2000, granted parental leave to fathers and mothers for up to
six months during the first eight years of the child's life, with fathers eligible for
an extra month as an incentive. If the leave was taken in the first three years of
the baby's life, parents received 30 percent of their salary. In the old days, the
term used for a man who cared for children was *mammo,* an "almost insulting"
term that defined fathers as derivative of mothers (Cavallieri 2003). In 2003,
men in Italy still expected that work outside the home was their main role. In
one study, they were found to be "the least collaborative" husbands in Europe,
and Italian women to be the busiest, working outside and inside the home an
average of eleven hours per day. For men to do full-time fathering, even if only
for a few months, they had to radically change their self-expectations and
habits. Yet because there were few models for engaged modern fathering in Italy,
men ran into prejudice, feelings of inadequacy, and ambivalence from women
about relinquishing power over children's upbringing (Cavallieri 2003).

Youth and Changing Cuisine

Because men were reluctant to help around the house and with child care,
there was a real strain on working women—the strain to get everything done
that Caterina and Sandro spoke about previously. Inevitably this strain
affected cuisine, as the following comments by twenty-two-year-old Maria

showed: *I don't cook often, but when I set myself to it, I like it; I like it. It's not that I follow recipes very much; however, I like to experiment on my own. Usually it comes out pretty well. I haven't watched my mother cooking very much because I've always been at school or work. I don't shop for her because I'm not really familiar with her foods and I won't satisfy her. But I go to the supermarket, look around, and get some ideas and buy these little things that maybe my father doesn't eat. He eats foods that don't change, so it's best if my mother does the shopping.* Maria did not shop at the neighborhood stores that her mother frequented and was unfamiliar with the subtleties of choosing the right cut of meat for the traditional recipes her father preferred. She and other young people like her favored supermarkets over small specialty stores.

The changes in shopping paralleled changes in cuisine. Maria said, *I like many processed foods, canned foods. That's what I eat when I don't feel like cooking anything. I eat **sofficini**—frozen pastry turnovers, and **bastoncini**—frozen fish sticks.[3] If I were to cook, I would make different dishes from my mother. I would avoid the boiled dishes—**lesso** (inexpensive meat for boiling), **zampa** (foot)—those are things I would never make, for sure. I don't like them and I only eat them at home because my mother makes them. If I'm making **pastasciutta**, sometimes I buy ready-made pesto sauce and dress the spaghetti with that. I like to make not just a tomato sauce, but I always add some cream, some hot pepper, or some cheese if I have some, or processed cheese slices (**sottilette**). I melt them and eat them with the spaghetti.*

Maria ate and cooked processed foods that older people disdained, and her recipes deviated from the **cucina casalinga** of her mother and mother-in-law: *I like to make **spaghetti con panna e pomodoro** (spaghetti with cream and tomato). You put some **pomarola** (tomato sauce) into a pan. I usually use the sauce my mother puts up, but if not, I buy ready-made **pomarola** sauce at the COOP supermarket. I put it in a pan with a little olive oil or butter, depending, and I put in right away some **peperoncino** so that it starts boiling and gives up its flavor to the sauce. When it is well seasoned, I stir some cream into it. Sometimes I use basil, which gives it a different taste, or else ginger (**zenzero**), which makes it have a bite. Or else mushrooms. If we have some dried mushrooms in the house, I soak them, I sauté them, and I add them to the **pomarola** and cream sauce. Or else without tomato, just cream and mushrooms and olive oil or butter. We call sauce made with cream, **peperoncino**, and tomato: **sugo rosé***—pink sauce. Look, in my house, my mother either makes meat sauce or else tomato sauce, but ever since I started eating tomato with cream, tomato alone doesn't seem to have much flavor.*

Maria described significant changes in cuisine. She used new and processed ingredients like cream, processed cheese slices, and ready-made spaghetti sauces. She bought **pomarola,** the most basic tomato sauce, or used her mother's, but did not make it herself. Caterina did the same: *Do I know how to make **pomarola**? Listen, we made it one year when we were camping—a friend* *and I. However, if I had to say that I was going to make a **pomarola** now, I wouldn't know how. Sincerely, if my mother doesn't give me some **pomarola** to take home, then I buy it ready-made. I don't make meat sauce either, because it's too much bother to make just for two people. It's more likely that we eat spaghetti with cream and ham—**spaghetti con panna e prosciutto***—than with meat sauce, understand? I like spaghetti with cream or with pomarola and cream— **sugo rosé***—or with garlic and hot pepper—**spaghetti aglio olio e peperon- cino***—or with four cheeses—**spaghetti ai quattro formaggi***; and other things like this that maybe come from cookbooks and aren't based on home cooking. But **pomarola**, I never make it. I don't know how.* In contrast to what her uncle Raf- faele said in Chapter 2, **pomarola** was not always **pomarola** in Caterina's life. Like her future sister-in-law Maria, she did not produce the home cooking (*la cucina casalinga*) that she ate at her mother's, but introduced new, high-fat milk products and processed foods.

This was partly because Caterina did not learn Tuscan home cooking: *I don't know how to cook very well. When I lived at home and my mother cooked, I never wanted to watch her. She was ready to teach me, but I really wasn't at all in- terested. I always thought I would have plenty of time to learn. Now if I want to make something—a chicken dish, for example—I take my cooking encyclopedia and I look up a recipe, and if I have the necessary ingredients, I try to make it. I like to experiment and cook new things, but only when I have the time.*

Caterina was attracted to culinary innovation, but lack of time hindered her efforts in the kitchen: *I would love to have time to cook, to dedicate myself to it. But I realize that I am never home. When I get home in the evening, it's late, and even if I wanted to make something good to eat, to experiment, I don't have time. I'd love to make a dessert, a pie, but I'm tired in the evening, and by the time I get home, it's too late. Sometimes I realize that I would like to stay at home and have the liberty to say, "Today I feel like making this; I'm going to make it." Instead, I don't have this liberty, because I'm not here in the daytime, and when I get home, it's late. If I fuss around very long in the kitchen, it's eleven o'clock or midnight before we eat. You can't eat that late, because afterwards you go to bed and you feel sick; you don't digest your food. Then, of course, after making dinner, I have to clean up the house. In short, there are still so many things left to do. So I realize that my situation is not wonderful.*

Caterina appreciated home cooking, but working made it difficult: *If you compare the cooking of a working woman to the cooking of the woman who stays home, in my opinion the latter's is much better. I would go eat with the housewife. It's not that I have anything against the working woman, because sure, she might cook really well too; however, it's a more rapid cooking. The housewife can say, "We'll eat at eight," and set herself in the kitchen at seven to take her time and prepare everything. . . . But the working woman arrives home and takes whatever she has at hand that's quick and throws something together. This has an effect on the family diet, of course. Take, for example, **melanzane alla parmigiana**—egg- plant Parmesan—if I don't eat it at my mother's, I'm not going to eat it at all. I* *don't have time to make it—get the eggplant, slice it, salt it, drain it, fry it. Then I have to make the sauce, put the eggplant in the sauce, and cook it in the oven. How long would it take? When would I do it? So if I feel like eating it, I either buy it ready-made or I eat it at my mother's. Sure, it could happen that on my day off I make it, but when I have a day off, I have so many other things to do.* Caterina did not have time to cook, had not learned from her mother because she was always too busy, cooked faster new recipes that she learned from cookbooks, used processed ingredients, and ate out often.

She sacrificed cuisine to keep her job: *I would be sorry to leave my job, because I think that a woman too should have her independence and her own activity. However, I realize that mine is a situation that doesn't work. I get home at nine, and even if I'm tired, I still have to cook. I absolutely can't put only a sandwich on the table. Better to go and eat at a* pizzeria; *at least then we can choose what we want and it's all ready and we eat better. It's not right that we live a life like this—a life full of sacrifices. Our life consists only of work, and we don't even have time to enjoy this thing or to eat that thing, because we reach home exhausted and still with so much to do.*

Caterina's cousin Piera also prioritized work outside the home over passing time in the kitchen. When I asked her what she knew about cooking, she said, *Nothing. I am the desperation of my father. I will learn when I apply myself to it. . . . I see what my parents do, and if I were home alone, I too would cook, but if I had to put myself to cooking out of pure desire, I'd never do it.* Changes in cuisine were inevitably deriving from the changes in the household economy and especially the fact that women were working outside the home and had less time for and interest in cooking.

The younger males preferred the home cooking of their mothers, but they recognized that change was inevitable and that their girlfriends and wives were not the cooks their mothers were. Twenty-one-year-old Arturo said, *I don't really like processed foods. I really like the traditional cooking that my mother makes at the stove. But I think that we will tend increasingly towards these half-cooked foods, these processed foods, for reasons of time.*

Twenty-five-year-old Piero was working two jobs and thought he and his future wife would have to manage somehow: *I'm convinced that if I get married, we will both work. So we'll have to look at how much time we have. If I have little time—for example, if I keep working my afternoon job as well as my morning job—she will cook. If she is busy all day, I will do it. If not, we won't eat or we will go out to a restaurant every day. But that doesn't seem normal to me, and furthermore, it costs a lot and it means you're never home.* Even though he knew times were changing, he did not welcome the demise of home cooking.

While Piero was speculating about what his future might be like after he married, his cousin-in-law Sandro spoke about the challenges to working couples from experience: *Having a wife that works influences the eating regimen at home. If you have the possibility of having a wife who doesn't work, I think you can ask for something more in the meals, no? But if you have a wife who works, you always have the minute steaks, the* **bracioline**—*more often than not, it's minute steaks. I accept the minute steaks. I accept them willingly—it's not that I make a big deal about eating them. If one day we have minute steaks with mushrooms, so much the better. If it is Caterina's day off, maybe she sets herself to cooking, but she's not really into it. And when we get home at nine or nine-thirty in the evening, as I already told you, there isn't much time for cooking.* Sandro loved his mother-in-law Valeria's home cooking, but somewhat begrudgingly was willing to accept a lesser and more modern cuisine typified by the ubiquitous, quick-fried thin slices of beef called **braciole** or **bracioline.**

Young couples faced a dilemma in the 1980s to which *it will be difficult to find a solution*, said Piera. With women working outside the home, the household chores had to be reduced, and one important way was by streamlining cooking. They ate more processed foods and more one-course meals, and ate out more often at quick restaurants like **pizzerie, spaghetterie, birrerie,** and **rosticcerie,** featuring pizza, spaghetti, beer, and quick foods like cold cuts, sandwiches, roasted meat, and cooked vegetables. Eating out introduced them to new foods. As twenty-one-year-old Piero said, *At the* **spaghetteria** *they make spaghetti with crabmeat, with shrimp, with spinach, with salmon and cream. They make simple dishes that take little time, because they can't be there doing really complicated things. But they are dishes that I don't eat at home. When I eat out, I usually order something different, because, for example, if I ordered spaghetti with* **pomarola** *sauce, I wouldn't like it there, because I like how we have it at home.* Due to lack of time, the **cucina casalinga** based on complex meals with a **primo** of pasta or soup and a **secondo** of meat and vegetables was becoming more rare, and dining on quick pastas, processed foods, and new ingredients was increasing.

Women were cooking less, but they still felt that cooking was essential to their identity as women. Men and women were talking about inaugurating greater sexual equality in the home but had not reached it. Men were able to feel fully men simply by working outside the home, but women were in deep conflict between their traditional role of housewife and their modern role as salaried worker. They eased this conflict by relying on their parents, especially their mothers, to help with meals, domestic chores, and children. Raffaele cooked for Piero and Piera, and their mother did all their washing and ironing. Even after Caterina and Sandro married and moved to their own apartment, they continued to eat with their natal families for most of their meals. Caterina's mother and mother-in-law helped with her washing and mending, and both were prepared to help care for eventual grandchildren. Many Italian couples were reducing family size, and Italy has the lowest birthrate in the world.[4] It remains to be seen if my younger subjects raised their children to share household chores and pave the way toward maintenance of traditional diets by forging new gender balances.

10
Conclusion:
Molto, Ma Buono?

Foodways in the New Millennium

In the last chapter, six younger Florentines spoke about gender and food in the 1980s and gave an idea of where things were headed. The quality of the diet was changing along with content of meals, habits of eating, and meanings of consumption. In this final chapter, I summarize Florentines' perspectives on changing cuisine in the 1980s and place them in the context of foodways in the new millennium. Older people particularly emphasized three major changes: abundance, taking consumption for granted, and the loss of desire due to excess. I suggest that these changes could be summarized as a movement from *poco ma buono*—"only a little, but let it be good"—to *molto, ma buono?*—"a lot, but is it good?"

My subjects felt that it was important to talk about the transformation from *miseria* (poverty) to *benessere* (well-being) and to keep cultural memories alive. Baldo commented: *Oh, things are very different today. I think we parents should have talked more to our children about how things were in the past. They only know the improvements of today. . . . Yes, I think we should have told our children more about how things used to be, just as my father did for me. Many times my father said, "As a young peasant, I had to go 7 kilometers to get to work and 7 to return home. And do you know what I had in my lunch box? I had a piece of cold polenta, and that was all. They had rubbed it with a piece of herring, but the herring wasn't there, just the faintest flavor of it, and that was all. Maybe we had a half a glass of wine and some bread, and we had to make do with that." I hardly believed him, but in short, it was the truth.*

From "**polenta** to crackers" (Sorcinelli 1998), from *baccalà* to *bastoncini* (dried cod to fish sticks), the Florentine diet reflected the social and economic changes of the twentieth century, whose meaning and value were contested, as seventy-five-year-old Massimo suggested: *As I look back on my life, I see sacrifices, sacrifices. I was always working. I had to work so much. But the old days were better than today, first of all because we were younger, we were healthier, even if we ate less. But we were more tranquil. Today there are more worries, worries about the end. We have a great deal of well-being today. We have food, we have clothes, we have everything. . . . Well, let's hope for the best. It seems to me that it's like when you go up a staircase, you go up and you go up, and when you reach the top, either* *you go back down or you hit the ceiling—am I right? Well, that's the way it is today. Up until now, we have always gone up, ever higher, ever higher, always doing better. When we reach the top of this staircase, what will we do?*

Abundance, Variety, and Surfeit

Massimo's rising staircase was a good metaphor for the most important trend in twentieth-century Italian foodways: overcoming the persistent hunger, malnutrition, and privation that plagued Italy's masses for millennia (Zamagni 1998, 203). At the end of the century, economic development meant that most Italians lived with a greater amount and variety of foods than they had even dreamed of in the first half of the century. Fifty-four-year-old Baldo described how the increase in material well-being affected his diet: *I've learned to eat dishes that my mother never cooked. Of course, she never made chicken breasts in white wine! Of course, she never made stuffed roast chicken—forget it! You have to value the foods of the time. Today, we are able to spend more than in the old days. No matter what you say, it revolves around money. There were tortellini in the old days, but today, we say, "Let's have tortellini with cream sauce." This came later, because in the old days, first of all, you had to buy the tortellini and then think about the cream and the sauce. It just didn't happen. For me, there is economic progress that has changed things. Families passed from one economy to another more affluent one.*

Along with affluence, according to Baldo, came the loss of longing replaced by nostalgia, and the depletion of pleasure: *Maybe we appreciated food more in the old days than now, because today we have no desire for anything. We reach the holidays, and, yes, we have our traditional foods, but we eat these same foods so many times during the year. How many times do we eat these things—chicken, special desserts, either made at home or purchased in the store? Who even dreamed of these things in the old days?* Baldo linked the surfeit of food to the surfeit of sex among the younger generations, as he continued: *The young people have this freedom—they go out, they have fun, they go to the movies, they go here, they go there. Everything culminates; they do everything. I just want to say one thing. When a man has obtained so easily what he wants from a woman and then he comes to marry her, well I just don't think that is a marriage. I don't say this to be backward and imply that things were so great in the old days—no, for the love of God, let's not even talk about it. But today desires are nothing like they were before. What kind of desires do they have today? A man has none for sure, and neither does a woman.*

Seventy-three-year-old Renzo also noted that consumption standards in the 1980s were much higher than in his youth in the 1920s: *Progress has brought us so many things, interesting things. Everything. The way of life. The foods. Now we go out, we get a pastry, a coffee—all these things were just dreams in the old days. Today there is more cleanliness, better health care, medicine—all*

Fig. 10.1 *Fagioli gentili dall'occhio* ("nice beans with an eye" or black-eyed peas) with the brand name of *Sapore Antico*—"Taste of the Old Days," March 2003

these things. In the old days, there were none of these things. So this is progress. In the old days, water—what we use today to brush our teeth, then would have been enough for three days—I tell you, that's the truth.

While glad for the increased consumption, Renzo lamented the decline of desire and food quality:[1] *Today we eat much better, with more variety. However, in the old days (see Figure 10.1), the food was more desired—Sunday, because we ate better; holidays, because we ate capon. In contrast, today every day is Sunday. Then we longed for things. Today, instead, pretty much every day, we have everything we want, but the taste of food is worse. Today the food has no more taste. Today, if you eat, let's say spinach, or Swiss chard, or beet greens—everything tastes the same.*

*But in the old days, if you ate spinach, it had a distinct flavor. If you ate meat—pork, let's say—it had its own flavor. It was completely different from other meat. In the old days, we always raised two pigs—they ate the overripe fruit, all the kitchen scraps, all that good stuff. They fattened up on those things. They had a different taste. You know how meat is produced today, right? In feedlots. And the same thing for chickens, but they're even worse. They give them all that junk, and they don't do anything except drink and drink—because their feed is really salty—and they get filled up with water and they have no taste. However, today everything is available. Back then, there was nothing. At the store there was **mortadella** (bologna), and there was gorgonzola cheese, but there was nothing else, not even salame, in a normal grocery store. Very few people could buy anything.*

Renzo underscored how the quantity of food had increased but the quality decreased—a fact at odds with the traditional Tuscan belief in *poco ma buono.* By linking glut of food to glut of sex, he extended the bounds of the question "a lot, but is it good?" *In my opinion, the sexual freedom that exists today between men and women has no taste—**non sa di nulla.** This is my belief. Because there is no desire, no effort. It's like going out for coffee. Anytime is good—you lean against a wall and it's done. Well, then, it loses everything, eh. You laugh, but that's the way it is. It's like dancing—in the old days, you longed for it, it was an event, with your girlfriend—oh, you looked forward to it. Now they stop at the corner and it's all done. Look, today there's no more flavor to it. It's like eating. I used to wait for Christmas, the holidays, or Easter to eat well. That was when we ate sweets, only then. But now it is different. Yes, there are beautiful things, but every day is a holiday, and so there is no desire.*

Some of the older people welcomed culinary change, like Berta, who said, *Yes, the food was very good in the old days, but it's better today, right? But it's completely different, eh?* But many of the older people thought that the new diet was inferior in taste and quality, like Berta's husband, seventy-five-year-old Massimo: *I remember those trays of pork we used to cook for the **trattoria** in Trespiano . . . and sometimes when pork loin is available, I say to myself, "I'll get a little piece." But its taste is not even close to the old days. It's because of the animals. Where they raise the pigs, they give them all this animal feed—who knows what it is? We have no idea what they put in the animal feed. I have relatives up there in the country, and they raise pigs and cattle, and I can tell that their meat isn't like what I get down here. Sometimes they say meat is good for you, but we have no idea what those animals eat—maybe it's better for you to eat potatoes than a steak. Today everyone eats a lot of meat. But that's why there are all these diseases, because of the foods that those animals eat. I'd rather eat vegetable foods. It's rare that I eat meat, just a little. I don't like it. I used to like **lesso** (boiled meat) so much. But now, no, I don't like it; it has no taste. I still eat the broth willingly, but just that. The meat, especially the cuts we use for boiled meat, has bad-tasting*

Fig. 10.2 *Esselunga* ("Long S") supermarket in Via Pisana, Florence, March 2003

fat; it tastes of sawdust. Instead, in the old days, if you had tasted that fat, it was really good.

Massimo prized the old, cheap, delicious, and filling foods: *I like* **baccalà** *a lot, the way we used to eat it in the old days—the whole fish, with the bones and all. Nowadays, people can't be bothered to clean the fish, so they buy these fillets—what kind of flavor do these fillets have? They have no taste. If you cook a baby's diaper, it has a better taste. You laugh? Listen to what I say.* **Baccalà,** *the whole dried cod, has a great taste when you cook it at home. Fish fillets? A baby's diaper has a superior flavor. Unfortunately, I eat them. Oh, I like them all right, but* **baccalà** *is a whole different thing, a whole different taste, there's no question.*

Although several of the older people lamented the loss of taste, many recognized the vast increase in the amount and variety—of a certain kind—of food. It was no longer solely the temporal variety of the seasons but the synchronous variety of consumer society. As Giovanna said in 2003, *It's amazing how much food you can find—whether it's prepared food or fresh food. The variety of vegetables, the variety of meats, it's just unending. It's funny, because the Italians seem to take it all for granted now. They seem to have forgotten the days of scarcity. . . . I think Italians consume more meat now than they did before, and fish. . . . But they obviously, according to the displays that you see, consume a good amount of vegetables.*

Variety was particularly evident at the supermarket, part of its appeal, according to Giovanna (see Figure 10.2): *At the supermarket, they have a great turnover, because they sell so much stuff that everything's always replenished fresh. Everything is fresh. They must have forty-five types of prosciutto at the deli. They have the prosciutto from all over Italy, San Daniele, Parma—any kind of exotic name of prosciutto that you want. You go to that store and you see that deli and it leaves you speechless. It's incredible. . . . When you go to a supermarket, you don't see just a case of oranges—you see twenty cases of oranges, twenty cases of apples, an aisle full of pasta. Such abundance. . . . And variety, the different brands, the different types of things, the different choices.*

Brand and type variety was replacing the local and seasonal variety of the Tuscan past, though these were not entirely gone, of course. In the last two decades of the twentieth century, variety also involved increased consumption both at home and outside the home of processed, "half-prepared or ready-to-eat dishes" (Turrini et al. 2001, 586). Giovanna noted: *I have seen a lot more consumption of prepared foods—whether they would be deli foods, whether they would be frozen, prepared things. . . . The prepared foods have been excellent over there [in Italy]. I don't buy prepared foods over here [in the United States], hardly ever, because I never feel as though they're that good. But over there [in Italy], I think that there's great stuff.*

Vegetables constituted an important category of pre-prepared foods, and Turrini et al. (2001) found a significant increase in frozen vegetable consumption between 1980–84 and 1994–96. Besozzi (1998) claimed an increase in consumption of frozen foods from 9 kilograms/capita/year in 1994 to 12 kilograms in 1998, with vegetables, potatoes, and fish the main items, and sales highest in large supermarket chains and franchises. Giovanna commented on vegetables in 2003: *I saw people buying vegetables liberally, which was nice. The supermarket also boils the vegetables, like spinach and Swiss chard, and they squeeze the water out, and they sell it so that you don't have to wash it. All you do when you go home is you open the container, then you fry olive oil and garlic, and you sauté the vegetables. . . . They're in little containers—sealed and dated so that you know they are fresh. A lot of that is being consumed . . . as well as frozen vegetables. They have a wonderful **minestrone** in the bag, frozen. If you don't know how to do anything else, you just put that in water and you boil it—it has fourteen or fifteen different kinds of vegetables. . . . It is labor-saving and good quality, very good.* Middle-aged Giovanna looked at quality differently from her older uncle Renzo, and was more satisfied than he.

Leonardo summarized the pluses and minuses of variety: *If you are talking about variety in cooking, yes, there are twenty-five ways to cook risotto, thirty-five ways to cook pasta, like with cream, things that didn't exist before. But variety from the starting point, I don't see it. In short, the person who sold **raveggioli**[2] (fresh ewe's milk cheese)—where is he? The one who sold little fish from the Arno[3]—where is he? These things—who sees them anymore? The variety of fruit, all the local kinds, they don't exist anymore.*

Some of the old foods were disappearing and new ones were entering— products showing wider provenance and greater elaboration. In a study of Ital-

ian eating habits in the last two decades of the twentieth century, Vercelloni
(2001, 144) found an expansion in "the request for service" in the food system
demonstrated in increased consumption outside the home and of prepared
foods inside the home. He attributed this increasing reliance on others' labor
in one's own food to "the speeding up of life's rhythms, the intensification of
social obligations, women's claims for 'private time' for themselves, rising female occupation, and increasing nuclear families." My subjects expressed all of
these trends except "women's claims for 'private time,'" which were not mentioned by the women I interviewed in the early 1980s or in 2003.

Processing, Experimentation, and Innovation

Vercelloni (2001, 141–145) found increasing gastronomic innovation and ex-
perimentation in Italian foodways. Florentines were eating quick prepared
foods more often because of the speeded-up lifestyle, as described by Baldo: *In
the families where both the husband and wife go off to work, you tell me what they
eat. I don't know. Either they go to the **rosticceria**, or they have a slice of roast beef
or a slice of prosciutto or a slice of head cheese (**soprassata**), and that's it—with a
couple of fried potatoes. Maybe they buy a little container of lasagna or cannel-
loni, but in short, that's all. On Saturday and Sunday, they would have time to
cook, but they go out; they want to eat out.*

*One solution might be to completely revolutionize Italian eating habits and eat
more in the morning, eat only a sandwich at lunch, then eat a big supper. But that's
not the Italian system. I don't think we'll ever change.* Yet even as Baldo spoke, Italians were changing. At the end of the twentieth century, Vercelloni (2001, 141)
found a significant "meal destructuring" manifest in four trends: (1) a decline in
"the canonical tripartite division of the meal" (into *primo, secondo,* and *frutta*);
(2) a multiplication of meals; (3) a growing importance of breakfast; and (4) "a
sudden growth in eating outside of meals" (145). At lunch, Italians were increasingly eating a rapid meal of a sandwich, a pizza, or a *piatto unico* (one-plate meal)
in bars, *pizzerie, trattorie,* or quick-service restaurants. With the increase in meal
simplicity was a reduction in wine and bread consumption (Vercelloni 2001,
145). In 2003, several of my Florentine subjects confirmed Vercelloni's findings
by saying that *il pranzo non si fa più*—"no one eats a big lunch anymore."

In my university focus group interviews, students from outside of Florence
reported eating in the university *mensa* (cafeteria), in their apartments, and in
fast-food restaurants if, as one said, "there's no food at home or if the *mensa* is
closed (Sundays)." Another student reported that when he was at the university he ate *una serie infinitia di panini o focacce o frutta* ("an infinite series of
sandwiches or fruit"), but when he ate with his family, they had the first and
second courses with dessert and coffee. My interviews in Florence in 2003 indicated that "meal destructuring" seemed to be experienced particularly by
students and working people whose work was too far from their home to make
return for lunch feasible. Although declining in numbers, some Florentine

families still had a big *pranzo* with several family members present, and many had a substantial tripartite *cena.*

One study of 10,000 Italian teenagers found that they usually had a rushed lunch held 36 percent of the time in a bar or *tavola calda* (quick-service restaurant) and 14 percent of the time in a fast-food restaurant (*"La metà delle ragazze si vede grassa,"* 2002). When I conducted my interviews in 1982–84, there was not a single McDonald's fast-food outlet in Italy. In 2000, there were approximately 300, with four in Florence, including one inside and one right outside the main train station ("Symbols of U.S. Capitalism" 2001).[4] In March 2003, this McDonald's showed the complexity of food globalization, for this quintessential U.S. fast-food chain was featuring Mexican food—hence the sign "Bienvenidos in Mexico"—"Welcome to Mexico"—in Spanish, in Florence.

People were frequenting restaurants and other informal eating establishments outside the home in 2003, sometimes consciously choosing traditional cuisine and at other times experimenting far more widely than they did in the early 1980s. One proof of this was the mushrooming number of foreign or ethnic restaurants. In the early 1980s, the only foreign restaurant widely known in Florence was *il ristorante Cinese*—the Chinese restaurant. In 2003, I counted twenty-nine Chinese restaurants in the Florence yellow pages (see Figure 10.3). There were also restaurants featuring at least nine other international cuisines including Mexican, Cuban, Egyptian, Vietnamese, Japanese, Indian, Spanish, French, and Brazilian.

Home-cooked Tuscan foods were waning because young people did not have the time or desire to make them. Delicatessen foods, processed foods, and restaurants were increasingly filling the gap. Fifty-four-year-old Raffaele, the man who in Chapter 2 extolled *minestra di pane* as representing centuries of Tuscan identity, encapsulated the changes in foodways: *Our cuisine has been passed down from generation to generation, but I think that right now it is going to end. Why? Because the young people no longer have the inclination to cook in the old ways. They're content to eat a pizza or something out of a can. Oh, God, when they find a good bean soup or a bread and cabbage soup, they eat it willingly, or a delicious pan of baccalà in sauce, they love it. But these things take hours, they demand a certain preparation, and the young people don't have the time to make them. If a person goes off to work, he or she can't do it. In fact, you see many at the rosticceria picking up foods already cooked, or else they base their cooking around the evening meal. But there's a problem with that too. When two people have worked all day, they just don't feel like going to the trouble of cooking every night, and spending hours at the stove. . . . They just don't have the desire to do it. It's not there. They prefer to go to the rosticceria, because everyone is working and has the money. . . . That's why I predict that little by little the traditional ways of cooking are going to die out and disappear. For reasons of time.*

One important change in the cuisine noted by Raffaele's brother-in-law Baldo was the waning consumption of once important animal innards: *Cheap*

Fig. 10.3 Chinese restaurant in Via dei Servi, Florence, March 2003

foods can be delicious—for example, beef intestines or chicken gizzards. If you know how to cook them in a nice dish with potatoes, well, they can be better than a steak. However, today there aren't many women who can lose themselves in cooking, so all those foods are disappearing. Take tripe, tripe is good—when it is made well, it is really good. Certainly if you just throw it in the pot and boil it, it's nothing. I don't like it. For me, it needs to be cooked in sauce, nicely, so it takes up the flavor of the sauce, and so you have to cook it slowly, slowly. You can't just toss it in there and bum, bum, bum, and it's done. Then it just has no taste at all. But if it is made right with the time it needs, it is really good and can surpass more select foods. . . . Well, it's natural that the newlyweds of today are either going to eat tripe at their parents' house, or they aren't going to eat it at all—there's no other way.

Raffaele also used tripe to make a similar point about the inevitability of culinary change: *My children might ask for **trippa alla fiorentina**—tripe Florentine style. You have to go and buy the tripe, cut it up, wash it, wash it again, boil it, drain it, and then put it in the sauce you've made, and let it boil there very slowly for hours and hours and hours. Oh, it is delicious. But it's a very humble dish because tripe costs almost nothing. They feed it to dogs, they feed it to cats. . . . But, instead, a lot of people think it is an exquisite dish—a skillfully cooked plate of tripe is absolutely delicious. How could the young people of today make it? To cook a pot of tripe right takes at least four hours. Who is willing to pass four hours in front of the stove? Someone like me who doesn't have anything else to do and who enjoys doing it, that's who. But if someone really considered the fact that people today earn twenty-five thousand lire an hour and it takes four hours to make that tripe, and they think that they would spend four hours cooking something that cost two thousand lire to buy, those four hours equal one hundred thousand lire of work lost. Forget it. They won't eat tripe anymore. They will buy it in cans, which tastes truly disgusting.*

*Today it's different. The women say, "You have a hole in your sock? Throw it away and buy another." Understand? So today the women find time to go out with their husbands. They say, "Let's go out, but what will we eat? Oh, we'll find something to eat." That's what they say today, eh. On their way home, they stop in a **pizzeria**, a **rosticceria**; they buy a little bag of stuff and they take it home and eat it. Then they go out again. In this way they don't even have any dishes to wash, they don't have to clean up, they don't get anything dirty. But in the old days, people didn't have the means to live like this.*

The consumer society generated demands that forced both husband and wife to work for money, and cooking inevitably changed because people had less time for it. Raffaele explained: *In my opinion, life today demands a great deal of work. People have to work very hard because they are no longer used to poverty. People are used to having the car at the doorway, along with all kinds of motorbikes and motorcycles. . . . To buy all these things, everybody has to be working. This is having a huge effect on Tuscan cuisine, and perhaps on other cuisines as well. In the old days, when the woman was a housewife, she did the cooking from morning until night and it was a way to pass the time; it was a diversion.*

Increasing Scale of Production and Distribution

Though few women in my study defined cooking as a diversion, it had been a time-consuming part of their lives that was shrinking due to the increased penetration of industry into the food system. There was an agricultural, industrial, and consumer revolution in food in Italy in the last half of the twentieth century that ended the longstanding grounding of foodways "on local agriculture production in every part of the country" (Taddei 1998, 25). Food production and distribution have become increasingly delocalized and Italy has seen the rise in multinational corporations in agriculture and food processing, such as the enormous global Ferruzzi corporation involved in sugar beets, cereals, seed oils, fruits, and vegetables (Grassivaro 1991).

The changes in scale have affected landscape and memory. Seventy-three-year-old former peasant Renzo described a visit to his former home in Santa Lucia del Trespiano: *Today, all that bounty that I used to see there on that land is gone. There are no more fruit trees. There are no more grapes. A well that I thought we had up there—a beautiful well—not even that is still there. I almost can't recognize the land any more.* Renzo's remarks encapsulate some of the losses that have come with modernity in Florence. Ironically, while much of the twentieth century has been a movement toward bounty for all, Renzo remarked on the loss of some of the land's bounty.

Economies of scale were manifest in changes in food shopping. While in the 1980s most Florentines shopped daily in small stores, several also shopped at least some of the time at a supermarket. By the close of the century, supermarkets had almost doubled while small stores were declining (see Chapter 7). In 2003, some local stores continued to flourish and sell a good selection of local goods, but others were closing up because supermarkets were proliferating. Giovanna in 2003 remarked on *the disappearance of the small shops. . . . Oh, yes, you can see it. Oh, yes,* **con il bandone chiuso,** *with the metal gate down. . . . The single store is slowly disappearing.* Concomitantly, Giovanna noted the striking *appearance of larger stores and supermarkets.*

Diet, Health, and Resistance

In the year 2000, Italians still ate a relatively nutritious Mediterranean diet:[5] 87.3 percent of the population ate bread, pasta, or rice on a daily basis and 76.8 percent ate fruit, 51.5 percent ate greens, 38.1 percent ate vegetables, and 60.2 percent drank milk (ISTAT 2001). The population was fairly healthy, although 31.5 percent of the population still smoked. That 9.1 percent were classified as obese, with a body mass index (BMI) of 30 or more (ISTAT 2001), confirmed Massimo's predictions in 1984: *You know the children are getting fat with all this*

food that they are eating—milk, pastries, all these things—they have no sub-
stance. Instead, in the old days, you had some **caffelatte** *and some toasted bread,*
like I still eat. But today if you eat a pastry, you feel like you haven't eaten any-
thing, because what does it do for you? Two hours later, you're hungry, yet you ate.
Children and adolescents were eating more snack and "junk" foods and their
food habits "seem to go in the opposite direction to healthy behavior" (Turrini
et al. 2001, 586).[6] Italy's obesity rate was nonetheless significantly lower than
U.S. obesity rates of 31 percent for adults (Variyam 2002, 16).

Some Italians pursued health food fads, like two old friends of mine, a middle-class couple in their early fifties who practiced *trofologia*—"trophology."
They said that in general the big midday dinner was declining, but they had
lunch every day together since the husband had retired and the wife worked at
home. They ate bread with a lot of raw vegetables like celery, artichokes, cabbage, cauliflower, broccoli, asparagus, and even avocado if they could get it.
They ate the vegetables with *gomaso*—toasted sesame ground up with salt, or
with brewer's yeast, oil, and cumin, or oil and mustard. Sometimes they ate
pasta with vegetables cooked in a little water, and they ate lots of legumes, usually boiled with just some sage or another herb.

Their consumption of this atypical diet supported Vercelloni's (2001, 145)
findings that Italians were evincing a growing interest in dieting and health.
They seemed to be as concerned about the harmful effects of food additives as
of fats and sugars. In the new millennium, health concerns led Italians to an
increasing consumption of *prodotti biologici*—"organic foods." Italians did
not allow the import of hormone-raised beef, and the majority of them had
unfavorable attitudes toward genetically engineered foods (Saba et al. 2000).
With the bovine spongiform encephalopathy (BSE) or *mucca pazza* (mad-cow
disease) scare in the late 1990s and early 2000s, Italians significantly cut their
beef consumption except for cold cuts (*insaccati*) because of their image of
traditionalism and artisanry (Vercelloni 2001, 148). Italy was one of the last
European countries to report BSE, but as of April 2001 had eleven official cases
with many more predicted. Growing numbers of Italians joined other Europeans in reducing beef consumption and turning to locally produced or Ar-
gentinian beef. Others became vegetarians or experimented with alternative
meats such as horse, ostrich, and local products, leading to a resurgence of the
traditional Piedmontese cattle (*Economist* 2000, Hale 2001, Stille 2001). In
March 2003, however, beef was widely available and consumed in Florence.

Of my subjects, only Sergia, Rinaldo, and their two daughters still lived on
the land and ate the old homegrown foods in the old places, but both were
transformed by money. Whereas in the past, traditional cuisine was rooted in a
peasant tradition of scarcity and subsistence, for them it was an elite product,
produced by wage labor and consumed in a farmhouse transformed into a
tasteful upper-middle-class home. For all Florentines, eating the traditional

food necessitated effort: having lots of money, having networks of family or friends still farming the land, or seeking local producers who sold at open-air markets all around the city or in the neighboring hamlets, such as the one in Galluzzo frequented by Sergia.

New technologies and communication systems have stimulated wider interest in and markets for traditional products that were consumed mainly locally in the past (Hundley 2000). Florentines were participating in an increasingly industrialized global food economy but were also resisting global homogenization by revitalizing and appreciating traditional foods. An example of this came from my friend Beppe Lo Russo, who talked about how most beans consumed in Italy came from North and South America. He gave me some beans that they have been rediscovering and reproducing in Tuscany—for example, *lo zolfino,* the yellow bean from Pratomagno; the *fagioli del purgatorio* ("beans of Purgatory") that were traditionally cooked during Lent; the *fagioli Toscanelli,* that are like the traditional Tuscan white beans but smaller and traditionally used in *fagioli all'uccelletto* with tomato and sage; and the *fagioli gentili dall'occhio* ("nice beans with an eye"), which look like black-eyed peas and were purported to have deep Tuscan roots (see Figure 10.1).

Friends in Florence gave another example of how Italians resisted and capitalized on globalization through a highly successful restaurant in Naples that uses the golden arches M from McDonald's but is called *Merenne 'e Mammà,* Neapolitan for "Mamma's Snacks"—delicious *pane* and *compantico* of all kinds. Many Florentines supported local production by continuing to buy oil and wine in bulk (*vino sfuso*) from the farmer. They said that there were no young *contadini*—farmers in the old sense—anymore, but there were young entrepreneurs producing wine, oil, and organic and artisanal foods like *pecorino* (sheep's milk) and *caprino* (goat milk) cheeses.

In 1986, Italians started the Slow Food Movement—"an organization for the defense of vegetable, animal, and cultural diversity" (Petrini 2001, xii). By 2000, it had 70,000 members in more than forty-five countries and was publishing an innovative quarterly called *Slow* in five languages (Kummer 2002, Leitch 2000, Stille 2001). About half of the worldwide members are Italian, and there are 340 local groups (*condotte*) or convivia scattered throughout the country. The goals of the Slow Food Movement are to take pleasure in food, to promote sustainable agriculture, to protect the environment, and to promote regional products and cuisines. Slow Food has brought attention to local endangered products through its Ark project. "The aim of this massive project is to identify and catalogue (alas increasingly often) products, dishes and animals that are in danger of disappearing. The operational offshoots of the project are the so-called Slow Food Presidia, through which the association provides economic support and a media back-up to groups and individuals pledged to saving an Ark product."[7] In Italy, marketing and government supports sustain regional food products like the renowned *parmigiano reggiano* (Roest and Menghi 2000) or *lardo di Colonnata*—the lard of Colonnata— some of which are honored with the DOP (*Denominazione di Origine Protetta*) label similar to the DOC (*Denominazione di Origine Controllata*) label given to fine wines (Leitch 2000).[8]

Food, Family, and Gender in the Twenty-First Century

In 2003, many Florentines continued to eat regularly the traditional foods of their ancestors, either out of habit or out of self-conscious desire. I had dinner with two old friends, a comfortable middle-class couple who were members of the Slow Food Movement and who did everything they could to purchase the most genuine Tuscan foods. For hors d'oeuvres, they served some delicious local Tuscan *finocchiona* and some *lardo di Colonnata* produced in Tuscany near the Carrara marble quarries that supplied not only the stone for Michelangelo's famous statues in Florence, but also the surface on which the lard was cured.[9] The husband made a delicious bean soup with broth and *cavolo nero* (Tuscan kale). He cooked the broth with the *carnici di prosciutto* (ham scraps), onion, and the *odori*: carrot, celery, basil, and parsley. After he cooked the broth, he cooled it, defatted it, then cooked the beans in it. He steamed separately the *cavolo nero* and cooked triangular lasagne in boiling water, then mixed them both into the soup. Then for *secondo* we had *stracotto* (pot roast) with tomato sauce. We also had a delectable local pecorino cheese and, of course, Tuscan bread. Although a special occasion, this meal was not untypical of the foods this couple regularly ate.

At the end of the twentieth century, meals were still the foundation of the family, and Raffaele defined the older generations as bearers of the traditional cuisine and nurturers of their children into old age: *Today, the young people eat differently. I see that they don't have any desire to pass hours at the stove. So I predict that my son and my daughter, even after they are married and on their own, if they want to eat something good, something genuine, they will have to return home and have their father and mother make it. Just the way it happens now. Piero comes and says, "Daddy, will you make me"—I don't know—"bean soup, it's been so long." He feels the need to have this soup, no? Surely he wouldn't know where to begin to make it himself. Imagine if he marries one like himself and Piera marries one like herself, understand? How will they manage to make these dishes? It won't happen. So I predict that even at eighty years old, it will still fall to me to make them bean soup when they desire it. Otherwise, they won't eat it.* The fact that the younger generations were relying on their parents to prepare the traditional foods for them contributed to the continuing strength of the family.[10]

In 2003, food was still at the heart of social occasions. One student reported that eating together was the "core" of their parties because they were "always hungry, and then comes the wine." The Sunday meal with extended family continued to be important, and I attended one meal in Florence in March 2003 with some of my Florentine subjects. I ate with Valeria (69), her sister Laura (67) and her husband Raffaele (73), Caterina (45) and Sandro (47) and their son (12) and daughter (17), and Arturo (40) and Maria (39) and their daughter (13) and son (8). We had lunch in the usual living room around the same old table with all its leaves out and we had the usual huge meal—a *primo* of two kinds of lasagna, one with a meat sauce and the other with a pesto and white sauce; a *secondo* of grilled steak, *salsicce* (sausages), and ribs. Then for *contorno,* peas, and radicchio salad, and finally a *dolce* of sweets brought by Raffaele and Laura left over from the previous day's birthday party of their grandson. The table was lively, with everyone talking at once, and the feeling was very upbeat. Raffaele said that he and his group of friends, six couples, still go every Thursday into the country to a place called La Torre where they have a big feast that they all cook together.

I asked Caterina what she thought about her comment of twenty years earlier, **La parità dei sessi non c'è**—"sexual equality does not exist." She responded, **non c'è ancora**—"it still does not exist." Then she said that among the younger generations things were improving, but slowly, and sexual equality had not yet been reached. She said that the girls seemed to be doing much better in school than the boys, and were pulling ahead. Several people remarked that young women put career before marriage and were increasingly intolerant of men who did not pull their weight. Giovanna said, *I think that the girls are trying to have the guys share in the household burden. . . . A lot of the young girls—they haven't spent a lot of time trying to cook because they didn't feel as though they had to be married by twenty-one and entice some guy with their good cooking like perhaps we were led to understand. . . . Right now they're too interested in their careers, and, you know, you can't blame them, because life is so expensive . . . People want things, and in order to get things, you have to work and make money. . . . You have to support yourself. This idea is well rooted among young women now and they all want to support themselves. . . . Fidanzamento is not quite as formal anymore. I think people eat in people's houses much more casually, and, of course, a lot of people live together rather than getting married. For example, look at my cousin's daughters, both living together without getting married. . . . So, it's a different world. It's a different world.*

The food-centered narratives of the twenty-three Florentines I interviewed in the early 1980s, along with the information and observations made in 2003, reveal how central food was to their lives, their families, and their gender relations. It remains to be seen how Florentine cuisine will evolve in the new millennium, in the "*different world.*" Their long tradition of valuing fresh, varied, locally produced food means that they may be able to sustain these against the forces pushing toward quicker and more convenient processed foods. But the increasing entry of women as well as men into the workforce, the shrinking of families and reduction in females to share the domestic workload, and the failure of gender parity in the home have all produced challenges to cooking traditional ways. As foodways change, so does the culture. This book has sought to use Florentines' words to present the richness of their food and culture, and to document the traditions that are so rapidly changing.

Life Synopses of Subjects in 1984

Arturo. Born in Florence in 1963 to Baldo and Valeria. Finished high school and was working at manual labor jobs looking for a permanent position. Engaged to Maria.

Baldo. Born in Empoli in the province of Florence in 1930. Married Valeria in 1955. Learned cabinet-making from his father but abandoned it in 1958 to become a sales representative for the same Florentine textile firm that later employed his cousin Leonardo. Worked until 1980 when disabled with spinal paralysis. Had two children: Caterina in 1958 and Arturo in 1963.

Berta. Born near Montorsoli in the hills northwest of Florence in 1908 into a poor *mezzadria* peasant family of eleven. Married Massimo in 1933, moved to Trespiano, Prato, and finally Florence, where she and Massimo ran a flower shop on Via dei Bardi next to the Ponte Vecchio from 1958 to 1974. Had two daughters: Valeria in 1934 and Laura in 1936.

Caterina. Born in Florence to Baldo and Valeria in 1958 and married Sandro in 1981. Received a high school diploma as a certified kindergarten teacher but could not find a teaching job, so she clerked in a supermarket.

Elena. Born in Fiesole in 1918 to parents who ran a grocery store. Moved to Florence when she was six in 1924, where her parents ran a bakery in Piazza Donatello until 1964. She worked there from age 16 until it closed. Married Giorgio on leave from combat in 1943 and had Giovanna in 1946.

Eugenia. Born to Rinaldo and Sergia in 1970. Attended a private girls' high school.

Giovanna. Born in Florence in 1945 to Elena and Giorgio. Became a tour guide in Florence in 1965, met her American husband Joseph on a tour, and married him in 1967, whereupon she moved to a Boston suburb in Massachusetts, had two daughters, Georgia in 1967 and Susan in 1970, graduated Phi Beta Kappa from college in 1976, and received a master's degree in 1985.

Laura. Born in Trespiano to Berta and Massimo in 1936. Worked at a fancy dressmaker's shop in Florence until she married Raffaele in 1958.

Moved to Empoli, sewed pieces, had Piero in 1959 and Piera in 1964, and started working full-time in a garment factory in 1970.

Leonardo. Born during the German occupation of Florence in July 1944 to Renzo and Grazia. Received a high school accounting degree and worked several years as a sales representative for the same Florentine textile firm that employed his cousin Baldo. In 1974 he went to the United States and earned a BFA in 1978 and an MFA in 1981, after which he returned to Florence.

Marco. Born in Florence in 1912 to an artisan family. Father was a silversmith, he was silversmith until he took over his wife's family's bakery in 1947 and ran it until 1964. Married Tommasa in 1942 and had Sergia in 1943.

Maria. Born in Florence in 1962. She was engaged to Arturo, working temporarily in a factory, and looking for a permanent job so they could save up for marriage.

Marianna. Born in 1923 in the city of Florence to a disabled father who had to give up his wine shop and a mother who ran a newspaper kiosk in Via dei Neri. Grew up in public housing as a member of the urban proletariat. Worked from age eighteen to fifty-eight as a clerk in the Florence city hall, Palazzo Vecchio. Remained single until 1980, when she married the widower Renzo.

Massimo. Born in 1909 in Trespiano into a *mezzadria* peasant family. Married Berta in 1933 and had two daughters: Valeria in 1934 and Laura in 1936. Worked as a cemetery groundskeeper, a truck driver, and finally ran a flower shop with his wife on Via dei Bardi next to the Ponte Vecchio from 1958 to 1974.

Ondina. Born to Rinaldo and Sergia in 1972. Attended a private girls' middle school.

Piera. Born to Laura and Raffaele in Empoli in 1964. Received an accounting high school degree in 1982. Was working in a small accounting firm in Empoli and was engaged to be married.

Piero. Born to Laura and Raffaele in Empoli in 1959. Was a nurse employed by the Tuscan region and was working part-time at a radio station in Empoli.

Raffaele. Born in Empoli in 1930 to a father who was a manual worker in a glass factory and a mother who sewed piecework at home. Was a member of the urban proletariat and went to work at age fourteen in the glass factory, working his way up to master glass blower before he quit in 1964 to become a factotum for a Catholic nursing home.

Renzo. Born in 1911 in Trespiano into a *mezzadria* peasant family. Married Grazia in 1938 and moved to Florence. Became a city policeman (*vigile urbano*) and later held a desk job in the police department. Simultaneously ran an in-home artisanal handbag business with his wife that employed several women and earned a solid upper-middle-class income. Had one son, Leonardo, in 1944. Became widower in 1973, married Marianna in 1980.

Rinaldo. Born in 1939 in Prato to parents who ran a fruit and vegetable business. Started and ran a dyeing factory (*tintoria*) outside of Florence. Married Sergia in 1968 and had two daughters: Eugenia in 1970 and Ondina in 1972.

Sandro. Born in Scandicci in 1956 to a father who was a butcher and a mother who was a *casalinga* (housewife). Became a dental technician and eventually started his own business. Married Caterina in 1981.

Sergia. Born in Florence in the middle of World War II (1943) to Marco and Tommasa. Received a high school teaching degree in physical education in 1963 and taught until she married Rinaldo in 1968. Had two daughters: Eugenia in 1970 and Ondina in 1972.

Tommasa. Born in Fiesole in 1920 to parents who ran a grocery store. Moved to Florence when she was four, where her parents ran a bakery in Piazza Donatello until 1964. She worked there from age sixteen until she married Marco in 1942. Had Sergia in 1943.

Valeria. Born in Trespiano to Berta and Massimo in 1934. Worked for a fancy dressmaker in Florence until she married Baldo in 1955. Lived with her parents Berta and Massimo in public housing in Florence, ran the household, sewed pieces, and had Caterina in 1958 and Arturo in 1963.

Glossary of Italian Terms

Most Italian nouns end in *-a* (usually feminine), *-o* (usually masculine), or *-e* (feminine or masculine) and form plurals by converting *-a* to *-e*, *-o* to *-i*, and *-e* to *-i*.

Florentine Italian makes great use of suffixes to alter the meaning of words. The endings *-ina/o, -etta/o, -uccia/o,* and *-ella/a* are diminutives; the endings *-ona/e* and *-otta/o* are augmentatives; and the endings *-accia/o* are depreciatives.

Articles are *il, la, lo, i, le, gli, uno, una.*

I have consulted *Il Nuovo Dizionario Italiano Garzanti* and *Mondadori's Pocket Italian-English, English-Italian Dictionary.*

abbuffarsi: to throw oneself into eating, to "pig out."

acqua cotta: thin soup, literally "cooked water."

acqua pazza: acquarello.

acquarello: water tinted with wine; or a product made from grape stems, seeds, and skins left over from making wine, mixed with water, fermented for a couple of weeks; also called *mezzone.*

alimentari: foods; general food store.

ammasso: government store of food during war.

andavano a far pane: they went to seek bread; refers to hungry children during World War II.

antipasto: hors d'oeuvre, literally "before the meal."

artigianato artistico: artistic craftwork.

baccalà: dried, salted codfish.

baccello/i: pod(s) of fava beans or peas.

ballocca: boiled chestnut.

bandone: metal gate that pulls down over storefronts.

bastoncini di pesce: fish sticks.

battaglia del grano: battle for grain, Mussolini's plan to reach self-sufficiency in grain production.

battuto: literally "the chopped up"; the diced basic ingredients used in many Florentine dishes: a carrot, a celery stalk, a small bunch of parsley, and a leaf or two of basil. These are called *gli odori,* "the flavors." They are usually sautéed in olive oil before other ingredients are added, often with an onion. Sometimes the *battuto* is just parsley and garlic.

benessere: well-being, especially economic well-being.

birreria: quick-service restaurant specializing in beer and ready-to-eat foods.

bischerata, bischero/a: Florentine slang for idiocy, idiot.

bistecca alla fiorentina: Florentine-style T-bone steak.

bosci-bosci: Florentine slang for Bolsheviks.

braciola, braciolina: very thin slice of meat (about a quarter-inch) that is cooked in various ways.

brodo: broth.

bruciata: roasted chestnut (literally "the burned thing").

calmiere: price control.

calorosa/o: heat-producing, from *calore,* heat.

campanalismo: provincialism, from *campanile,* bell tower.

cannellini: white beans.

capoccia: male head of the Tuscan *mezzadria* family (from *capo,* head), usually husband of the *massaia.*

capoluogo: capital.

caprino: goat's milk cheese.

carciofaia: artichoke bed, from *carciofo,* artichoke.

carpaccio: cured meat.

casa colonica: farmhouse.

casalinga: housewife.

case popolari: public housing.

casotto: brothel.

castagna: chestnut, also called *marrone.*

castagnaccio: sweet cake made of chestnut flour; also called *migliaccio.*

cavolo nero: Tuscan or lacinato kale.

cena: evening meal, dinner or supper.

cenci: sweets made from fried flour dough, literally "rags."

Centro: Center, the name for the historic center of Florence *(centro storico).*

coda: tail.

cognata/o: sister/brother-in-law.

colazione: morning meal, breakfast.

collanina d'aglio: little necklace of burned garlic, worn in the old days to ward off worms.

compagni: comrades, companions.

companatico: that which accompanies bread.

comune: municipality.

contadina/o: peasant, farmer.

contorno: vegetable accompanying a meat dish (literally, hem or border).

cotenna del maiale: pork rind.

crème caramel: flan.

criticone: big critic.

crostata: fruit tart.

crostini: "crusts," an appetizer made of bread and some substance, especially chicken liver pâté.

cucina: kitchen, cuisine, or cooking.

cucina casalinga: home cooking.

cucina economica: soup kitchen.

cucina fiorentina: Florentine cooking or cuisine.

cucina semplice: simple cooking or cuisine.

cucina toscana: Tuscan cooking or cuisine.

damigiana: demijohn, used for storing wine.

dolce: sweet, a dessert.

doppia pesata: double weighing, the habit of weighing babies before and after nursing to ensure they had adequate milk.

erba da paura: herb for fear, used to make an infusion to wash a person who suffered a fright.

fagioli: white beans, an important staple of Tuscan cuisine.

falegname: cabinet-maker.

fame da morire: deathly hunger.

farina: flour.

farina dolce: "sweet" or chestnut flour.

farinata: pap made from flour and water, sometimes with olive oil.

fasci: literally bundles, the name given to the Fascist groups.

fascio di combattimento: Fascist fighting group.

fattoria: estate, farm.

femminista: feminist.

femminista sfegatata: an ardent feminist, literally "without a liver."

festa: holiday (including Sunday), feast day.

fettunta: literally "greasy slice," made of salt-free, thick Tuscan bread toasted and rubbed with raw garlic, then drenched in fresh, extra-virgin olive oil.

fiasco: flask, usually covered in straw and filled with Chianti or other wine.

fidanzamento, fidanzato/a: engagement, fiancé(e).

figli maschi: male children.

filastrocca: children's poem.

filone: loaf of bread.

finocchiona: typical Florentine salame flavored with fennel seeds.

forno: oven, bakery.

frenarmi: "to brake myself," sometimes used in regard to limiting one's food desires.

frittata: cooked beaten eggs, like an omelet, but cooked on both sides.

frittella: fritter, a fried sweet.

frittelle di riso: rice fritters.

fritto: (n.) dish of fried foods; (adj.) fried.

fritto misto: dish of mixed fried foods that could be composed of fish, vegetables, or meat.

frutta: fruit, fruit course.

frutti-vendolo: greengrocery.

garzoni: young farmworkers who boarded with and worked for *mezzadria* peasant families.

genero: son-in-law.

ghiotta/o: ravenous or gluttonous.

gnocchi: dumplings, made of wheat of corn flour, eaten with sauce as a first course.

goderecciona/a: someone dedicated to enjoyment in a really big way, from *godere*—to enjoy.

gola: literally throat, but also desire or longing for food.

golosa/o: desiring or craving food.

guancia: cheek, an inexpensive cut of meat eaten by the poor in the old days.

guerra quindici-diciotto: First World War (literally, the war of [nineteen] fifteen–eighteen).

imboscato: one who shirked conscription, literally "in the woods."

impiegato: clerk, white-collar worker.

in gamba: in fine fettle, capable.

insaccati: cold cuts.

interiora: entrails and other "interior" parts of the butchered animal.

in umido: cooking term meaning "in sauce," usually tomato sauce.

labbro leporino: harelip.

lampredotto: cooked lining of the cow's stomach.

lardo: lard.

lattaio: milkman.

latteria: milk and cheese store.

lavoro nero: "black work"—that is, work outside the formal economy and without benefits.

lesso: boiled meat.

lesso rifatto: leftover boiled meat fried with onions and possibly potatoes and/or tomatoes.

libretti colonici: mezzadria account books (also called *quadernucci* in Tuscany).

lingua: tongue.

macchinetta: "little machine," usually meaning a small, stove-top espresso coffee maker.

macelleria: butcher shop.

magazziniere: warehouse supervisor.

mamma mia: mother of mine, a common Italian expletive.

mangiare: (n.) cuisine; (v.) to eat.

mangiare fiorentino: Florentine cuisine.

mangiare in bianco: to eat "in white,"—that is, to eat bland foods, usually when ill.

mangiare toscano: Tuscan cuisine.

mangionae: big eater.

mansarda: attic space.

maschilismo, maschilista: male chauvinism, male chauvinist.

massaia: senior female in the *mezzadria* family, usually the wife of the *capoccia.*

mensa: cafeteria.

mensile: monthly allowance.

mercato, mercatino: market, little market.

merenda: snack.

mezzadria: sharecropping system typical of Tuscany.

mezzaluna: half-moon-shaped knife with handles on each end used in a rocking motion to make the finely chopped *battuto.*

mezzone: see *acquarello.*

migliaccio: chestnut cake, *castagnaccio.*

migliacciola: chestnut fritter.

minestra: soup.

minestra di pane: bread soup, usually made with beans, vegetables, and old bread.

minestrina: "little soup," usually a broth with small-size pasta in it.

minestrone: "big soup," vegetable soup.

minestruccia: meager, watery soup.

miseria: poverty, misery.

mollica: soft inner part of bread (distinguished from the crust).

molto, ma buono?: a lot, but is it good?

mortadella: bologna with large chunks of white lard in the pink meat.

mucca pazza: mad-cow disease (bovine spongiform encephalopathy or BSE).

nastroni: homemade pasta cut into wide strips.

nuora: daughter-in-law.

nutrimento psicologico: psychological nurturance.

odori: essential Florentine flavors: celery, carrot, parsley, basil, often joined by either an onion or a few cloves of garlic.

Oltrarno: zone "on the other side," the south side, of the Arno River.

orario spezzato: broken-up workday (e.g., 8 A.M. to 1 P.M. and 3 to 6 P.M.).

orario unico: continuous workday (e.g., 8 A.M. to 2 P.M.).

ortolano: greengrocer.

padrone: landlord or boss.

pane: bread.

panettone: holiday yeast cake, usually with raisins and dried fruit in it (literally "big bread").

panforte di Siena: Christmas fruitcake traditionally made in Siena (literally "strong bread").

panificio: bakery.

panino: bread roll or sandwich.

panzanella: summer salad usually made of old bread, tomatoes, cucumber, basil, and onions.

pappina, pappuccia: pap, gruel, made from flour and water, perhaps with a little olive oil.

parità dei sessi: sexual equality.

pastasciutta: "dry" pasta—that is, pasta with sauce.

pasticciere: pastry chef.

pasto: meal.

pattona: polenta-like substance made out of chestnut flour.

pecorino: sheep's milk cheese commonly made in Tuscany and called *pecorino toscano.*

pelliccia: fur coat or animal skin.

peperoncino: hot pepper.

pesci di campo: "fish of the field"—that is, fried zucchini flowers.

piatto unico: one-course (or plate) meal.

piccante: spicy hot.

pignoleria: pickiness.

pinzimonio: dressing for raw vegetables made of olive oil, salt, and lots of pepper.

pizzeria: restaurant specializing in pizza and other light meals.

pizzicheria: delicatessen.

poco ma buono: Florentine saying, "Only a little, but let it be good."

podere: farm.

polenta: cornmeal mush, sometimes hardened into a cake, cut into slices and fried in olive oil.

pomarola: tomato sauce.

porca miseria pig misery! (a common Florentine expletive).

porchetta: roast pork, a Florentine specialty.

pranzo: midday meal, dinner or lunch.

primo: first course, usually soup, pasta, or rice.

prodotti biologici: organic products.

prosciutto: ham.

prosciutto cotto: cooked ham.

prosciutto crudo: uncooked cured ham.

radicchio: wild greens.

ragù: meat sauce.

raveggioli: fresh ewe's milk cheese, sold in balls.

ricamo antico: embroidery in the old style.

richiamo: recalling, calling back, remembering.

rigirata: the turnaround, Italy's break with the Axis in World War II, join-
ing with the Allies.

riso: rice.

risotto: rice dish cooked in many different ways served as a *primo.*

ristorante: restaurant.

rosticceria: "roasting restaurant," selling roast chicken, pork, and beef;
fried and roast potatoes; baked pasta; and cooked greens.

roventini: fried pigs' blood, a Florentine dish.

sacrificata/o: literally "sacrificed," overburdened.

salacca, salacchina: generic name for fish, similar to herring, eaten dried
and smoked.

saporoso: rich in flavors, tasty.

scampagnata: excursion to the country centering around a feast.

schiacciata alla fiorentina: Florentine sweet yellow cake eaten especially
during Carnival.

sciocco: lacking salt, insipid, stupid.

secondo: second course.

segnare bachi: to cast a spell on worms (to get rid of them).

semelaio: man who used to bring the *sémele* rolls door-to-door.

sémele: hexagonally shaped roll.

semolino: pasta in tiny granules.

sfoglia: pasta made by hand.

sistemata/o: set up, settled.

sistemazione: act of getting set up or settled, usually including marriage,
house, and children.

sofficino: literally "soft little thing," the name for processed filled pastries.

soprassata: head cheese.

sorella di latte: "milk sister," a girl who has nursed from the same woman;
also *fratello di latte*—"milk brother."

sott'aceti: pickled vegetables (literally, "things under vinegar").

sottilette: literally "thin things," the name for processed cheese slices.

spaghetteria: a quick-service restaurant specializing in spaghetti, usually
having other quick or prepared foods such as cold cuts and sandwiches,
cooked greens, salad, and fruit.

sperluzzicare: to snack or nibble at food, to eat sporadically.

spumante: Italian champagne, from *spuma,* meaning foam.

stracchino: a soft, mild, white cheese.

stracotto: stew, literally "the overcooked."

sugna: aged pig fat, rubbed on body for muscle pain in the old days.

sugo: meat sauce for pasta.

sugo rosé: pink sauce, a tomato sauce with cream.

sugo scappato: "escaped sauce"—that is, sauce without meat.

suocera/o: mother/father-in-law.

tavola calda: quick-service restaurant, literally "hot table."

tegamata: panful—that is, one-pot meal; from *tegame,* meaning pan.

tegamino: small portable pot used to carry workers' lunches.

tirchio: stingy.

tocco, il: "the touch," 1 P.M.

torta di riso: rice cake.

trattoria: simple restaurant usually featuring home-style cooking.

trecciaiola: female straw braider.

trippa: tripe.

trippaio: tripe vendor.

uova: eggs.

ventosa/o: wind-producing.

vigile urbano: city policeman.

vinaio: wine seller.

vinello: watery or light wine.

vino nero, vino rosso: red wine.

vivandiera: food person, from *vivande,* meaning provisions.

vizi: vices; money for *vizi* is pocket money spent on nonnecessities.

viziata/o: spoiled, overindulged.

voglia, voglie: desire, desires; during pregnancy, *le voglie* refer both to the woman's food cravings and the birthmarks on the child that are believed to result from unsatisfied cravings.

voglia delle chiocciole: craving for snails during pregnancy, dangerous to boy babies because it causes the penis to curl up like a snail.

zampa: calf or pig foot boiled with herbs and spices.

zenzero: ginger.

zuppa: soup.

zuppa inglese: "English soup," a sweet dessert like a trifle.

Recipe List: Recipes Collected from All Subjects

Recipes with no name are from Sergia's handwritten cookbook. Those with M are from Marianna's handwritten cookbook. Those with names were collected orally. Recipes in italics lacked names in Marianna's cookbook; I invented names based on main ingredients.

Anatra o piccione con le olive, M
Aringhe marinate
Arista arrosto, Valeria
Arista arrosto e agnello arrosto
Asparagi lessi e conditi
Baccalà alla livornese, Elena
Baccalà, coda di rospo, palombo triglia ecc. alla livornese
Bietola, Marianna e Renzo (see verdura cotta)
Bistecca alla fiorentina
Bistecchine di maiale, Elena
Braciola al sugo, Maria
Braciola ripiena
Braciola al limone
Braciola in salsa di pomodoro
Braciole al forno, M
Braciole fritte
Braciole rifatte, Marianna
Braciole rifatte con acciughe e capperi, Marianna
Braciole ripiene, M
Cacciucco
Capriolo in umido, Valeria
Carciofi all'olio
Carciofi fritti
Carciofi lessi
Carciofi sott'olio, Valeria
Carciofi ziti ripieni
Cavolini Bruxelles
Cavolo nero, Massimo

Cetriolo condito, Valeria
Collo ripieno
Coniglio dissossato, M
Coniglio in umido, Marianna
Coppa gelata
Coppe di panna e prugne, M
Crostini
Crostini, Sergia
Dolce di uova, M
Dolce di riso, M
Dolce di mascarpone (1), M
Dolce di mascarpone (2), M
Dolce di mascarpone (3), M
Fagioli all'uccelletto
Fagioli all'uccelletto, Marianna
Fagioli conditi all'olio, Marianna
Fagioli freschi, Marianna
Fagioli freschi in umido, Marianna
Fagioli lessi secchi o freschi
Fagiolini al sugo, Marianna
Fagiolini in umido, Valeria
Fagiolini in umido
Fave al pomodoro, Marianna
Fegato alla salvia, Marianna
Fegato al burro
Fett'unta, Sergia
Frittata alla pomarola
Frittata di fagiolini e prosciutto, Valeria
Frittata di zucchini
Frittatine alla Fiorentina, M
Frittelle, M
Frittelle con l'uvetta
Funghi all'olio
Funghi fritti
Funghi trifolati, Marianna e Renzo
Gnocchi o penne alla gorgonzola, M
Gobbi gratinati, M
Hamburger, Marianna
Insalata di radicchio e cetriolo, Marianna e Renzo
Lesso, Marianna e Renzo
Lesso rifatti alla francesina
Lesso rifatto, Marianna
Lesso rifatto con le cipolle

Lingua sott'olio, Marianna e Renzo
Marmellata di limoni, M
Merluzzo al brandy, Marianna
Minestra, Marianna
Minestra di brodo (see lesso), Marianna e Renzo
Minestra di dado con burro e parmigiano, Marianna
Minestra di fagioli, Marianna
Minestra di pane, Berta e Massimo
Minestra di pane al cavolo nero o bianco
Minestra di verdura
Minestrina, Marianna
Mozzarella col pomodoro, Marianna
Muscoli marinati
Olive nere, Sergia
Ossibuchi
Palombo lesso, Elena
Pancetta di vitella arrotolata, Elena
Pane al pomodoro, Raffaele
Pane fritto, Berta e Massimo
Panzanella
Pappa al pomodoro, Raffaele
Pasta ai quattro formaggi, Caterina
Pasta alla boscaiola, Raffaele
Pasta alle vongole
Pasta con l'ortica, Marianna
Pasta con panna e pomodoro, Maria
Pasta e fagioli
Pasta o bavette ai porri, M
Pastasciutta alla fornaia
Pasticcio di pasta verde
Patate al forno, M
Patate lesse condite
Penne al sugo coniglio, Marianna
Penne al sugo di cipolla di pollo, Elena
Penne con la ricotta, M
Penne strapazzate al sugo con ricotta, Marianna
Peperonata
Peperoni e melanzane in umido, Marianna
Pesce lesso (palombo, trota)
Pesci di campo fritti, Marianna
Petti di pollo con funghi, Marianna
Petti di pollo, Valeria
Piccione arrosto con patate, Sergia

Pinzimonio
Piselli all'olio
Pizza
Pollo al cognac, Marianna and Renzo
Pollo, anatra, faraona, piccione arrosto
Pollo a pezzi, M
Pollo fritto, Marianna e Renzo
Pollo ripieno, Valeria
Pollo–zorra, costoline, spicchio, petto–lessi
Pollo, coniglio, agnello fritto
Polpette fritte
Pomarola
Pomarola, Elena
Pomarola, Marianna
Pomarola conserva, Valeria
Pomodori al forno, Marianna
Purè di patate
Radicchio, Marianna e Renzo
Ragù alla Bolognese, Elena
Rape, bietole, spinaci all'olio
Ravioli (per minestra o contorno)
Ribollita Renzo
Riso al salmone, M
Riso col cavolo, Marianna
Risotto alla Milanese
Roast beaf (sic)
Rosbif
Salame dolce, M
Salsa verde
Saltimbocca alla romana
Schiacciata alla fiorentina, M
Seppie con i piselli
Serpentelle in umido
Spaghetti ai quatro formaggi
Spaghetti aglio e olio
Spaghetti ai quattro formaggi
Spaghetti alla fantasia di Raffaele
Spaghetti alle cozze Giovanna from Elena
Spaghetti come ci pare, Raffaele
Spaghetti con le acciughe, Elena
Spaghetti con limone, Marianna
Spaghetti con panna e pomodoro, Maria
Spaghetti con panna e proscuitto

Spaghetti con prosciutto, pomodoro e uova, M
Spinaci, Marianna e Renzo
Spinaci e fegatini al forno, M
Stracciatella in brodo
Stracotto, Elena
Stufato pelliccia
Sugo, Marianna
Sugo rosé, Maria
Sugo scappato
Tacchino alla cipolla
Tacchino alla Milanese, Elena
Tacchino al limone, Valeria
Tacchino arrotolato con pancetta, Elena
Tagliatelle al sugo di melanzane e peperoni, Leonardo
Tartine: 1. mozzarella, acciuga, cappero, origano, pomodoro, M
      2. groovier [sic] e salame, M
      3. gruviera e salsiccia, M
      4. gorgonzola e mascarpone con sopra noce, M
Torta di riso, Elena
Tortellini alla panna, Raffaele
Tortellini panna e prosciutto, M
Trippa
Trippa alla fiorentina, Raffaele
Trippa condita, Elena
Trotta, Elena
Uccellini e fegatelli in forno
Uova al pomodoro
Uova al pomodoro, Marianna
Uova e formaggio al forno, M
Verdura cotta, Marianna e Renzo
Verdura cotta, Valeria
Vitella arrotolata arrosto
Vitella di latte in quaretto
Vitella di latte, M
Zucchine ripiene
Zucchini, aglio, prezzemolo, Elena
Zucchini all'olio o trifolati, Marianna e Renzo
Zucchini fritti
Zucchini fritti, Marianna
Zucchini fritti, Raffaele
Zucchini ripieni, Valeria
Zuppa di verdura, Marianna e Renzo
Zuppa lombarda, Marianna

Recipes

The recipes here were collected from my Florentine subjects in the early 1980s. They are some of the many variants of common Florentine dishes and reflect the preference of the person who gave me the recipe. Florentines argue constantly among themselves about how to prepare any given dish, and variations are infinite. The key to good Florentine cooking is fresh, top-quality ingredients, especially extra-virgin olive oil. Quantities are approximate, since Florentines do not ordinarily measure, use more or less of any ingredient depending on preference, and constantly improvise. To cook pasta, use a large (8–10 quart) pot of rapidly boiling salted water. Cook the pasta *al dente*—"to the tooth"—until it still resists when you bite into it, but is no longer hard in the middle. Tomatoes appear in many recipes; fresh are best, but only if vine-ripened; otherwise, use canned and experiment with quantity. In most of these recipes, three to five fresh tomatoes or a 28–32 ounce can of tomatoes will do nicely.

Baccalà alla livornese (dried codfish Leghorn style)

1 dried codfish
1 handful flour
2–3 tablespoons olive oil
1 small bunch parsley
3 cloves garlic
hot red pepper to taste
canned or fresh tomatoes

Soak the salted dried cod in fresh water for several hours to remove the saltiness. Dredge the fish in flour. Fry in olive oil until just done, about 5 minutes per side. Remove fish and add chopped parsley, garlic, and red pepper to the pan drippings. Sauté 5 minutes. Add tomatoes and simmer 10 minutes. Add the fish and simmer 5 more minutes. Elena said, *it is superlative!*

Bistecca alla fiorentina (Florentine steak)

Take a thick T-bone steak and grill it on the charcoal. Some people say to coat it lightly with olive oil, salt, and pepper before cooking, but some—including the famous food writer Pellegrino Artusi (1985)—abhor anything on the meat before cooking, and advocate salt and pepper only after cooking, perhaps with a pat of butter placed on the steak still hot from the grill.

Crostini (liver pâté Tuscan style)

1 onion
2–3 tablespoons butter (or olive oil)
½ pound chicken livers
1 can anchovies, drained
2 tablespoons capers, drained
good bread, sliced thin

Chop the onion and sauté it in the butter or olive oil. Boil the chicken livers until just brown and firm, drain but keep the water, and chop fine with a *mezzaluna* knife. Chop the anchovies and capers. Add chicken livers, anchovies, and capers to the onion when translucent. Sauté for 10 minutes, adding the chicken liver broth as necessary to keep mixture moist. Spread on thin bite-size slices of bread and serve as an hors-d'oeuvre.

Fagioli all'uccelletto (beans little-bird style)

1 pound dried white beans soaked overnight or fresh beans
1–3 cloves garlic
1–2 fresh sage leaves
olive oil
canned or fresh tomatoes

Cook the beans in lots of slowly boiling water until done, an hour or two. Sauté the garlic and sage in the olive oil and add the tomatoes. Cook 10 minutes, then add the beans. Cook the beans in the tomato sauce for 5–10 minutes.

Fagioli conditi (beans with oil)

1 pound dried white beans soaked overnight or fresh beans
olive oil
salt
pepper

Cook the beans in slowly boiling water until done, an hour or two. Drain and dress with olive oil, salt, and pepper.

Fave al pomodoro (fava beans with tomato)

1 onion
olive oil
canned or fresh tomatoes

1 cup fresh, tender fava beans

Chop the onion fine and sauté it in the olive oil until transparent. Add two or three fresh or canned tomatoes and their juice and cook a couple of minutes. Then add the fresh fava beans and cook a few more minutes until they are tender but not mushy.

Fett'unta ("oily slice")

bread
several cloves fresh garlic
extra-virgin olive oil

Fettunta comes from the words *fetta*—slice—and *unta*—oily. Use thick, dense white or whole-wheat bread and slice it about three-quarters of an inch thick. Toast it well on both sides—over coals on a fire if possible, or in the toaster. Then take a peeled clove of garlic and rub it over one side of the bread. The garlic grates into the bread with a release of pungent fragrance. Dribble or drench olive oil on the bread, according to taste. Florentines sprinkle salt on the bread because their bread is unsalted. Use only excellent quality, extra-virgin olive oil. *Fettunta* is good as a snack or as an accompaniment to soup.

Frittata

1 egg per person
olive oil

Beat the eggs well while you heat olive oil in a cast iron or nonstick frying pan. When the oil is hot, turn the flame down and pour in the beaten eggs. Cook slowly until firm, lifting the edges and letting the uncooked egg slide under. Flip over and cook on the other side until done.

Frittata di zucchini

2–3 small zucchini
1 small onion
1 peeled ripe or canned tomato (optional)
3 eggs
olive oil

Slice the zucchini, chop the onion, chop the tomato, and beat the eggs. Fry the onion in the olive oil until soft and add the zucchini and fry some more. When lightly browned, add the chopped tomato if desired and cook a few minutes. Then add the beaten eggs and cook slowly, lifting the edges to let the uncooked egg slide under. Flip over and cook on the other side until done.

Frittelle (rice fritters)

1 cup rice
1 pint milk
½ cup raisins
½ cup sugar
1 teaspoon vanilla
1 tablespoon rum
3 eggs, separated
flour
vegetable oil
confectioners sugar

Boil the rice in the milk until it is cooked and let it cool. Add the raisins, sugar, vanilla, and rum. Stir in the egg yolks. Whip the egg whites until they form stiff peaks and fold them into the rice mixture. Stir in a little flour until the mixture is dense, but not too thick; a tablespoon or two of flour should suffice. Heat the oil in a large frying pan and drop tablespoons of batter into the hot oil, fry them, and turn them. When cooked, put the fritters on absorbent paper and sprinkle with confectioners sugar. *Frittelle* are traditional in Florence for the Feast of St. Joseph, March 19, when many women make them at home and all the pastry shops sell them.

Lesso (boiled meat)

2 pounds good stewing beef (optional: calf's foot, beef tongue, and ox-tail)
1 onion
odori: parsley, celery stalk, carrot, basil
salt and pepper to taste

Boil the beef, onion, and *odori* for 2–3 hours in just enough water to cover beef. Salt and pepper to taste at the end of cooking. Remove the meat to a plate and strain the broth. Bring it to a boil and cook some kind of small pasta in it, making a watery soup. If you have a lot of broth, you can save it to cook rice for *risotto.* Eat the soup as a first course and the meat as a second course. If any meat is left over, make *lesso rifatto.* (If the broth is very fatty, cool it and skim off the fat before cooking the pasta in it).

Lesso rifatto (refried meat)

1 large onion
4–6 potatoes
olive oil
leftover boiled meat *(lesso)*

Slice the onions and potatoes thinly and fry them together in olive oil until the potatoes are cooked, 20 minutes or so. Chop the *lesso* and add it to the pan; fry for 5 more minutes.

Lesso rifatto alla francesina (French-style refried meat)

1 large onion
olive oil
canned or fresh tomatoes
leftover boiled meat *(lesso)*

Slice the onion and fry in olive oil until soft. Add the tomatoes and cook 10 minutes until a sauce forms. Chop the *lesso* and add it to the mixture, cooking until the meat and sauce are mixed, about 5 minutes.

Minestra di pane (bread soup)

1 pound dried white beans
1 onion
odori: chopped parsley, celery stalk, carrot, basil
olive oil
canned or fresh tomatoes
some or all of the following:
   chopped green cabbage
   chopped Tuscan kale
   string beans with string removed
   spinach
   Swiss chard
several slices of stale, thick, dense bread

Soak the beans overnight in water. Cook the beans in lots of water for an hour or two until done, then add salt to taste. In a frying pan, sauté the onion and *odori* in the olive oil until soft, then add the chopped tomatoes and cook until they form a sauce. Then add this mixture to the beans along with the cabbage and other vegetables and cook 30–40 minutes. Take a big soup tureen or individual bowls and put a layer of bread, then a layer of soup, then bread, soup, bread, soup, until it is all used up. Let sit until thoroughly soaked and eat.

Minestrina

broth or water
olive oil or butter or bouillon cube
small pasta like Ave Maria or spaghetti broken into 1-inch pieces

Boil the broth or the water with a few drops of olive oil or a pat of butter or a bouillon cube, drop in the pasta, and cook until done, serving as a watery soup.

Minestrone (**hearty vegetable soup**)

1 onion
1 small bunch parsley
1 carrot
1 celery stalk
olive oil
1 zucchini, sliced
1 cup sliced green cabbage
½ cup string beans, chopped into small pieces
2–3 potatoes
2 cups Swiss chard and/or spinach
1 cup cooked or canned white beans
any other vegetables according to availability and preference
Optional: ½ cup small pasta or rice

Chop onion, parsley, carrot, and celery, and sauté in olive oil until soft. Add 3–4 cups of water, the zucchini, cabbage, and string beans, and bring to a boil. Cook about an hour. Add the potatoes and Swiss chard/spinach and cook half an hour. Add the cooked white beans and bring to a boil. Then add pasta or rice and cook until done, about 15 more minutes. Or you can omit the pasta or rice and eat with lots of bread. There are as many minestrone recipes as there are women with kitchens, and most vegetables go well in this soup.

Olive (**olives**)

Olives must be cured because they are extremely bitter. Forty-year-old Sergia learned to cure olives from a farmer who worked her land. Pick the olives when they are just turning from green to black and are still firm. Soak the olives for forty-eight days in well water. Remove them and put them in new salted well water. Let this sit for a year or so and then eat. The olives will form a skin on the surface of the water, a sort of mold. Do not remove or break this skin, for it protects the olives; just push it aside and spoon out the olives from underneath.

Panzanella (**summer salad**)

1 pound stale, dense white or whole-wheat bread
1 onion
1 cucumber
2 fresh ripe tomatoes
4 fresh basil leaves
4 tablespoons olive oil
2 tablespoons vinegar
salt and fresh ground black pepper to taste

Soak the bread in water for a short while, squeeze it dry, and crumble it into small pieces. Put it in a big salad bowl. Slice the onion thinly. Peel and slice the cucumber. Slice the tomatoes. Cut the basil with scissors into small pieces. Toss all these ingredients with the bread, olive oil, vinegar, salt, and pepper.

Pappa al pomodoro (tomato pap)

4 fresh ripe tomatoes
3–4 tablespoons olive oil
4 cloves garlic
4 fresh basil leaves
1 cup broth
4 slices stale, dense bread

Chop the tomatoes and cook them in the olive oil in a frying pan over a medium heat for 10 minutes. Slice the garlic into slivers and cook with the tomatoes for 5 minutes. Add the whole basil leaves and cook 5 more minutes. Add the broth so that the mixture is fairly liquid and bring to a boil. Chop the stale bread into small pieces and add to the tomato broth mixture. Cook for 5 more minutes until it is a fairly solid mass.

Pasta e fagioli (pasta and bean soup)

1 pound dried white beans soaked overnight, or fresh white beans
3–5 cloves garlic
1–2 fresh sage leaves
1 small bunch parsley
olive oil
canned or fresh tomatoes
small pasta, like ditalini, or spaghetti broken into 1-inch pieces
salt and pepper to taste

Cook the beans in lots of slowly boiling water with 1–2 cloves garlic and the sage until done, an hour or two. Chop 2–3 cloves garlic and the parsley and sauté in the olive oil for a few minutes, then add the tomatoes and cook slowly for 10 minutes. Add some of the beans to the tomato mixture and mash with a potato masher until they form a thick paste. Add this paste to the bean soup and cook 10 minutes. Then add pasta and cook until the pasta is *al dente.* Add salt and pepper.

Pinzimonio (piquant dressing)

extra-virgin olive oil
salt
fresh ground pepper

Pinzimonio is a dressing for raw vegetables, especially artichokes, which in Tuscany are harvested while still tender enough to eat raw. Other vegetables commonly eaten in *pinzimonio* in Tuscany are celery, carrots, radishes, fennel, and spring onions, though any vegetable you like can be used. Put some olive oil in a small bowl. Stir an abundant amount of salt and fresh ground black pepper into the oil. Dip the vegetables. For Rinaldo, this is "*a meal from God.*"

Pomarola (tomato sauce)

1 onion
1–2 tablespoons olive oil
canned or fresh tomatoes
4–5 fresh basil leaves

Chop the onion and sauté it in the olive oil. When the onion is translucent, add the tomatoes and basil and cook until thick. Put mixture through a food mill, add fresh olive oil, and cook a bit more. There are many ways to make *pomarola,* and every Italian cook has her own "right" way. This is Elena's recipe for the "true" *pomarola.* Marianna gave me two other recipes for *pomarola,* one identical to Elena's, but with garlic instead of onion. The second contains the *odori*—chopped carrot, celery stalk, basil, and parsley—in addition to the onion and tomatoes.

Ribollita ("reboiled" soup)

Ribollita is made from leftover minestrone "reboiled" the second day and ladled over bread to produce a thick pap eaten hot or cold, which is "reboiled" until it is all eaten.

Riso col cavolo (rice with cabbage)

6–8 cups broth
½–1 chopped green cabbage
1 cup rice

Boil the broth and toss in the chopped cabbage. Boil for 30 minutes, then add the rice and cook 15 minutes or so until the rice is just *al dente.* Eat as a brothy soup rather than as a dense rice dish.

Risotto alla Milanese (Milanese-style rice)

1 small onion
olive oil
1 cup uncooked rice
2 cups broth
pinch of saffron
grated Parmesan cheese

Chop the onion very fine and fry it in a large frying pan in the olive oil until it is slightly browned. Toss the rice in and stir it over medium flame until very lightly browned. Then add the broth little by little, keeping it simmering, stirring frequently, adding more broth when it is absorbed. When the rice is almost cooked, add a pinch of saffron. Serve with grated Parmesan cheese.

Saltimbocca ("jump-in-the-mouth")

1 pound thinly sliced steaks
¼ pound sliced bologna
¼ pound sliced mozzarella
1 clove garlic
1–2 fresh sage leaves or ¼ teaspoon dried sage
olive oil
canned or fresh tomatoes

Roll up each steak with 1 piece of bologna and 1 slice of mozzarella and fasten with a toothpick. Sauté the garlic, sage, and rolled meat in the olive oil until the meat is browned on all sides. Add the tomatoes and cook 10–15 minutes until the sauce thickens and the meat is cooked.

Saltimbocca alla romana ("jump-in-the-mouth" Roman style)

Substitute ham or prosciutto for bologna in the above recipe.

Spaghetti aglio e olio (spaghetti with garlic and olive oil)

1 pound spaghetti
1 small bunch parsley (optional)
3–5 cloves garlic
3–5 tablespoons olive oil
grated Parmesan

Cook the spaghetti in rapidly boiling salted water. Finely chop the parsley and the garlic, and sauté over a low flame in the olive oil for 5 minutes, stirring constantly and being careful not to burn the garlic. Toss the cooked, drained spaghetti in a large bowl with the olive oil mixture and sprinkle with grated Parmesan to taste.

Spaghetti aglio, olio, e peperoncino (spaghetti with garlic, olive oil, and hot pepper)

1 pound spaghetti
1 small bunch parsley
3–5 cloves garlic
hot pepper to taste
3–5 tablespoons olive oil
grated Parmesan

Cook the spaghetti in rapidly boiling salted water. Finely chop the parsley, garlic, and hot pepper. Sauté them over a low flame in the olive oil for 5 minutes, stirring constantly and being careful not to burn the garlic. Toss the cooked, drained spaghetti in a large bowl with the olive oil mixture and sprinkle with grated Parmesan to taste.

Spaghetti ai quattro formaggi (spaghetti with four cheese)

1 pound spaghetti
3 tablespoons butter
¼ cup grated Parmesan
¼ cup grated pecorino cheese
¼ cup crumbled gorgonzola cheese
¼ cup grated Swiss or gruyère cheese

Cook the spaghetti *al dente* in boiling water, then toss in a large bowl with the butter and the four cheeses. You can use penne or other short pasta or rice instead of spaghetti.

Spaghetti come ci pare (spaghetti as we like it)

2–4 cloves garlic
1 small bunch of parsley or basil
hot pepper (*pepperoncino*) to taste
olive oil
canned or fresh tomatoes

Finely chop the garlic, parsley or basil, and hot pepper. Sauté in olive oil briefly, being sure not to burn it. Add tomatoes and simmer for 10 minutes. Serve with spaghetti *al dente.*

Spaghetti con panna e prosciutto (spaghetti with cream and ham)

¼–½ pound sliced ham
¼–½ cup heavy cream
1 pound spaghetti
½ cup grated Parmesan
pepper

Cut the ham into small pieces and stir into the cream in a big bowl. Cook the spaghetti *al dente* in boiling water and drain and toss with the cream and ham, then add the grated Parmesan and pepper to taste.

Stracotto ("the overcooked," i.e., pot roast)

5–6 cloves garlic
rosemary

salt and pepper to taste
2–4 pounds beef suitable for pot roast
1 small bunch parsley
optional:
    1 celery stalk
    1 onion
    1 carrot
1–2 tablespoons olive oil
flour
canned or fresh tomatoes

Push bits of half the garlic and the rosemary with salt and pepper into the meat. Chop up the remaining garlic and parsley (with the celery, onion, and carrot if desired) and sauté in olive oil until soft. Dredge the meat lightly in flour and brown in the oil on all sides. Add tomatoes and water to cover. Boil on stove for 2–3 hours, allowing the water to reduce itself into a thick sauce that can be used with pasta.

Sugo rosé (pink sauce)

1–2 cups *pomarola** sauce (homemade or purchased)
2 tablespoons olive oil or butter
pinch of hot pepper, ginger, or basil
optional: dried mushrooms, soaked
¼–½ cup heavy cream

Heat the pomarola in some butter or olive oil, add the hot pepper, ginger, or basil, and the soaked dried mushrooms if desired and simmer for 10 minutes. Then stir in the cream and heat thoroughly, but do not boil. Use as a sauce for spaghetti or penne.

Sugo scappato

1 onion
1 celery stalk
1 carrot
1 small bunch parsley
3–4 fresh basil leaves
olive oil
peeled ripe or canned tomatoes
salt and pepper to taste

Finely chop together the first five ingredients. Sauté them in the olive oil until soft. Add the tomatoes, salt, and pepper and cook a long time until a thick sauce emerges. Use with spaghetti cooked al dente and sprinkle with Parmesan cheese. Codacci (1981, 49) calls this *sugo finto* (fake or pretend sauce) or *sugo scappato.* He says, "A 'thing' emerges that is neither meat nor sauce, but a genuine amalgam that will make an excellent impression when you put it on your pastasciutta."

Torta di riso (rice cake)

½ pound uncooked rice
1 quart milk
4 eggs, lightly beaten
½–1 cup sugar
dash of any liqueur
¼–½ cup candied fruits
½ teaspoon grated lemon peel

Cook the rice *al dente* in the milk. Mix it with all the other ingredients. Bake in a buttered 9-inch square baking pan at 325 degrees for 30–40 minutes until a toothpick inserted in the center comes out clean.

Uova al pomodoro (eggs with tomatoes)

canned or fresh tomatoes
1–2 fresh basil leaves
olive oil
1 egg per person
salt and pepper to taste

In a small frying pan, cook the tomatoes and basil in the olive oil for 5–10 minutes into a fairly wet sauce. Then crack the eggs into the sauce, being careful not to break the yolk, and cook until the white is hard and the yolk is still runny. Season with salt and pepper.

Zuppa lombarda (Lombard soup)

1 pound dried white beans soaked overnight or fresh
1–2 fresh sage leaves
3 cloves garlic, crushed
canned or fresh tomatoes
olive oil
several slices of thick white or whole-wheat bread, toasted

Cook all the ingredients except the bread in a pot with a lot of water until the beans are done, 1–2 hours. Crumble the toasted bread into individual bowls and ladle the beans and broth over it.

Notes

Chapter 1

1. The catalyst to thinking about food as voice was Joan Jacobs Brumberg's (1988) chapter "Appetite as Voice" reprinted in Counihan and Van Esterik (1997). This book emerges out of a quarter-century of exploration of how ethnographic interviews centered on food can be a way for people to talk about history, culture, relationships, and identity. I have collected food-centered life histories with Pennsylvania college students and pregnant women (Counihan 1999), with Mexican-Americans in southern Colorado (Counihan 2002), and with the Florentines presented here. My work is embedded in feminist anthropology, which places women at the center, defines gender as a crucial category in social life and social analysis, and challenges gender oppression (Moore 1988). Feminist ethnography has made recuperating the lost voices of women a central goal, and has struggled mightily to find ways of presenting those voices in empowering ways (Behar 1993, Behar and Gordon 1995, Wolf 1992). Some feminist studies of food as women's voice are Adams 1990, Avakian 1997, Bordo 1993, Brumberg 1988, Bynum 1987, Charles and Kerr 1988, Chernin 1981, 1985, Counihan 1999, DeVault 1991, and Thompson 1994. Some women who have found a voice through food writing are Esquivel 1989, Fisher 1954, and Randall 1997.
2. Some important recent works on Italian foodways are Alberini 1992; Alexander 2000; Bevilacqua 1989, 1990, 1991; Bonfili 1993; Camporesi 1980, 1996, 1998a, 1998b, 2000; Camporesi and Woodhall 1998; Capatti, De Bernardi, and Varni 1998; Capatti and Montanari 1999; De Clercq 1990, 1995; Grammatico and Simeti 1994; Helstosky 1996, 2003, 2004; Serventi and Sabban 2002; Sorcinelli 1992, 1998; Teti 1976, 1995. On Tuscany and food, see Apergi and Bianco 1991; Bianchi 1995; Codacci 1981; Costantini 1976; Da Monte 1995; Jenkins 1998; Lo Russo and Pratesi 1999; Mayes 1996, 1999, 2000; Meis 1993; Perticoni 1979; Petroni 1974, 1991; Romer 1984; Taddei 1998; Vesco 1984. On breast-feeding in Italy, see Olivi 1997; Whitaker 2000.
3. All names are pseudonyms.
4. I know Italian well, not only from having studied it in college and lived for six years in Italy in almost totally monolingual environments, but also from Florentines' constant linguistic didacticism, which sometimes reached an extreme of pickiness that Florentines call *pignoleria*. Willy-nilly, I was constantly taught the subtleties of their language. I thank Christine Streit Guerrini for helpful translating advice on several occasions.
5. I learned this style from Stack's (1996) *Call to Home: African Americans in the Rural South*.
6. Richard Flores (1998, 2–3) provides a succinct definition: "Modernity . . . refers to a complex, uneven, and multifaceted process of transformation through which earlier social and cultural complexes are dislodged from the habitats of their making and are reconstituted, under the weight of rationalized, technocratic forces, into distinct and qualitatively new forms. . . . One of the primary engines of modernity is capitalism, with its incessant drive toward the creation of new markets and its incorporation of earlier productive practices and relations into its guiding principles of wage labor, surplus value, and commodity fetishism."
7. Italy has always been and still is a diverse nation where regional differences are highly important. What I describe here pertains to the foodways of Florence and Tuscany, which although characteristically their own also shared attributes with other areas of Italy, particularly with the contiguous regions of central Italy: Umbria, Emiglia-Romagna, and Le Marche.
8. See Lamphere 2000, Moore 1988, Rosaldo 1974, Rosaldo and Lamphere 1974, Sacks 1974, Sargent 1981.
9. Engels (1972, 120) said that the privatization of women's labor in the monogamous nuclear family led to the "world historical defeat of the female sex." Feminist anthropologists have carried Engels's analysis in several directions. Rosaldo (1974) found the public/private, production/reproduction gender dichotomy related to the widespread subordination of

women. Sacks (1974) emphasized how the privatization of women's labor robbed them of "social adulthood." Riddiough (1981) and Harding (1981) linked the production/reproduction split to how family structure, child rearing, and domestic practices reinforced male power inside and outside the home. Later feminist anthropologists looked at gender relations worldwide, found much variability in how men and women defined and participated in production and reproduction, and argued for a more culturally and historically grounded conception of the two spheres (Lamphere 2000).

10. Bates (1975, 352) defines Gramsci's concept of hegemony as "political leadership based on the consent of the led, a consent which is secured by the diffusion and popularization of the world view of the ruling class." See Counihan 1986.

11. Camera di Commercio 1958, Barucci 1964, and ISTAT 1990.

12. Prato was separated from the province of Florence and became capoluogo of its own province in 1992.

13. These data come from Camera di Commercio 1958, Barucci 1964, ISTAT 1990, and the ISTAT Web site: http://demo.istat.it/pop1/selback1.htm, consulted February 13, 2002. In 1999, 34,423 foreigners from 140 countries were officially resident in Florence, with the top five countries being China (5,114), Albania (4,374), the Philippines (2,787), Morocco (2,158) and Yugoslavia (1,358) (http://demo.istat.it/stra1999/quey.php, consulted May 21, 2003).

14. Any bibliographic search on Florence will call up endless titles on Florentine history, art, architecture, and politics focusing mostly on periods before the twentieth century—for example, Cochrane 1973, Fei 1971, Levey 1996, Lewis 1995, Schevill 1961. There is also a considerable amount of travel literature written about Florence. On recent Florence and/or Tuscany, see Clemente 1980, Epstein 1994/1995, Falassi 1980, Hellenga 1994, Lewis 1995, Mayes 1996, 1999, 2000, Mori 1986, Origo 1947, Plattner n.d., Rotelli 1980, Silverman 1975, Vannucci 1986. Anthropological writing on Italy has concentrated on the south and islands, usually on small towns—for example, Angioni 1974, 1976, 1989, Assmuth 1997, Banfield 1958, Blok 1974, Brögger 1971, Chapman 1971, Cornelisen 1969, 1976, Davis 1973, Magliocco 1993, Pitkin 1985, Schneider 1998, Schneider and Schneider 1976, 1996, White 1980. There are a few ethnographic studies of Italian cities, though none of Florence: Belmonte 1979, Goddard 1996, Kenny and Kertzer 1983, Kertzer 1980, 1983, Pardo 1996, Romanucci-Ross 1991, Shore 1990. On Italy, see also Blim 1990, Cole and Wolf 1975, Holmes 1989, Horn 1994, Kertzer 1984, 1998, Kertzer and Hogan 1989, Kertzer and Saller 1991, Whitaker 2000.

15. All names are pseudonyms. Ages throughout the book refer to how old subjects were in 1984 when I completed the interviews. The kinship chart shows names, relationships, and birth, death, and marriage dates. Appendix A shows life synopses of subjects.

16. Three were Americans—Giovanna's husband and daughters, Joseph, Georgia, and Susan—and although I interviewed them, I have not used their narratives here.

Chapter 2

1. This also appears in Pecori (1981). Thanks to Christine Streit Guerrini for help on translation.

2. Weismantel (1988, 87) defines *cuisine* as "the cultural construction of meals, the structures that organize knowledge about foods, and the pattern of their preparation and combination." Other anthropological discussions of cuisine include Appadurai 1988, Barthes 1997, Douglas 1975, Goody 1982, Lehrer 1969, 1972, Lévi-Strauss 1966, Mintz 1997, and Soler 1973.

3. For the cuisine of the elites, see Louis Monod's early-twentieth-century cookbook *La Cucina Fiorentina* (Lo Russo and Pratesi 1999). For the debate over the definition of "traditional" *Florentine cuisine,* see Lo Russo (1999). For a discussion of Italian cookbooks and nation-building, see Helstosky (2003).

4. See Vesco 1984 on Florentine cuisine in the late Middle Ages. See Helstosky (1996, 175) on how Mussolini extolled whole-wheat bread over white *bread.*

5. See Appadurai 1988, Goody 1982, Mintz 1997.

6. See Lo Russo and Pratesi (1999) on the different diets of the *Florentine* elites and masses. Apergi and Bianco (1991, 87–88) confirm that for *mezzadria* peasants beef was expensive and rarely purchased except for holidays. See Zamagni 1998 and Helstosky 1996 on Italian

dietary studies in the late nineteenth and early twentieth centuries, which found class differences in food consumption.

7. *Mollica* was a commonly used term describing the soft inner part of the bread, as opposed to the crustier outer part. Often Italians removed some of the *mollica* when making a sandwich.

8. In Vicchio di Mugello (Florence), peasants spoke of "making the cross" (*fare la croce*) with olive oil to indicate how sparingly they used it. Lard was the main cooking fat, and they ate little butter (Apergi and Bianco 1991, 60).

9. I have translated this Tuscan expression loosely. *Pelliccia* is a fur coat or the skin of an animal with long hair—in either case, nothing very edible—and *ciccia* refers to meat. Codacci (1981, 105) suggests the origin of the *stuffato di pelliccia:* "The story of the little stew of Signor Pelliccia . . . has peasant origins. It was born from the desire of the ancient Tuscan mothers to spur their children to eat with good appetite. Because these women knew how influenced their children were by the eating habits of the upper class, they used the strange and curious name of Signor Pelliccia to induce their children to eat this stew. But the name also contained a bitter irony because the stew of Signor Pelliccia has so many potatoes and so little meat."

10. Bananas were imported from Ethiopia after the Italian invasion in 1935 (Helstosky 1996, 208).

11. The word *semelaio*—bread man—comes from the word *sèmele* or *sèmelle*—a small, hexagonally shaped roll made out of fine white flour. Raddi (2001, 256) says the word comes from the German word for roll, *semmel.* Thanks to Beppe Lo Russo for confirming this etymology.

12. For a discussion of food and memory among Greek villagers from Kalymnos, see Sutton 2001.

13. Sutton (2001, 17) calls food's ability to unite multiple sensory domains "synesthesia" and links this to its role in memory.

14. Taddei (1998, 33) confirms that bread with wine and sugar was a common snack in Tuscany.

15. See "The Body as Voice of Desire and Connection in Florence" (Counihan 1999, chap. 10) for a more extended discussion of food, body, and *gola.*

16. These and all translations from Italian are mine unless otherwise noted.

17. In *A Hunger So Wide and So Deep,* Thompson (1994) reflects on the protective and dangerous dimensions of eating for consolation among diverse women in the United States.

18. Florentine beliefs were similar to those found by Romanucci-Ross (1991, 140) in the central Italian province of Ascoli Piceno: "The psychosomatic system must be kept in balance. Specifically, extremes in temperatures should be avoided; food must be consumed with an eye toward balance among meats, fish, vegetables, salads, fruits, grains ('heavy' and 'light' are classifications to be balanced)." None of my informants mentioned the concept of *calore* or heat in regard to food. Apergi and Bianco (1991, 114) found that in Vicchio di Mugello (Florence) pregnant women avoided herring because it was "*troppo calorosa*" but said no more.

19. See Apergi and Bianco (1991, 110–111) on the use of the fats called *lardo, sugna, sego,* and *retìna* for pulmonary illness and muscle injury.

20. Romer (1984, 89) describes one Tuscan woman "eating in white" after giving birth, with a diet "consisting mainly of rice and pasta with grated *pecorino* to flavour it, and fresh ricotta or *ravigiolo* [sic] that they made at home."

21. Cantagalli (1981, 105) calls it the "*l'erba della paura.*" He says, "It is *Stachys recta,* a rather bristly plant with yellow flowers. In the countryside it is known as the herb for fear because the grandmothers used it to make an infusion to wash children who had had a fright that they feared might cause boils or an alteration to the nervous system."

22. Researchers have found a value on plump bodies in many cultures; see, for example, Becker 1995, Counihan 1999, De Garine and Pollock 1995, Powdermaker 1997, Sobo 1997, Teti 1995.

23. On Florentines who are keeping alive traditional vegetable varieties, see Nabhan (1993, 35–54).

24. Raffaele demonstrated the fact that he had never worked the land by mixing up the harvest times of vegetables. Artichokes matured first, then asparagus, then peas, then string beans.

Chapter 3

1. See Apergi and Bianco (1991, 43–52) for a thorough description of "the culinary cycle of the pig" among *mezzadria* peasants, including a discussion of all the products made and used.

2. On the Tuscan *mezzadria* system, see Anselmi 1990, Clemente et al. 1980, Falassi 1980, Origo 1947, Sereni 1968, Signorelli 1990; Silverman 1975, Sabbatucci Severini 1990, Snowden 1989. See also Kertzer 1984 and Kertzer and Hogan 1989 on the neighboring Emilia Romagna region. On Tuscan *mezzadria* foodways, see Apergi and Bianco 1991 and Taddei 1998. On the history of Italian foodways, see Camporesi's many books; Capatti et al. 1998; Capatti and Montanari 1999; Helstosky 1996, 2003, 2004; Prezzolini 1948; and Sorcinelli 1992.

3. Law 756 of September 15, 1964, instituted the demise of *mezzadria* by prohibiting any new contracts and encouraging the establishment of peasant-proprietors in various ways (Silverman 1975, 71–72). By 1982, barely more than 3 percent of Italy's cultivated land was worked under *mezzadria* (Fanfani 1990, 436).

4. Most Italians in the nineteenth and first half of the twentieth century had a scarce and monotonous diet, defined politically as *il problema dell'alimentazione,* which was linked to a widespread cultural value on parsimony (Helstosky 2003, 2004). See also Capatti et al. 1998, Capatti and Montanari 1999, Sorcinelli 1992, 1998, Taddei 1998, Zamagni 1998.

5. *Mezzadria* shared characteristics typical of peasant systems documented by many scholars. See Marx 1964 and Engels 1966, 1972. On the European peasantry, see also Blok 1974; Franklin 1969; Hobsbawm 1959, 1964; Landsberger 1974; Schneider 1998; Schneider and Schneider 1976, 1996; Sereni 1968; Shanin 1973; Silverman 1975; Wolf 1966, 1969, 1982.

6. The next closest region was Lazio, with 39.2 percent of the land in plots of 100 hectares or more (Preti 1986, 606–607).

7. Snowden 1989, chapter 1. See Clemente 1980, 117–123, for an example of a *mezzadria* contract detailing the numerous obligations of the peasant family to work and provide for the landlord's family. Festa (1980) collected several folk songs of the Tuscan peasants lamenting their burdens of feeding others while never having enough for their hungry families.

8. Coppi and Fineschi (1980, 192) define *garzoni* as young men whose families were too poor to maintain them and sent them to work in families where they received room and board in exchange for their labor. See also Apergi and Bianco (1991, 66–67), who say that *garzoni* were children of both sexes who were sometimes orphans and were often exploited in *mezzadria* families, where they were fed less well than family members.

9. "The birth of male children was generally welcomed with more joy and celebrated more excessively than the birth of girls" (Coppi and Fineschi 1980, 196).

10. Coppi and Fineschi 1980, 197. Apergi and Bianco (1991, 28) collected several examples of the books or *libretti colonici* kept by *mezzadri* which in the Mugello region were called *quadernucci.*

11. "The peasants produced oil, wine; they cultivated the garden; they raised courtyard animals and a pig; all this is true, but of all this goodness of God they ate very little. Almost all of it was sold to profit the *padrone*" (Lo Russo 1999, 29).

12. On Prato, see Cerpi-Censis 1974, Faccioli 1991, Nigro 1986.

13. See Helstosky 1996, 2004; Sorcinelli 1992, 1998; and Zamagni 1998 on the very low levels of meat consumption all over Italy.

14. Another well-known proverb is *"essere come pane e cacio,"* meaning "to be like bread and cheese"—that is, to get along well together.

15. The cheese readily accessible to the poor in Tuscany and elsewhere was *ricotta,* called such because it was made by "recooking" the whey after the fatty curds had been made into cheese. See Romer 1984, 44, on *ricotta*-making in Tuscany, and Counihan 1981 on making *ricotta* in Sardinia.

16. Ferrali (1979, 5) gives a longer version, which he says comes from Montalbano near Pistoia: *"Marzo: chi non ha scarpe, vada scalzo, e chi ce l'ha ne tenga ben di conto, per andare alla festa di San Baronto"*—"March: who does not have shoes, barefoot he goes, and he who has them keeps them dear, to go to the festival at San Baronto." San Baronto was a mountain hamlet known for its church and its annual May 1 celebration.

17. The shirkers were called *imboscati*—"the ones hiding in the woods."

18. During and after World War I, the *calmieri* or price controls were off and on, and most often struck wheat flour, corn flour, bread, rice, pasta, meat, eggs, lard, cheese, butter, oil,

sugar, coffee, and milk. A major challenge to the Italian government was ensuring adequate wheat supplies; imports increased almost 300-fold from 15,329 quintals in 1914 to 4,349,632 in 1918. The government mandated a *tipo unico* bread that was at least 80 percent of the milled wheat and thus coarser than the preferred and prestigious white bread (Helstosky 1996, chapter 1).

19. Socialist historian Salvemini (1973, 210) observed the Florence food riots, and he claimed that not the Socialists but the "ultra-conservative" Florence *La Nazione* newspaper launched them by attacking war profiteers in its July 3 report on the previous days' riots in Forlì. According to Salvemini, the food riots were really the spontaneous actions of a mob incited by the Right. But in some people's minds, like Marco's, the Left was responsible.

20. On fascism, food, and gender, see Caldwell 1986; Capatti et al. 1998; De Grazia 1992; Helstosky 1996, 2004; Morgan 1995; Salvemini 1973; Snowden 1989; Sorcinelli 1992, 1998; and Tannebaum 1972. Avati's (1989) lush film *The Story of Boys and Girls*, set in 1936 at the height of fascism, portrays the culinary culture of the Tuscan *mezzadria* family.

21. Tannenbaum (1972, 107) said, "The Battle of Grain was typically Fascist not only in its name . . . but also in the ballyhoo that accompanied it, in its effort to mobilize millions of people in a common undertaking and in its emphasis on national prestige at the expense of sound economics." See also Hestosky 1996, 2004; Preti 1986; and Segre 1982.

22. Helstosky 1996, 157; Morgan 1995, 98–101. In addition to promoting bread production and consumption, the fascist government also encouraged consumption of rice, fish, vegetables, grapes, and wine—all domestic products (Helstosky 1996, 176–205).

23. "The stereotype of Mussolini's new man tried to assert himself in factory canteens, at the tables of patriarchal families, and in the kitchens of the emerging white collar classes" (Sacchetti 1999, 114).

24. See Preti 1986 on the straw-braiding industry in the province of Florence in the interwar years.

25. Law 1514 of September 5, 1938, set a quota of 10 percent for women in large and medium-size businesses and proposed their exclusion from firms smaller than ten employees, although this law had limited effects in practice. Women were prohibited from being heads of middle schools and from teaching history, philosophy, or economics in high schools in 1923. Women who remained employed lacked representation in the fascist trade unions that dominated labor negotiation (De Grazia 1992, 175–179; Caldwell 1986, 125–126).

26. Girls were discouraged from schooling and few went further than fifth grade. Only one-fourth of the university-track high school students in 1935 were women, and most women in the university were in teaching tracks (De Grazia 1992, 149–153).

27. Fascist pro-natalist policies included lowering the legal ages of marriage for women from fifteen to fourteen and for men from eighteen to sixteen, "the criminalization of abortion, . . . family allocations, maternity insurance, birth and marriage loans, career preferences for fathers of big families, and special institutions established for infant and family health and welfare" (De Grazia 1992, 46; see also Caldwell 1986; Whitaker 2000).

28. Gibson (1986) describes Italy's "regulation" of prostitution. The Legge Merlin, passed in 1958, abolished brothels and banned registration of prostitutes.

29. Quoted in De Grazia 1992, 192.

30. See Whitaker (2000) for a detailed discussion of fascism's oppressive legacy of birth and breast-feeding policies.

31. Historian Ginsborg (1990, 10) said, "Mussolini's decision to enter the Second World War on Hitler's side proved fatal for Italian fascism."

32. Lindberg (1946). In the immediate postwar period, the average nonfarm consumer in Italy still had less than 1,500 calories a day.

33. See Helstosky (2004, chapter 4) on Germans' appropriation of Italian food.

34. See Helstosky (2004, chapter 4) on the deportation of Italian civilians to Germany to work.

35. Wilhelm (1988, 234) describes the Germans' control of Florence in early August 1944: "In the city they had now secured a position that extended from the Arno to the Cascine Park, along the Mugnone to Piazza delle Cure and from there, along the Florence–Rome railway line."

36. In Tuscany, land cultivated in *mezzadria* dropped from 31 percent to 6 percent of the total between 1961 and 1982. Sabbatucci Severini (1990) describes the processes by which *mezzadria* peasants left the land. Generally the young people left first; some started businesses, often based on traditional crafts, which employed other family members; often they kept some land that was worked by the older family members or part-time by the younger ones.

37. Marianna referred to the devastating flood of the Arno River on November 4, 1966, which struck the center of Florence with a vengeance. Hellenga's (1994) novel contains vivid descriptions of the flood, as does Lewis's (1995) memoir.

Chapter 4

1. On Tuscan cuisine, see Bianchi 1995; Codacci 1981; Costantini 1976; Da Monte, 1995; Jenkins 1998; Lo Russo 1999; Meis 1993; Perticoni 1979; Petroni 1974, 1991; Romer 1984. I thank Samuela Ristori for sending me a copy of Da Monte's (1995) book on the traditional cuisine of the Casentino zone of Tuscany which arrived just as I was sending this book to the printer, too late to incorporate, but a rich source on Tuscan cuisine.

2. My subjects rarely ate fresh fish or game, although residents of coastal Tuscany consumed fish, and those living in the country, especially near the border with Umbria, ate game (Romer 1984).

3. Massimo used *"farina,"* which usually refers to wheat flour. His brother Renzo said *migliacciole* were made with chestnut flour, a fact confirmed by Costantini (1976). Raddi (2001, 175) says that migliaccio "is a tasty mixture made with chestnut flour, also called sweet flour (*farina dolce*), and pine nuts, cooked in the oven and served in pieces, very hot. Elsewhere it is known as *castagnaccio* and its inventor seems to have been a certain Pilade da Lucca, who lived in the sixteenth century. When the above-mentioned mixture is maintained in a more liquid form and instead of in the oven is cooked in a pot . . . it is the so-called *pattona* or chestnut polenta. In the same family, the tasty *migliacciuole* [sic] a kind of round fritter of small size." Apergi and Bianco (1991, 55) write, "*Migliaccio* is normally used to define a sweet made with chestnut flour (but in the nearby Romagna region the same term designates a sweet made with pig's blood). *Migliacciòla* is defined as a [wheat] flour dough cooked in oil," probably only consumed by better-off peasants because oil was scarce (1991, 57). Codacci (1981, 137–138) describes how to make *pattona* and *castagnaccio.* See also Romer (1984, 148–150).

4. Codacci (1981, 37) gives a different recipe for *acqua cotta di Maremma,* which he suggests originated with the cattle herders of the Maremma region who gathered wild greens while herding and cooked them in soup with olive oil, bacon, onion, green grapes, dried cod, and potatoes.

5. In 1980–84 in Italy, the average per-capita intake of meat was 129.9 grams; of bread, pizza, pasta, rice, and other cereals, 229.9 grams; of vegetables and legumes, 210.3 grams; of fruit and nuts, 195.8 grams; of olive oil, 19.8 grams; of vegetable oil, butter, and other fats, 8.1 grams; and of sugar, honey, cakes, biscuits, pastries, etc., 76.8 grams (Turrini et al. 2001, 584).

6. According to Vesco (1984, 64), *cenci* dated back to Saturnalia festivals of ancient Rome. See Perticoni 1979 for a collection of traditional Tuscan dessert recipes.

7. See Apergi and Bianco 1991, chapter 4, on foods for Sundays and holidays under *mezzadria.* The *feste grosse* (big holidays) were Christmas, Carnival, and Easter. See Falassi 1988 and Toschi 1963.

8. Codacci 1981, 23–27, has a list and brief description of the principal Florentine herbs. See also Lo Russo 1999, 33–34.

9. According to Raddi (2001, 200), the word *panzanella* comes from *pane,* bread, and *zanella,* diminutive of *zana,* meaning valley or hollow, and by implication, bowl.

10. On the first page of the Florentine cookbook *Con poco o nulla* (Costantini 1976) is the following list of foods to eat with bread: red onion, walnuts, dried black olives, herring, *salacche,* green onions, tomato and salt, pecorino cheese and garlic, grapes, and pecorino cheese and pears. Just two pages later, the book lists the following ways to have *pane condito,* "flavored bread": bread, olive oil, and salt; bread with a drop of vinegar, olive oil, and salt; bread with tomato, olive oil, salt, and pepper; bread dampened with broth and eaten with hot tripe, salt, and pepper; bread with water or red wine and sugar; bread with butter and salt or sugar; bread with ricotta and sugar.

11. See Bonfili (1993); and Console (1993, 23), who reports that bread recalled the body and blood of Christ and that grain "contained the oppositions and the contradictions of life and death."

12. See Cirese et al. 1977; Console 1993; Counihan 1999; Kanafani-Zahar 1997; Kaplan 1996, 1997, 2002; Teti 1976.

13. Massimo does not mention his mother or his grandmother, but surely they ate too.

14. Raddi (2001, 176) gives a longer version: *"Fiorentin mangia fagioli, lecca piatti e romaioli, e per farla più pulita, poi si lecca anche le dita"*—"Bean eater is the Florentine, licks the plates and ladles clean, and to make it even cleaner, he even licks his fingers." See also Pecori 1980, who reprints two versions. Cantagalli (1981, 129) says that although beans were once considered a "vulgar food of poor people," they have always been integral to the Florentine diet. He presents *"L'Inno al fagiolo"*—"Hymn to the Bean"—sung at a banquet entirely of beans at the Artists Club in Via de' Servi: *"Ave o fagiolo/divinamente fiorentino/cui natura diede forma di cuore/come del fatal viscere umano./Cosparso l'edulio con olio soave dei colli toscani/battezzandolo al chianti generoso e al pomino soave./Leviam fratelli di mensa/ l'inno secolare:/Ave o fagiolo."* "Hail to the bean/Divinely Florentine/To which nature gave a heart shape/Just like the fateful human organ./Covered deliciously with the sweet oil of the Tuscan hills/ Baptized with generous Chianti and sweet fruit/Brothers of the table let us raise/The centuries-old hymn:/Hail to the bean" (translation mine).

15. *Cavolo nero* is a loose-leaf member of the *Brassica* family and a dark purple red color. In English it is called Tuscan kale, black cabbage, or Lacinato kale. I thank Sharon Peters, Nancy Jenkins, Alessandra Guigoni, and Beppe Lo Russo for information about *cavolo nero*.

16. See Codacci (1981, 41) for the origins of the name Lombard soup.

17. Zamagni (1998, 189) estimates that Italian dried bean consumption stayed at around 5 kg per capita in the second half of the twentieth century.

18. For an exhaustive history of pasta in Italy and China, see Serventi and Sabban (2002).

19. On making the *sfoglia* and the various kinds of flat noodles such as *nastrini, maccheroni, nastroni,* and *pappardelle,* see Apergi and Bianco (1991, 58).

20. See Codacci (1981, 56–8) for how to cook *pappardelle sulla lepre* (pappardelle over hare) as well as *pappardelle sul sugo di conigliolo* (pappardelle over sauce of rabbit).

21. Per-capita potato consumption in Italy rose slightly between 1951 (42 kilograms) and 1992 (45 kilograms), tomato consumption tripled from 20 to 58 kilograms, and overall vegetable consumption rose from 73 to 102 kilograms per capita (Zamagni 1998, 189).

22. So common were dried figs that a Tuscan saying implying excessive thrift and even avarice was *"far le nozze coi fichi secchi"*—"to have a wedding with dried figs" (Raddi 2001, 125).

23. Codacci (1981, 95) said, "Wrongly steak has become the symbol of Florentine gastronomy. I say wrongly because the value of the culinary arts is not shown with steak but with the valorization of the so-called humble dishes."

24. Codacci (1981) has recipes for pig's ribs, liver, rinds, feet, stomach, and tail; and for cow's tripe, feet, and stomach lining—*centopelle* ("one hundred skins").

25. Friends told me that fears of mad cow disease put an end to the *trippaio* in the late 1990s, but there was one at work in Piazza di Porta Romana in March 2003.

26. I have come across no other references to eating guinea pigs in Tuscany. Apergi and Bianco (1991, 90–91) say that peasants raised geese, especially for the meals they had to provide for workers who helped with grape and grain harvests, because geese reached 13 to 18 pounds and could feed many people, even though Tuscans did not particularly like the meat, which they defined as *dolcina* (slightly sweet), *calorosa* (heat-producing or heavy), *la peggiore delle carni* (the worst of all meats), and *troppo grassa* (too fatty).

27. See Codacci (1981, 114–119) and Costantini (1976, 18–21) for diverse ways of cooking eggs in Florentine cuisine.

28. See also Codacci (1981, 108–109) and Costantini (1976, 33–34).

29. Between 1951 and 1992, Zamagni (1998, 189) estimates butter consumption increasing from 1.5 to 2.2 kilograms per capita, lard from 3.3 to 3.8, olive oil from 5.7 to 11.2, and seed oil from 2 to 13.1.

30. *Quaderni di controinformazione alimentare,* October 1978, 13–17.

31. See Apergi and Bianco (1991, 60). Many of Monod's recipes contain butter, probably imported from his French-Swiss background, and more typical of elite than humble Florentine cuisine (Lo Russo and Pratesi 1999).

32. In some regions of Italy, only men drank wine—Sardinia, for example (Counihan 1981, 285).

33. Codacci (1981, 39–40) described *acquarello* or *mezzone:* "It was a drink made out of the grapes right after they were pressed. Left behind were stems and seeds and a little substance. All this was put to boil with lots of water and then it was hermetically sealed into a big ter-

racotta vase. After several days, the *acquarello* or *mezzone* was drunk just as it was, lightly effervescent." Taddei (1998, 33) describes *mezzone* in an identical manner. Apergi and Bianco (1991, 87) describe *acquarello* or *vinello* as "a watered down wine of second choice."

34. Wine "is by far the most common type of alcoholic beverage in Italy, and accounts for over 80% of alcohol intake" (Chatenoud et al. 2000, 177). Zamagni (1998) estimates wine consumption dropping from 97.4 kilograms per capita in 1951 to 60.5 in 1992, with beer rising in the same period from 3.5 to 23.3.

35. Lolli (1958, xiv) said, "For Italians drinking is a part of eating, even a form of eating, for wine is food; . . . the set of attitudes which does not separate drink from food is at least partly responsible for the relative sobriety of Italian drinking."

36. See Ferro-Luzzi and Branca 1991; Keys 1995; Nestle 1995; Turrini, Leclercq, and D'Amicis 1999.

Chapter 5

1. In 2000, the average monthly Italian household food expenditure was 18.6 percent of family income, whereas housing expenditure was 34.3 percent and clothing was 6.6 percent (ISTAT 2001).

2. Moore (1988, 53) wrote, "It is the relationship between women's reproductive and productive labor which is the crucial determinant of their position in society." See also Rosaldo 1974, Sacks 1974, Sargent 1981, and Zavella 1987. See Collier 1997 on changes in women's relation to production and reproduction in late-twentieth-century Spain.

3. See Counihan 1999, chapter 9, for a full discussion of how Tommasa and Sergia enacted the mother–daughter relationship through food.

4. Sergia generously photocopied her recipe notebook for me. Many of her recipes are included in this book, and a list of all the ones she collected is included in Appendix C.

5. Apergi and Bianco (1991, 101) found *frittelle* for St. Joseph's Day in Vicchio del Mugello (Florence) and report them made of apples and *semolino* as well as rice. See Codacci 1981, 142; Costantini 1976, 38; Perticoni 1979, 26; Jenkins 1998, 238–239.

6. Italy has had two different daily work schedules—*l'orario unico*—the continuous workday—and *l'orario spezzato*—the broken-up workday. State workers were the first to have *l'orario unico*—a workday from 8 A.M. to 2 P.M. six days a week, without a break for lunch. Laura's factory had the *orario spezzato*—a workday that went from 8 A.M. to 1 P.M. and from 3 to 6 P.M., and they were discussing whether to convert to a continuous workday.

7. The *macchinetta* was the coffee pot most commonly used in Italian homes. It has a hexagonally shaped top that screws onto a bottom part after a round metal filter piece full of coffee is inserted in the bottom. The *macchinette* come commonly in 1-cup, 3-cup, and 6-cup demitasse sizes.

8. In *An Italian Education*, Englishman Tim Parks (1995) describes with humor and awe the limited participation of many of his male neighbors in household chores or child rearing.

Chapter 6

1. My research sample unfortunately included no gay or lesbian Florentines, but on the role of food in homosexual relationships in the United States, see Carrington 1999.

2. In 2000, 47.9 percent of males and 26.4 percent of females were employed (ISTAT 2001).

3. On Florentines' body beliefs, see Counihan 1999, chapter 10.

4. On anorexia nervosa and eating and body attitudes in Italy, see Allegranzi et al. 1994, De Clercq 1990, 1995, Galli 1997, Orsatti 1997, Palazzoli 1963, Recalcati 1997, and Riva 1997.

5. On women's economic position in Italy, see Assmuth 1997, Balbo and May 1975–76, ISTAT 2001, and Saraceno 1992, 1998.

6. Whether the idea that women have to please men has existed "*from the beginning*" is debatable, but it certainly got an enormous boost during fascism through explicit policies and propaganda affirming women's duty to work long, hard, unremunerated hours to serve husbands and family (Caldwell 1986, De Grazia 1992, Horn 1994).

7. See DeVault 1991 for a discussion of how "feeding the family" in the United States reproduces women's subordination.

Chapter 7

1. Ochs, Potecorvo, and Fasulo (1996, 41) affirm, "The maintenance of a continuous culinary tradition across generations within the family is a crucial vehicle for maintaining an emotional relationship with one's roots."

2. Sharing the same food literally linked people in communion, the central ritual act of the Catholic mass, itself a reenactment of a meal. My subjects, although all nominally Catholic, took their religion for granted and said little about food in their religion or its rituals. On commensal rituals, see Counihan 1981, 1999; Douglas 1984; Feeley-Harnik 1981; Freud 1918; Kahn 1986; Mauss 1967; Ortner 1975; Weismantel 1988; Young 1971.

3. Parks (1992, 1995) describes the Italian phenomenon of getting the children set up at marriage.

4. Freud (1918, 174–175) commented that eating together "was at the same time a symbol and a confirmation of social community and of the assumption of mutual obligations," especially of kinship. In many cultures, the family consists of people who eat together. See Bossard 1943, Charles and Kerr 1988, DeVault 1991, Douglas 1975, Pitkin 1985, Siskind 1973, Weismantel 1988, Wood 1995, Young 1971.

5. *Semolino* is a kind of pasta in tiny granules that might be eaten in broth or just in a kind of wet pap with butter. It might be given to toddlers or people who are sick or without much appetite.

6. The city hall established a cafeteria or *mensa* for workers soon after World War II that was in use until it was destroyed in the Arno Flood of 1966. See Chapter 3.

7. I counted food stores in the area from the corner of Borgo S. Frediano and Via Serragli south on Via Serragli to Porta Romana (a stone's throw from my old apartment in Via S. Ilario a Colombaia, 2), and then back north up Via Romana to Via Guicciardini to Borgo San Jacopo and then west to where I started.

8. *Panettone* is yeast cake made with flour, butter, eggs, sugar, and various flavorings—vanilla or lemon or anise principally. Today, its most famous form is as the ubiquitous and highly commercialized Christmas cake that is sold all over Italy in boxes around the holidays.

9. See Apergi and Bianco 1991, 95–98, on commensality in peasant marriages in the Mugello area.

10. *Le Cascine* is a large park along the Arno River northwest of Center city. Massimo is perhaps referring to the fact that it is a renowned locale for street-walkers.

11. *Suocera,* mother-in-law; *suocero,* father-in-law; *nuora,* daughter-in-law; *genero,* son-in-law; *cognato,* brother-in-law; and *cognata,* sister-in-law.

12. Rinaldo used the word *privasie*—an Italianization of the English word privacy, because there is no Italian word for privacy, a concept that has not existed for Italians until very recently. The closest Italian words are *solitudine, intimità*—solitude, intimacy.

13. Both eating and sex are fundamental human drives that ensure the continuance of the species; both are pleasurable; both involve crossing body boundaries; and both connote intimacy. On commensality and sexuality, see Counihan 1999, Farb and Armelagos 1980, Gregor 1985, Herdt 1987, Kahn 1986, Meigs 1984, Murphy and Murphy 1974, Pollock 1985, Tambiah 1969.

Chapter 8

1. See especially Chodorow 1974, 1978; Flax 1978; Harding 1981; Riddiough 1981.

2. Some sources on feeding as a form of socialization and personality formation are Bossard 1943; Bruch 1973; Counihan 1999; Du Bois 1941; Farb and Armelagos 1980; A. Freud 1946, 1968; S. Freud 1962; Holmberg 1969; D. Shack 1969; W. Shack 1971.

3. See Counihan 1999, chapter 3, for further discussion of food and women's power.

4. See Counihan 1999, chapter 9.

5. See Parks's (1995) humorous observations about how little Italian men do in the home in regard to either child rearing or domestic chores.

6. On *le voglie,* see Apergi and Bianco (1991, chapter 5), Olivi (1977, 85), and Whitaker (2000, 39–40).

7. In her study of pregnant Sardinian women, Ketler (1997) showed that they struggled to negotiate a balance between the nutritional admonitions of health care professionals, their own food cravings, and their desire not to gain too much weight.

8. Feeding with breast milk and other foods defined kinship in Florence and in other cultures (see, e.g., Young 1971). Wet-nursing other women's babies seems to have been fairly com-

mon in Italy in the first half of the twentieth century and established kinship between "the milk child and the mother, and their wider families" (Whitaker 2000, 14). Perhaps during the war and immediate postwar period, more women than usual lacked breast milk due to malnutrition.

9. In the 1950s and 1960s, some Italian pediatricians told women "that it was better not to breast-feed because it ruined the figure" (Whitaker 2000, 249), but in fact breast-feeding actually helps women get back their prepregnancy shape because it uses so many calories (up to 1,000/day).

10. See Whitaker 2000 for a detailed discussion of Italian breast-feeding practices and beliefs throughout the twentieth century. See also Olivi 1997.

11. Interestingly, when I interviewed her in 2003, Giovanna said that she had come to love *baccalà*. Some friends had prepared the boiled *baccalà* with finely sliced onions, green olives, capers, olive oil, and vinegar, and she had found it so delicious that she was able to overcome her previous antipathy.

12. See Ochs, Pontecorvo, and Fasulo (1996, 41): "The Italian predilection towards catering to individual tastes comes at a price, however. When Mamma or Papà buys ingredients and prepares them to satisfy particular tastes, a deep relationship of emotional dependence is created. The individual child comes to rely on that parent (and in some cases on a grandparent) to know how to make him/her happy by fulfilling his/her tastes. The Italian child is expected to express gratitude and strong positive feelings about these individualizing attentions and labor. And the parent (or grandparent) comes to depend on such praises to foster their self-esteem. In this way, there develops a reciprocity of emotional need fulfillment. Here the socialization of individuality is achieved through interdependence rather than through the fostering of autonomy [as in the American case]."

13. See Whitaker (2000, 290): "Today, maternity continues to be valued as the supreme self-sacrifice and evident expression of women's devotion to the husband and family."

Chapter 9

1. Now with the universal price symbol and electronic scanners, clerks do not even need to know prices anymore.

2. See Passerini 1996a.

3. Besozzi (1998) notes that frozen food consumption in Italy was steadily rising in the 1990s, with frozen vegetables and fish the top sellers.

4. *USA Today*, April 17, 1997, Istat 2000.

Chapter 10

1. Florentines' ambivalent feelings about the changing diet were similar to of the former *mezzadria* peasants studied by Apergi and Bianco (1991, 38), who called their olden-day foods "simple," "genuine," and "better than today's foods," but also "poor and insufficient." They frequently commented, *si mangiava pane e miseria*—"we ate bread and misery."

2. My dictionary (Garzanti 1984) uses the spelling *raveggiolo*. Jenkins (1998, 242) describes *raviggiolo* [sic] as "a barely curdled and thickened whole milk cheese eaten very fresh before the cheese is salted, no more than a day old, maximum."

3. Costantini (1976) gives a recipe for *frittura di pesciolini*—fried little fish (up to 5–6 centimeters long): Wash them, dry them, and dredge them briefly in flour, then fry them in a frying pan with abundant, smoking hot olive oil for a couple of minutes.

4. Thanks to Beppe Lo Russo for information on McDonald's in Florence.

5. See Turrini, Leclercq, and D'Amicis 1999 for information on the Mediterranean diet in Italy and national dietary improvement campaigns in Italy in 1975, 1981, 1986–88, and 1997.

6. Greco et al. (1998) studied childhood feeding practices in Italy with children six to thirty-two months old and found few legumes and vegetables, lots of dairy and grains, and fat content close to the recommended 35 percent of the diet. They recommend that Italians "recover the positive choices of the time of scarcity in the time of abundance: reduction of processed milk products and use of skimmed milk and dairy products has to be seriously considered" (256).

7. Information comes from the Slow Food Web site: www.slowfood.com.
8. Multiproduct farm butcheries were thriving in nearby Umbria (Ventura and Milone 2000) and sustainable agriculture was a viable endeavor in Italy; between 1990 and 1999, hectares farmed directly by farmers have stayed the same, though the number of farms has decreased by 13 percent to 2,215,000 (Tellarini and Caporali 2000, ISTAT 2001).
9. See Leitch 2000 for a description of the curing process and politics of *lardo di Colonnata.*
10. See Pontecorvo and Fasulo 1999.

Bibliography

Adams, Carol J. 1990. *The Sexual Politics of Meat: A Feminist-Vegetarian Critical Theory.* New York: Continuum.

Alberini, Massimo. 1992. *Storia della cucina italiana.* Casale Monferrato: Piemme.

Alexander, David. 2000. The geography of Italian pasta. *Professional Geographer* 52:3553–3566.

Allegranzi, P., et al. 1994. La variazione nel tempo dell'immagine corporea: risultati di un approccio sperimentale. *Medicina Psicosomatica* 3, 4:309–319.

Angioni, Giulio. 1974. *Rapporti di produzione e cultura subalterna: Contadini in Sardegna.* Cagliari: EDES.

Angioni, Giulio. 1976. *Sa Laurera: Il lavoro contadino in Sardegna.* Cagliari: EDES.

Angioni, Giulio. 1989. *I pascoli erranti: Antropologia del pastore in Sardegna.* Napoli: Liguori Editore.

Anselmi, Sergio. 1990. Mezzadri e mezzadria nell'Italia centrale. In *Storia dell'agricoltura italiana in età contemporanea,* a cura di Piero Bevilacqua. Venice: Marsilio, vol. 2, pp. 201–259.

Apergi, Francesco, and Carla Bianco. 1991. *La ricca cena: Famiglia mezzadrile e pratiche alimentari a Vicchio di Mugello.* Firenze: Centro Editoriale Toscano.

Appadurai, Arjun. 1988. How to make a national cuisine. Cookbooks in Contemporary India. *Comparative Studies in Society and History* 30, 1:3–24.

Artusi, Pellegrino. 1985. *La scienza in cucina e l'arte di mangiar bene.* Milano: Rizzoli.

Assmuth, Laura. 1997. *Women's Work: Women's Worth: Changing Lifecourses in Highland Sardinia.* Saarijärvi: Transactions of the Finnish Anthropological Society, 39.

Avakian, Arlene Voski, ed. 1997. *Through the Kitchen Window: Women Explore the Intimate Meanings of Food and Cooking.* Boston: Beacon Press.

Avati, Pupi. 1989. *La storia di ragazzi e ragazze (The Story of Boys and Girls).* Film. RAI.

Balbo, Laura, and Marie P. May. 1975–76. Woman's condition: The case of postwar Italy. *International Journal of Sociology* 5:79–102.

Banfield, Edward. 1958. *The Moral Basis of a Backward Society.* Glencoe, IL: The Free Press.

Barbagli, Marzio, and David I. Kertzer, eds. *Storia della famiglia italiana, 1750–1950.* Bologna: Il Mulino.

Barthes, Roland. 1997. Toward a psychosociology of contemporary food consumption. In *Food and Culture: A Reader,* eds. C. Counihan and P. Van Esterik. New York: Routledge.

Barucci, Piero. 1964. *Profilo Economico della Provincia di Firenze.* Firenze: La Nuova Italia.

Bates, Thomas R. 1975. Gramsci and the theory of hegemony. *Journal of the History of Ideas* 36, 2:351–366.

Becker, Anne E. 1995. *Body, Self, and Society: The View from Fiji.* Philadelphia: University of Pennsylvania Press.

Behar, Ruth. 1993. *Translated Woman: Crossing the Border with Esperanza's Story.* Boston: Beacon.

Behar, Ruth, and Deborah A. Gordon, eds. 1995. *Women Writing Culture.* Berkeley: University of California Press.

Belmonte, Tom. 1979. *The Broken Fountain.* New York: Columbia University Press.

Besozzi, Vanda. 1998. Italy Opts for Frozen Food Convenience. *AgExporter* 10, 11: 7–9.

Bevilacqua, Piero, ed. 1989, 1990, 1991. *Storia dell'agricoltura italiana in età contemporanea.* Venezia: Marsilio, vols. 1, 2, 3.

Bianchi, Anne. 1995. *From the Tables of Tuscan Women.* New York: Ecco Press.

Blim, Michael. 1990. *Made in Italy: Small-Scale Industrialization and Its Consequences.* New York: Praeger.

Blim, Michael. 2000. What is still left for the Left in Italy? Piecing together a post-communist position on labor and employment. *Journal of Modern Italian Studies* 5, 2:169–185.

Blok, Anton. 1974. *The Mafia of a Sicilian Village, 1860–1960. A Study of Violent Peasant Entrepreneurs.* New York: Harper Torchbooks.

Bonfili, Silvana, ed. 1993. *Alimentazione e ritualità. Produrre, consumare, comunicare.* Rome: Artemide edizioni.

Bordo, Susan. 1993. *Unbearable Weight: Feminism, Western Culture, and the Body.* Berkeley: University of California Press.

Bossard, James H. S. 1943. Family table talk: An area for sociological study. *American Sociological Review* 8:295–301.

Bravo, Gian Luigi. 2001. *Italiani: racconto etnografico.* Roma: Meltemi.

Brögger, Jan. 1971. *Montevarese: A Study of Peasant Society and Culture in Southern Italy.* Bergen: Universitetsforlaget.

Bruch, Hilde. 1973. *Eating Disorders: Obesity, Anorexia Nervosa, and the Person Within.* New York: Basic Books.

Brumberg, Joan Jacobs. 1988. *Fasting Girls: The Emergence of Anorexia Nervosa as a Modern Disease.* Cambridge: Harvard University Press.

Bynum, Caroline Walker. 1987. *Holy Feast and Holy Fast: The Religious Significance of Food to Medieval Women.* Berkeley: University of California Press.

Caldwell, Lesley. 1986. Reproducers of the nation: Women and family in Fascist policy. In *Rethinking Italian Fascism: Capitalism, Populism, and Culture,* ed. David Forgacs. London: Lawrence and Wishart, pp. 110–141.

Camera di Commercio. 1958. *La Provincia di Firenze e le sue caratteristiche economiche e sociali.* Firenze: Camera di commercio, industria e agricoltura.

Camporesi, Piero. 1980. *Alimentazione, Folclore, Società.* Parma: Pratiche Editrice.

Camporesi, Piero. 1996. *Bread of Dreams: Food and Fantasy in Early Modern Europe.* Chicago: University of Chicago Press.

Camporesi, Piero. 1998a. *Il pane selvaggio.* Bologna: Il Mulino.

Camporesi, Piero. 1998b. *The Magic Harvest: Food, Folklore and Society.* Cambridge, UK: Polity Press.

Camporesi, Piero. 2000. *Il paese della fame.* Milano: Garzanti.

Camporesi, Piero, and Christopher Woodhall. 1998. *Exotic Brew: The Art of Living in the Age of Enlightenment.* Oxford, UK: Polity Press.

Cantagalli, Renzo. 1981. *Guida ai detti toscani: Loro origini e significati.* Milano: SugarCo Edizioni.

Capatti, Alberto, Alberto De Bernardi, and Angelo Varni, eds. 1998. *Storia d'Italia: l'alimentazione* (Annali 13). Torino: Einaudi.

Capatti, Alberto, and Massimo Montanari. 1999. *La cucina italiana: storia di una cultura.* Roma-Bari: Laterza.

Carrington, Christopher. 1999. *No Place Like Home: Relationships and Family Life Among Lesbians and Gay Men.* Chicago: University of Chicago Press.

Cavallieri, Marina. 2003. Padri sull'orlo di una crisi di nervi tra biberon e pannolini da cambiare. *La Repubblica,* March 22, 2003, p. 32.

Cerpi-Censis. 1974. *Ricerca sul sistema socio-economico dell'area tessile di Prato.* Prato.

Chapman, Charlotte Gower. 1971. *Milocca: A Sicilian Village.* Cambridge, MA: Schenkman.

Charles, Nickie, and Marion Kerr. 1988. *Women, Food and Families.* Manchester: Manchester University Press.

Chatenoud, L., E. Negri, C. La Vecchia, O. Volpato, and S. Franceschi. 2000. Short communication: Wine drinking and diet in Italy. *European Journal of Clinical Nutrition* 54:177–179.

Chernin, Kim. 1981. *The Obsession: Reflections on the Tyranny of Slenderness.* New York: Harper and Row.

Chernin, Kim. 1985. *The Hungry Self.* New York: Times Books.

Chodorow, Nancy. 1974. Family structure and feminine personality. In *Women, Culture and Society,* ed. Michelle Zimbalist Rosaldo and Louise Lamphere. Stanford: Stanford University Press, pp. 43–66.

Chodorow, Nancy. 1978. *The Reproduction of Mothering: Psychoanalysis and the Sociology of Gender.* Berkeley: University of California Press.

Cirese, Alberto M., Enrica Delitala, Chiarella Rampallo, and Giulio Angioni. 1977. *Pani tradizionali, arte effimera in Sardegna.* Cagliari: EDES.

Clemente, Pietro. 1980. I 'selvaggi' della campagna toscana: note sull'identità mezzadrile nell'ottocento e oltre. In *Mezzadri, letterati, e padroni nella Toscana dell'ottocento.* Palermo: Sellerio editore.

Clemente, Pietro, Mirna Coppi, Gianna Fineschi, Mariano Fresta, and Vera Pietrelli. 1980. *Mezzadri, letterati, e padroni nella Toscana dell'ottocento.* Palermo: Sellerio editore.

Cochrane, Eric. 1973. *Florence in the Forgotten Centuries, 1527–1800.* Chicago: University of Chicago Press.

Codacci, Leo. 1981. *Civiltà della tavola contadina: 190 "ricette" e tanti buoni consigli.* Firenze: Sansoni.

Cole, John W., and Eric Wolf. 1975. *The Hidden Frontier.* New York: Academic Press.

Collier, Jane Fishburne. 1997. *From Duty to Desire: Remaking Families in a Spanish Village.* Princeton, NJ: Princeton University Press.

Console, Ester. 1993. Il cibo tra alimento e segno. In *Alimentazione e ritualità,* ed. Silvana Bonfili. Rome: Artemide edizioni, pp. 19–29.

Coppi, Mirna, and Gianna Fineschi. 1980. La donna contadina. Riflessioni sulla condizione della donna nella famiglia mezzadrile toscana. In *Mezzadri, letterati, e padroni nella Toscana dell'ottocento.* Palermo: Sellerio editore, pp. 187–214.

Cornelisen, Ann. 1969. *Torregreca: Life, Death, Miracles.* New York: Dell.

Cornelisen, Ann. 1976. *Women of the Shadows.* New York: Vintage.

Corti, Paola. 1998. Emigrazione e consuetudini alimentari. L'esperienza di una catena migratoria. In *L'alimentazione,* ed. A. Capatti et al. Torino: Einaudi, pp. 683–719.

Costantini, Costante, ed. 1976. *Con poco o nulla: ricette di cucina popolare toscana.* Florence: Libreria Editrice Fiorentina.

Counihan, Carole. 1981. Food culture and political economy: Changing lifestyles in the Sardinian town of Bosa. Doctoral dissertation, Anthropology, University of Massachusetts.

Counihan, Carole. 1986. Antonio Gramsci and social science. *Dialectical Anthropology,* 11, 1:3–9.

Counihan, Carole. 1999. *The Anthropology of Food and Body: Gender, Meaning and Power.* New York: Routledge.

Counihan, Carole. 2002. Food as Women's Voice in the San Luis Valley of Colorado. In *Food in the USA: A Reader,* ed. Carole Counihan. New York: Routledge, pp. 295–304.

Counihan, Carole, and Penny Van Esterik, eds. 1997. *Food and Culture: A Reader.* New York: Routledge.

Da Monte, Mario. 1995. *A tavola in Casentino.* Stia: Edizioni: Fruska.

Davis, John. 1973. *Land and Family in Pisticci.* London: Athlone.

De Clercq, Fabiola. 1990. *Tutto il pane del mondo.* Milano: Bompiani.

De Clercq, Fabiola. 1995. *Donne invisibili: l'anoressia, la sofferenza, la vita.* Milano: Rizzoli.

De Garine, Igor, and Nancy J. Pollock. 1995. *Social Aspects of Obesity.* Amsterdam: Gordon and Breach.

De Grazia, Victoria. 1992. *How Fascism Ruled Women: Italy, 1922–1945.* Berkeley: University of California Press.

DeVault, Marjorie. 1991. *Feeding the Family: The Social Organization of Caring as Gendered Work.* Chicago: University of Chicago Press.

Diner, Hasia R. 2001. *Hungering for America: Italian, Irish, and Jewish Foodways in the Age of Migration.* Cambridge, MA: Harvard University Press.

Douglas, Mary. 1975. *Implicit Meanings.* London: Routledge and Kegan Paul.

Douglas, Mary, ed. 1984. *Food in the Social Order: Studies of Food and Festivities in Three American Communities.* New York: Russell Sage Foundation.

Douglass, William. 1984. *Emigration in a South Italian Town: An Anthropological History.* New Brunswick, NJ: Rutgers University Press.

Du Bois, Cora. 1941. Attitudes towards food and hunger in Alor. In *Language, Culture, and Personality: Essays in Memory of Edward Sapir,* ed. L. Spier, A. I. Hallowell, and S. S. Newman. Menasha, Wisconsin.

Economist. 2000. The latest mad-cow panic. December 2, 2000, vol. 357, 8199, p. 50 (http://ehostvgw11.epnet.com/ accessed June 10, 2002).

Ellis, Rhian. 1983. The Way to a Man's Heart: Food in the Violent Home. In *The Sociology of Food and Eating,* ed. Anne Murcott. Aldershot: Gower Publishing, pp. 164–171.

Engels, Frederick. 1966. *The Peasant War in Germany.* New York: International Publishers.

Engels, Frederick. 1972 [1899]. *The Origin of the Family, Private Property and the State.* New York: International Publishers.

Epstein, Jason. 1994/1995. This side of paradiso. *The New Yorker,* December 26, 1994/January 2, 1995.

Esquivel, Laura. 1989. *Like Water for Chocolate.* New York: Doubleday.

Faccioli, Marina. 1991. *Città e industria tessile: il caso Prato.* Presentazione di Bernardo Cori. Milano: Franco Angeli.

Falassi, Alessandro. 1980. *Folklore by the Fireside: Text and Context of the Tuscan Veglia.* Austin: University of Texas Press.

Falassi, Alessandro. 1988. Feste e ciclo dell'anno/Toscana. In *La Festa: tradizioni popolari in Italia,* ed. Alessandro Falassi. Milano: Electa, pp. 104–117.

Fanfani, Roberto. 1990. Proprietà terriera e azienda agricola nell'Italia del dopoguerra. In *Storia dell'agricoltura italiana in età contemporanea,* a cura di Piero Bevilacqua. Venezia: Marsilio, vol. 2, pp. 415–466.

Farb, Peter, and George Armelagos. 1980. *Consuming Passions: The Anthropology of Eating.* New York: Houghton Mifflin.

Fei, Silvano. 1971. *Nascita e sviluppo di Firenze città borghese.* Firenze: G&G Editrice Firenze.

Feeley-Harnik, Gillian. 1981. *The Lord's Table: Eucharist and Passover in Early Christianity.* Philadelphia: University of Pennsylvania Press.

Ferrali, Sabatino. 1979. Di alcuni dolci popolari toscani. In *A bocca dolce: ricette di dolci popolari toscani,* ed. G. Perticoni. Firenze: Libreria Editrice Fiorentina, pp. 5–15.

Ferro-Luzzi, A., and F. Branca. 1991. Mediterranean diet, Italian-style: Prototype of a healthy diet. *American Journal of Clinical Nutrition* 61:1338S–1345S.

Festa, Mariano. 1980. Canti popolari ed evoluzione della coscienza mezzadrile. In *Mezzadri, letterati, e padroni nella Toscana dell'ottocento.* Palermo: Sellerio editore, pp. 161–186.

Fisher, M. F. K. 1954. *The Art of Eating.* New York: Morrow.

Flax, Jane. 1978. The conflict between nurturance and autonomy in mother–daughter relationships and within feminism. *Feminist Studies* 4, 2:171–189.

Flores, Richard. 1998. Mexicans, modernity and *Martyrs of the Alamo.* In *Reflexiones 1998,* ed. Yolanda Padilla. Austin, TX: Center for Mexican-American Studies Books, pp. 1–19.

Franklin, S. H. 1969. *The European Peasantry: The Final Phase.* London: Methuen.

Freud, Anna. 1946. The psychoanalytic study of infantile feeding disturbances. *The Psychoanalytic Study of the Child: An Annual* 2:119–132.

Freud, Anna. 1968 [1947]. The establishment of feeding habits. In *Indications for Child Analysis and Other Papers, 1945–56.* New York: International Universities Press.

Freud, Sigmund. 1918. *Totem and Taboo: Resemblances Between the Psychic Lives of Savages and Neurotics.* Authorized translation with an introduction by A. A. Brill. New York: Vintage.

Freud, Sigmund. 1962. *Three Contributions to the Theory of Sex.* New York: Dutton.

Galli, Chiara. 1997. Il corpo bello, sano e "truccato." In *Donne e microcosmi culturali,* ed. Adriana Destro. Bologna: Patron Editore, pp. 185–219.

Garbesi, Marina. 1999. Il miraggio pericoloso della "dieta estrema." *La Repubblica* 18 aprile 1999, p. 21.

Garzanti. 1984. *Il nuovo dizionario italiano Garzanti.* Milan: Garzanti Editore.

Gibson, Mary. 1986. *Prostitution and the State in Italy: 1860–1915.* New Brunswick, NJ: Rutgers University Press.

Ginsborg, Paul. 1990. *A History of Contemporary Italy: Society and Politics, 1943–1988.* New York: Penguin.

Goddard, Victoria. 1996. *Gender, Family and Work in Naples.* Oxford: Berg.

Goody, Jack. 1982. *Cooking, Cuisine, and Class: A Study in Comparative Sociology.* Cambridge: Cambridge University Press.

Grammatico, Maria, and Mary Taylor Simeti. 1994. *Bitter Almonds: Recollections and Recipes from a Sicilian Girlhood.* New York: William Morrow.

Gramsci, Antonio. 1955a. *Il materialismo storico e la filosofia di Benedetto Croce.* Torino: Einaudi.

Gramsci, Antonio. 1955b. *Gli intellettuali e l'organizzazione della cultura.* Torino: Einaudi.

Grassivaro, Francesco. 1991. Le multinazionali agricole. In *Storia dell'agricoltura italiana in età contemporanea,* a cura di Piero Bevilacqua. Venezia: Marsilio, vol. 3, pp. 223–251.

Greco, L., F. Musmarra, C. Franzese, and S. Auricchio. 1998. Early childhood feeding practices in southern Italy: Is the Mediterranean diet becoming obsolete? Study of 450 children aged 6–32 months in Campania, Italy. *Acta Paediatrica* 87:250–256.

Gregor, Thomas. 1985. *Anxious Pleasures: The Sexual Lives of an Amazonian People.* Chicago: University of Chicago Press.

Hale, Ellen. 2001. Europe's tastes are changing. *USA Today,* April 11, 2001. Consulted at http://www.usatoday.com/news/health/2001-4-11-foot-europe-food.htm consulted May 28, 2003.

Harding, Sandra. 1981. What is the real material basis of patriarchy and capital? In *Women and Revolution,* ed. Lydia Sargent. Boston: South End Press, pp. 135–163.

Hellenga, Robert. 1994. *The Sixteen Pleasures.* New York: Soho.

Helstosky, Carol F. 1996. *The Politics of Food in Italy: From Liberalism to Fascism.* Doctoral dissertation, History, Rutgers University.

Helstosky, Carol F. 2003. Recipe for the nation: Reading Italian History through *La scienza in cucina* and *La cucina futurista*. *Food and Foodways* 11, 2:113–140.

Helstosky, Carol F. 2004. *Garlic and Oil: Politics and Food in Italy*. New York, Oxford: Berg Publishers.

Herdt, Gilbert. 1987. *The Sambia: Ritual and Gender in New Guinea*. New York: Holt, Rinehart, Winston.

Hobsbawm, Eric J. 1959. *Primitive Rebels*. Manchester, England: Manchester University Press.

Hobsbawm, Eric J. 1964. *The Age of Revolution: Europe, 1789–1848*. London: Weidenfeld and Nicolson.

Holmberg, Allan R. 1969. *Nomads of the Long Bow: The Siriono of Eastern Bolivia*. Prospect Heights, IL: Waveland.

Holmes, Douglas R. 1989. *Cultural Disenchantments: Worker Peasantries in Northeast Italy*. Princeton, NJ: Princeton University Press.

Horn, David G. 1994. *Social Bodies: Science, Reproduction and Italian Modernity*. Princeton, NJ: Princeton University Press.

Hundley, Tom. 2000. Italian campaign urges people to slow down and smell the fragoline. *Chicago Tribune,* August 29, 2000. Consulted on http://web14.epnet.com/ June 5, 2003.

Ires Toscana. 1988. *Toscana che cambia. Economia e società nella Toscana degli anni '80*. Milano: Angeli.

ISTAT 1990. *Sommario storico di statistiche sulla popolazione 1951–87*. Roma: Istituto Nazionale di Statistica.

ISTAT 2000. http://demo.istat.it/pop1/ consulted February 13, 2002.

ISTAT 2001. http://www.istat.it/Anumital/italy2001/italy2001.pdf consulted February 13, 2002.

Italy Losing Mom-and-Pop Shops. 2003. http://www.cnn.com/2003/TRAVEL/02/15/ciao.mom andpop.ap/ consulted September 22, 2003.

Jenkins, Nancy Harmon. 1998. *Flavors of Tuscany: Traditional Recipes from the Tuscan Countryside*. New York: Broadway Books.

Kahn, Miriam. 1986. *Always Hungry, Never Greedy: Food and the Expression of Gender in a Melanesian Society*. Cambridge: Cambridge University Press.

Kanafani-Zahar, Aida. 1997. Whoever eats you is no longer hungry, whoever sees you becomes humble: Bread and identity in Lebanon. *Food and Foodways* 7, 1:45–72.

Kaplan, Steven Laurence. 1996. *The Bakers of Paris and the Bread Question, 1700–1775*. Durham, NC: Duke University Press.

Kaplan, Steven Laurence. 1997. Breadways. *Food and Foodways* 7, 1:1–44.

Kaplan, Steven Laurence. 2002. *Le Retour du Bon Pain: Une histoire contemporaine du pain, de ses techniques et de ses hommes*. Paris: Perrin.

Kenny, Michael, and David I. Kertzer. 1983. *Urban Life in Mediterranean Europe: Anthropological Perspectives*. Urbana: University of Illinois Press.

Kertzer, David I. 1980. *Comrades and Christians: Religion and Political Struggle in Communist Italy*. Cambridge and New York: Cambridge University Press.

Kertzer, David I. 1983. Urban research in Italy. In *Urban Life in Mediterranean Europe*, eds. Michael Kenny and David Kertzer. Urbana: University of Illinois Press, pp. 53–75.

Kertzer, David I. 1984. *Family Life in Central Italy, 1880–1910: Sharecropping, Wage Labor, and Coresidence*. New Brunswick, NJ: Rutgers University Press.

Kertzer, David I. 1998. Representing Italy. In *Europe in the Anthropological Imagination*, ed. Susan Parman. Upper Saddle River, NJ: Prentice Hall, pp. 70–79.

Kertzer, David I., and Dennis P. Hogan. 1989. *Family, Political Economy, and Demographic Change: The Transformation of Life in Casalecchio, Italy, 1861–1921*. Madison: University of Wisconsin Press.

Kertzer, David I., and Richard P. Saller. 1991. *The Family in Italy from Antiquity to the Present*. New Haven: Yale University Press.

Ketler, Suzanne. 1997. Separating mothering and motherhood: Women's changing maternity experiences and the normalization of post-partum depression in Cagliari, Italy, 1943–1994. Ph.D. dissertation, Anthropology, University of Pittsburgh.

Keys, A. 1995. Mediterranean diet and public health: Personal reflections. *American Journal of Clinical Nutrition* 61:1321S–1323S.

Kummer, Corby. 2002. *The Pleasures of Slow Food; Celebrating Authentic Traditions, Flavors, and Recipes*. San Francisco: Chronicle Books.

La metà delle ragazze si vede grassa. 2002. *Corriere della sera,* May 13, 2002. http://ricerca. corriere.it/Primo_Piano/Cronache/2002/05_Maggio/13/grasse.html consulted September 9, 2002.

Lamphere, Louise. 2000. The domestic sphere of women and the public world of men: The strengths and limitations of an anthropological dichotomy. In *Gender in Cross-Cultural Perspective*, eds. Caroline B. Brettell and Carolyn F. Sargent. Upper Saddle River, NJ: Prentice Hall, pp. 100–109.

Landsberger, Henry A., ed. 1974. *Rural Protest: Peasant Movements and Social Change.* London: Macmillan.

Latina Feminist Group. 2001. *Telling to Live: Latina Feminist* Testimonios. Durham, NC: Duke University Press.

Leacock, Eleanor Burke. 1972. Introduction to *The Origin of the Family, Private Property and the State* by Frederick Engels. New York: International Publishers, pp. 7–67.

Lehrer, Adrienne. 1969. Semantic cuisine. *Journal of Linguistics* 5:39–56.

Lehrer, Adrienne. 1972. Cooking vocabularies and the culinary triangle of Lévi-Strauss. *Anthropological Linguistics* 14, 5:155–171.

Leitch, Alison. 2000. The social life of *Lardo:* Slow food in fast times. *Asia Pacific Journal of Anthropology* 1, 1:103–118.

Levenstein, Harvey. 1985. The American response to Italian food, 1880–1930. *Food and Foodways*, 1, 1:1–24.

Levey, Michael. 1996. *Florence: A Portrait.* Cambridge: Harvard University Press.

Lévi-Strauss, Claude. 1966. The culinary triangle. *Partisan Review* 33, 4:586–595.

Lewis, R. W. B. 1995. *The City of Florence: Historical Vistas and Personal Sightings.* New York: Henry Holt.

Lindberg, John. 1946. *Food, Famine and Relief, 1940–1946.* Geneva: League of Nations.

Liuccio, Michaela. 1998. Il cibo nel postmoderno: Dalla gastronomia e dal convivialismo verso la gastro-anomia e il fast-food. *Sociologia*, 32, 2–3:265–271.

Lolli, Giorgio. 1958. *Alcohol in Italian Culture: Food and Wine in Relation to Sobriety Among Italians and Italian Americans.* Glencoe, IL: The Free Press.

Lo Russo, Giuseppe. 1999. Introduzione. *La cucina fiorentina par Louis Monod, 1914.* Firenze: Tipografia Coppini Editore, pp. 5–40.

Lo Russo, Giuseppe. 2003. Personal email communication.

Lo Russo, Giuseppe, and Mauro Pratesi, eds. 1999. *La cucina fiorentina par Louis Monod, 1914.* Firenze: Tipografia Coppini Editore.

Magliocco, Sabina. 1993. *The Two Madonnas: The Politics of Festival in a Sardinian Community.* New York: Lang.

Marx, Karl. 1964. *Precapitalist Economic Formations.* New York: International Publishers.

Mauss, Marcel. 1967. *The Gift: Forms and Functions of Exchange in Archaic Societies.* New York: Norton.

Mayes, Frances. 1996. *Under the Tuscan Sun: At Home in Italy.* San Francisco: Chronicle Books.

Mayes, Frances. 1999. *Bella Tuscany: The Sweet Life in Italy.* New York: Broadway Books.

Mayes, Frances. 2000. *In Tuscany.* New York: Broadway Books.

Meigs, Anna S. 1984. *Food, Sex, and Pollution: A New Guinea Religion.* New Brunswick, NJ: Rutgers University Press.

Meis, John Dore. 1993. *A Taste of Tuscany.* New York: Abbeville Press.

Mintz, Sidney. 1997. *Tasting Food, Tasting Freedom: Excursions into Eating, Culture, and the Past.* Boston: Beacon.

Moore, Henrietta. 1988. *Feminism and Anthropology.* Minneapolis: University of Minnesota Press.

Morgan, Philip. 1995. *Italian Fascism, 1919–1945.* New York: St. Martin's Press.

Mori, G., ed. 1986. *La Toscana.* Torino: Einaudi.

Murphy, Yolanda, and Robert Murphy. 1974. *Women of the Forest.* New York: Columbia University Press.

Nabhan, Gary Paul. 1993. *Songbirds, Truffles, and Wolves: An American Naturalist in Italy.* New York: Pantheon.

Nestle, Marion. 1995. Mediterranean diets: Historical and research overview. *American Journal of Clinical Nutrition* 61:1313S–1320S.

Nigro, Giampiero. 1986. Il "caso" Prato. In *La Toscana*, ed. G. Mori. Torino: Einaudi, pp. 821–865.

Ochs, Elinor, Clotilde Pontecorvo, and Alessandra Fasulo. 1996. Socializing taste. *Ethnos* 61, 1–2:7–46.

Olivi, Alessandra. 1997. Mangiare "per due" o mangiare "quel che c'è." Regimi alimentari della madre in Romagna (1930–1950). In *Donne e microcosmi culturali*, ed. Adriana Destro. Bologna: Patron Editore, pp. 77–106.

Origo, Iris. 1947. *War in Val D'Orcia: A Diary*. Harmondsworth: Penguin.

Orsatti, Cristina. 1997. A proposito del "proprio corpo." In *Donne e microcosmi culturali*, ed. Adriana Destro. Bologna: Patron Editore, pp. 155–184.

Ortner, Sherry B. 1975. Gods' bodies, gods' food: A symbolic analysis of a Sherpa ritual. In *The Interpretation of Symbolism*, ed. R. Willis. ASA Studies 3. New York, pp. 133–169.

Padovani, Gigi. 2000. *Gnam! Storia sociale della nutella*. Roma: Castelvecchi.

Palazzoli, Maria Selvini. 1963. *L'anoressia mentale*. Milano: Feltrinelli.

Pardo, Italo. 1996. *Managing Existence in Naples: Morality, Action and Structure*. Cambridge: Cambridge University Press.

Parks, Tim. 1992. *Italian Neighbors, or, a Lapsed Anglo-Saxon in Verona*. New York: Grove Weidenfeld.

Parks, Tim. 1995. *An Italian Education: The Further Adventures of an Expatriate in Verona*. New York: Grove Press.

Passerini, Luisa. 1996a. *Autobiography of a Generation: Italy 1968*. Translation of *Autoritratto di gruppo*. Hanover, NH: University Press of New England.

Passerini, Luisa. 1996b. Gender relations. In *Italian Cultural Studies: An Introduction*, eds. David Forgacs and Robert Lumley. New York: Oxford University Press, pp. 144–159.

Pecori, Giampaolo. 1980. *Blasoni Popolari Toscani e Luoghi Proverbiali*. Firenze: Libreria Editrice Fiorentina.

Pecori, Giampaolo, ed. 1981. *All'ombra del cupolone: proverbi fiorentini*. Firenze: Libreria Editrice Fiorentina.

Perticoni, Girolamo. 1979. *A bocca dolce: ricette di dolci popolari toscani*. Firenze: Libreria Editrice Fiorentina.

Petrini, Carlo, ed. 2001. *Slow Food: Collected Thoughts on Taste, Tradition, and the Honest Pleasures of Food*. With Ben Watson and Slow Food Editore. White River Junction, VT: Chelsea Green.

Petroni, Paolo. 1974. *Il libro della vera cucina Fiorentina: 230 ricette*. Firenze: Casa Editrice Bonechi.

Petroni, Paolo. 1991. *Il grande libro della cucina Toscana: ricette, consigli, tradizioni, curiosità*. Firenze: Ponte alle Grazie.

Pitkin, Donald S. 1985. *The House That Giacomo Built: History of an Italian Family, 1898–1978*. Cambridge and New York: Cambridge University Press.

Plattner, Stuart. n.d. Contemporary art in a Renaissance setting: The local art system in Florence, Italy. Unpublished manuscript.

Pollock, Donald K. 1985. Food and sexual identity among the Culina. *Food and Foodways* 1, 1:25–42.

Pontecorvo, Clotilde, and Alessandra Fasulo. 1999. Planning a typical Italian meal: A family reflection on culture. *Culture and Psychology* 5, 3:313–335.

Powdermaker, Hortense. 1997. An anthropological approach to the problem of obesity. In *Food and Culture: A Reader*, eds. C. Counihan and P. Van Esterk. New York: Routledge, pp. 203–210.

Preti, Domenico. 1986. L'economia toscana nel periodo fascista. In *La Toscana*, ed. G. Mori. Torino: Einaudi, pp. 603–673.

Prezzolini, Giuseppe. 1948. *The Legacy of Italy*. New York: S. F. Vanni.

Raddi, Renzo. 2001. *A Firenze si parla così: Frasario moderno del vernacolo fiorentino*. Firenze: Alessandro Falciani Libri.

Randall, Margaret. 1997. *Hunger's Table: Women, Food and Politics*. Watsonville, CA: Papier Mache Press.

Recalcati, M. 1997. *L'ultima cena: anoressia e bulimia*. Milano: Bruno Mondadori.

Riddiough, Christine. 1981. Socialism, feminism, and gay/lesbian liberation. In *Women and Revolution*, ed. Lydia Sargent. Boston: South End Press, pp. 71–89.

Riva, Giuseppe. 1997. Representations of eating among adolescent Italian girls. *Journal of Social Psychology* 137, 2:205–217.

Roest, Kees de, and Alberto Menghi. 2000. Reconsidering "traditional" food: The case of Parmigiano Reggiano cheese. *Sociologia Ruralis* 40, 4:439–451.

Romanucci-Ross, Lola. 1991. *One Hundred Towers: An Italian Odyssey of Cultural Survival.* New York: Bergin and Garvey.

Romer, Elizabeth. 1984. *The Tuscan Year: Life and Food in an Italian Valley.* New York: North Point Press.

Rosaldo, Michelle Zimbalist. 1974. Women, culture and society: A theoretical overview. In *Women, Culture and Society,* eds. Michelle Zimbalist Rosaldo and Louise Lamphere. Stanford, CA: Stanford University Press, pp. 17–42.

Rosaldo, Michelle Zimbalist, and Louise Lamphere, eds. 1974. *Women, Culture and Society.* Stanford, CA: Stanford University Press.

Rossi, Mario G. 1986. Il secondo dopoguerra: verso un nuovo assetto politico-sociale. In *La Toscana,* ed. G. Mori. Torino: Einaudi, pp. 675–707.

Rotelli, Ettore. 1980. *La ricostruzione in Toscana dal CLN ai partiti,* 2 vols. Bologna: Il Mulino.

Saba, Anna, Simona Rosati, and Marco Vassallo. 2000. Biotechnology in agriculture: Perceived risks, benefits, and attitudes in Italy. *British Food Journal* 102, 2:114–121.

Sabbatucci Severini, Patrizia. 1990. Il mezzadro pluriattivo dell'Italia centrale. In *Storia dell'agricoltura italiana in età contemporanea,* a cura di Piero Bevilacqua. Venezia: Marsilio, vol. 2, pp. 785–822.

Sacchetti, Giorgio. 1999. Blackshirts at the table. *Slow* 15:114–177.

Sacks, Karen. 1974. Engels revisited: Women, the organization of production, and private property. In *Women, Culture and Society,* eds. Michelle Zimbalist Rosaldo and Louise Lamphere. Stanford, CA: Stanford University Press, pp. 207–222.

Salvemini, Gaetano. 1973. *The Origins of Fascism in Italy.* Translated and with an Introduction by Roberto Vivarelli. New York: Harper Torchbooks.

Saraceno, Chiara. 1992. Le donne nella famiglia: una complessa construzione giuridica. 1750–1942. In *Storia della famiglia italiana, 1750–1950,* eds. M. Barbagli and D. Kertzer. Bologna: Il Mulino, pp. 103–127.

Saraceno, Chiara. 1998. *Mutamenti della famiglia e politiche sociali in Italia.* Con la collaborazione di Manuela Naldini. Bologna: Il Mulino.

Sargent, Lydia, ed. 1981. *Women and Revolution.* Boston: South End Press.

Schevill, Ferdinand. 1961. *Medieval and Renaissance Florence.* New York: Harper and Row.

Schneider, Jane, ed. 1998. *Italy's "Southern Question": Orientalism in One Country.* Oxford: Berg Press.

Schneider, Jane, and Peter Schneider. 1976. *Culture and Political Economy in Western Sicily.* New York: Academic Press.

Schneider, Jane, and Peter Schneider. 1996. *Festival of the Poor: Fertility Decline and the Ideology of Class in Sicily, 1860–1980.* Tucson: University of Arizona Press.

Segre, Luciano. 1982. *La "battaglia" del grano.* Milano: CLESAV.

Sereni, Emilio. 1968. *Il capitalismo nelle campagne (1860–1900).* Torino: Einaudi.

Serventi, Silvano, and Françoise Sabban. 2002. *Pasta: The Story of a Universal Food.* Translated by Anthony Shugaar. New York: Columbia University Press.

Shack, Dorothy N. 1969. Nutritional processes and personality development among the Gurage of Ethiopia. *Ethnology* 8, 3: 292–300. (Reprinted in *Food and Culture: A Reader,* eds. C. Counihan and P. Van Esterik. New York: Routledge, 1997, pp. 117–124.)

Shack, William A. 1971. Hunger, anxiety, and ritual: Deprivation and spirit possession among the Gurage of Ethiopia. *Man* 6, 1:30–45. (Reprinted in *Food and Culture: A Reader,* eds. C. Counihan and P. Van Esterik. New York: Routledge, 1997, pp. 125–137.)

Shanin, Teodor. 1973. The nature and change of peasant economies. *Sociologia Ruralis* 13, 2:141–171.

Shore, Cris. 1990. *Italian Communism: The Escape from Leninism: An Anthropological Perspective.* Concord, MA, and London: Pluto Press.

Signorelli, Amalia. 1990. Il pragmatismo delle donne: la condizione femminile nella trasformazione delle campagne. In *Storia dell'agricoltura italiana in età contemporanea,* a cura di Piero Bevilacqua. Venezia: Marsilio, vol. 2, pp. 625–659.

Silverman, Sydel. 1975. *Three Bells of Civilization: The Life of an Italian Hill Town.* New York: Columbia University Press.

Siskind, Janet. 1973. *To Hunt in the Morning.* Oxford: Oxford University Press.

Snowden, Frank M. 1989. *The Fascist Revolution in Tuscany, 1919–1922.* New York: Cambridge University Press.

Sobo, Elisa J. 1997. The sweetness of fat: Health, procreation, and sociability in rural Jamaica. In *Food and Culture: A Reader*, eds. C. Counihan and P. Van Esterik. New York: Routledge, pp. 256–271.

Soldani, Simonetta. 1986. La grande guerra lontano dal fronte. In *La Toscana*, ed. G. Mori. Torino: Einaudi, pp. 343–452.

Soler, Jean. 1973. Sémiotique de la Nourriture dans la Bible. *Annales: Économies, Sociétés, Civilisations* 28: 943–955. (Reprinted as The semiotics of food in the bible. In *Food and Culture: A Reader*, eds. C. Counihan and P. Van Esterik. New York: Routledge, 1997, pp. 55–66.)

Sorcinelli, Paolo. 1992. *Gli italiani e il cibo: appetiti, digiuni e rinunce dalla realtà contadina alla società del benessere*. Bologna: CLUEB.

Sorcinelli, Paolo. 1998. Per una storia sociale dell'alimentazione. Dalla polenta ai crackers. In *L'alimentazione*, ed. A. Capatti et al. Torino: Einaudi, pp. 453–493.

Stack, Carol. 1996. *Call to Home: African Americans Reclaim the Rural South*. New York: Basic Books.

Stille, Alexander. 2001. Slow Food: An Italian Answer to Globalization. *The Nation* 273, 6:11–16 (August 20/27).

Sutton, David E. 2001. *Remembrance of Repasts: An Anthropology of Food and Memory*. New York: Berg.

Symbols of U.S. Capitalism in Italy May Be Targeted. 2001. *USA Today*, October 2, 2001. http://www.usatoday.com/news/sept11/2001/10/02/italy-threat.htm consulted May 28, 2003.

Taddei, Francesca. 1998. Il cibo nell'Italia mezzadrile fra Ottocento e Novecento. In *L'alimentazione*, ed. A. Capatti et al. Torino: Einaudi, pp. 23–38.

Tambiah, S. J. 1969. Animals are good to think and good to prohibit. *Ethnology* 8, 4:423–459.

Tannenbaum, Edward R. 1972. *Fascism in Italy: Society and Culture, 1922–1945*. New York: Basic Books.

Tellarini, Vittorio, and Fabio Caporali. 2000. An input/output methodology to evaluate farms as sustainable agroecosystems: An application of indicators to farms in central Italy. *Agriculture, Ecosystems and Environment*, 77:111–123.

Teti, Vito. 1976. *Il pane, la beffa e la festa: cultura alimentare e ideologia dell'alimentazione nelle classi subalterne*. Firenze: Guaraldi.

Teti, Vito. 1995. Food and fatness in Calabria. In *Social Aspects of Obesity*, eds. I. de Garine and N. Pollock. Amsterdam: Gordon and Breach, pp. 3–30.

Thompson, Becky W. 1994. *A Hunger So Wide and So Deep: American Women Speak Out on Eating Problems*. Minneapolis: University of Minnesota Press.

Toschi, Paolo. 1963. *Invito al folklore italiano: le regioni e le feste*. Roma: Editrice Studium.

Turrini, Aida, Catherine Leclercq, and Amleto D'Amicis. 1999. Patterns of food and nutrient intakes in Italy and their application to the development of food-based dietary guidelines. *British Journal of Nutrition* 81, 2:S83–S89.

Turrini, A., A. Saba, D. Perrone, E. Cialfa, and A. D'Amicis. 2001. Original communication: Food consumption patterns in Italy: The INN-CA Study 1994–1996. *European Journal of Clinical Nutrition* 55:571–588.

Vannucci, Marcello. 1986. *Storia di Firenze: dal 59 a.C. al 1966*. Roma: Newton Compton Editori.

Variyam, Jayachandran. 2002. Patterns of caloric intake and body mass index among U.S. adults. *Food Review* 25, 3:16–20.

Ventura, Flaminia, and Pierluigi Milone. 2000. Theory and practice of multi-product farms: Farm butcheries in Umbria. *Sociologia Ruralis* 40, 4:452–465.

Vercelloni, Luca. 1998. La modernità alimentare. In *L'alimentazione*, ed. A. Capatti, et al. Torino: Einaudi, pp. 951–1005.

Vercelloni, Luca. 2001. Le abitudini alimentari in Italia dagli anni ottanta agli anni duemila. *Sociologia del Lavoro* 83:141–149.

Vesco, Clotilde. 1984. *Cucina fiorentina fra Medioevo e Rinascimento: usanze, ricette, segreti*. Lucca: Marina Pacini Fazzi Editore.

Weismantel, M. J. 1988. *Food, Gender and Poverty in the Ecuadorian Andes*. Philadelphia: University of Pennsylvania Press.

Whitaker, Elizabeth. 2000. *Measuring Mamma's Milk: Fascism and the Medicalization of Maternity in Italy*. Ann Arbor: University of Michigan Press.

Whitaker, Elizabeth. 2002. Written personal communication. July 23, 2002.

White, Caroline. 1980. *Patrons and Partisans: A Study of Politics in Two Southern Italian Comuni.* Cambridge: Cambridge University Press.

Wilhelm, Maria de Blasio. 1988. *The Other Italy: Italian Resistance in World War II.* New York: Norton.

Wolf, Eric R. 1966. *Peasants.* Englewood Cliffs, NJ: Prentice-Hall.

Wolf, Eric R. 1969. *Peasant Wars of the Twentieth Century.* New York: Harper and Row.

Wolf, Eric R. 1982. *Europe and the People Without History.* Berkeley: University of California Press.

Wolf, Margery. 1992. *A Thrice-Told Tale: Feminism, Postmodernism, and Ethnographic Responsibility.* Stanford, CA: Stanford University Press.

Wood, Roy C. 1995. *The Sociology of the Meal.* Edinburgh: University of Edinburgh Press.

Young, Michael. 1971. *Fighting with Food: Leadership, Values and Social Control in a Massim Society.* Cambridge.

Zamagni, Vera. 1998. L'evoluzione dei consumi fra tradizione e innovazione. In *L'alimentazione,* ed. A. Capatti et al. Torino: Einaudi, pp. 171–204.

Zavella, Patricia. 1987. *Women's Work and Chicano Families: Cannery Workers of the Santa Clara Valley.* Ithaca, NY: Cornell University Press.

Index